MW00604042

Women in Fundamentalism

Modesty, Marriage, and Motherhood

Maxine L. Margolis
University of Florida

ROWMAN & LITTLEFIELD
Lanham • Boulder • New York • London

Executive Editor: Rolf Janke
Assistant Editor: Courtney Packard
Senior Marketing Manager: Amy Whitaker

Credits and acknowledgments for material borrowed from other sources, and reproduced with permission, appear on the appropriate page within the text.

Published by Rowman & Littlefield
An imprint of The Rowman & Littlefield Publishing Group, Inc.
4501 Forbes Boulevard, Suite 200, Lanham, Maryland 20706
https://rowman.com

6 Tinworth Street, London SE11 5AL, United Kingdom

Excerpt from *The Handmaid's Tale* by Margaret Atwood. Copyright © 1986 by O.W. Toad, Ltd. Used by permission of Houghton Mifflin Harcourt Publishing Company. All rights reserved.

Brief quote from p. 6 of *The Prime of Miss Jean Brodie* by Muriel Spark. Copyright © 1961 by Muriel Spark. Reprinted by permission of HarperCollins Publishers.

British Library Cataloguing in Publication Information Available

Library of Congress Cataloging-in-Publication Data Available

Library of Congress Control Number: 2019949862

ISBN 9781538134016 (cloth) | ISBN 9781538134023 (pbk.) |
    ISBN 9781538134030 (electronic)

Contents

Preface and Acknowledgments

Jews who have made their scholarly reputations studying other peoples and communities sometimes return, in the autumn of their careers, to studying their own.

—Peter Beinart, *New York Times Book Review*, 2014

What a perfect statement of my interest in the Satmar! The Satmar are an extreme fundamentalist Hasidic community living in Brooklyn and upstate New York and they are one of the three fundamentalist groups that are the focus of this book. As an anthropologist, a feminist, and a non-practicing Jew who strongly relates to the religion culturally, I find that Peter Beinart's statement exactly reflects who I am and why I chose to examine the Satmar and two other communities in terms of their attitudes towards and treatment of girls and women.

In doing this I am exiting what anthropologist Virginia Dominguez (1993) calls "the Jewish closet in anthropology." She notes that many American anthropologists have Jewish backgrounds, yet very few of them have done any research on or writing about Jews. So here I am, emerging from the "Jewish closet" by including in my discussion of gender roles a zealous brand of Hasidism.

Most of my other books have been based on my field research both in Brazil and in the United States. Fieldwork has a long tradition in anthropology, but such research is close to impossible in the three communities that are the focus of this book. The Hasidic Satmar and the Fundamentalist Church of Jesus Christ of Latter-Day Saints are infamous for their extreme insularity and the walls they create prohibiting access to outsiders, to those who do not share their fundamentalist beliefs. Then there are the Pashtun who live in Afghanistan and adjacent areas of Pakistan. They also present huge barriers to field research not only because of the difficulty of reaching many of the areas where they live, but also because of the very dangerous conditions resembling civil war in some of these places. As a consequence, much of Pashtun territory is simply off-limits to foreigners.

Accordingly, nearly all of the information contained in this book comes from written sources: from books, articles, numerous Web sites, and blogs. The only "fieldwork" I did for this project were visits I made to Williamsburg, Brooklyn, and Kiryas Joel, the Satmar community in upstate New York. In Williamsburg I twice went on the Hasidic Tours run by Frieda Vizel, herself a former Satmar. The tours were very helpful in introducing me to the Hasidic milieu through visits made to various local businesses and other sites along with Frieda's deep knowledge of her own religious community. My visit to Kiryas Joel was a brief one. We drove around the community simply to see what it looked like, but I did not attempt to speak to any of its residents, knowing that it is an insular enclave not welcoming to outsiders.

I thank Rolf Janke, my editor at Rowman & Littlefield, for strongly supporting this project. I am also grateful to Courtney Packard, his editorial assistant, for her timely communications and general assistance as well as to Jehanne Schweitzer, senior production editor. Sarah Zink's meticulous copy editing of my manuscript is also very much appreciated. I also want to acknowledge the excellent job done by Patrick Payne, my graphics expert, on the photos in this volume.

Last but most certainly not least, as in all my writing projects, I owe an enormous debt of gratitude to my husband, Dr. Jerry Milanich. His help putting my manuscript in shape for publication, his tireless efforts to help select and get approval for the photos contained in this volume, and his warm unswerving support in all things involving the author were crucial to seeing this book to completion.

Chapter One

Gendered Fundamentalism

An Introduction

There is a single profile in all fundamentalism. All are patriarchal, anti-feminist, anti-pluralistic and anti-liberal, with a belief that God is male and that the man in the family is the ultimate authority.

—Andrea Moore-Emmett, *God's Brothel*, 2004

Jew, Christian, Muslim . . . all religions have their splinter radicals, and they all embrace the notion of shrouding women, controlling women, and making women little more than baby factories.

—Ginia Bellafante, "Educational Orthodoxy," 2016

The roles of men and women in cultures around the world have long interested me. For many years I taught a course on the subject at the University of Florida and I authored two books about the changing roles of women in the United States (Margolis 1984, 2000). Several years ago while pursuing this interest I began noticing the striking similarities among extreme fundamentalist religions in their views about and treatment of women. Whether Christian, Jewish, or Muslim, the fundamentalist offshoots of these world religions subject women to myriad restrictions in their daily lives. They try to maintain male control over women's bodies, women's activities, and the people with whom women associate. They also share common ideologies about women's "true nature" and proper place.

Wanting to learn more about these parallels and the underlying conditions that gave rise to them, I decided to explore women's roles and the treatment

1

of women among extreme representatives of three of the world's major religions. First, representing an offshoot of Christianity are the Mormon polygamists, specifically the Fundamentalist Church of Jesus Christ of Latter-Day
Saints (FLDS), who live in Utah, Arizona, Texas, and isolated enclaves in
other northern and western states and in Canada and Mexico. Representing
Judaism are the Satmar Hasidim of Williamsburg, Brooklyn; Kiryas Joel, a
village in Orange County, New York; and various settlements in Israel. Finally, Islam is represented by one brand of that religion as practiced by the
Pashtun ethnic group of Afghanistan and neighboring areas of Pakistan.

I realize that the inclusion of the Pashtun in this study is somewhat problematic not only because their population is many times larger than the
Jewish and Christian sects on which this book focuses, but also because they
are not a religious sect per se but rather a cultural entity, an ethnic community. There is another caveat about my use of the Pashtun here. Some of the
Pashtun practices described in the pages to follow stem from customs that are
part of Pashtun *tribal* culture rather than from their practice of Islam. Nevertheless, because the Pashtun's treatment of and beliefs about women are so
strikingly similar to those of the Satmar and the FLDS, I have included them
as one variant of Islamic belief and tradition. Moreover, the Taliban, a fundamentalist political movement and an offshoot of the Pashtun population proper, have exhibited many of the same severe attitudes and behaviors towards
women as the Satmar and the FLDS.

Why have I decided to do a study of these three religious communities?
As an anthropologist I have always been far more interested in similarities
among cultures than differences between them. Of even greater interest to me
are the conditions that underlie these similarities. The cases covered here
have provided me with a striking example of complex parallels in three
vastly different societies. Why, I wanted to know, have such similar treat-
ments of and ideas about girls and women evolved independently in each
case? What gave rise to this intricate and strikingly similar behavioral and
ideological repertoire?

The answer, I believe, is the enormous stress placed on women's role in
unending procreation. It is the insistence that women give birth to as many
children as possible that impacts their lives across multiple domains and
limits their participation in many spheres—social, economic, political, and
religious—limitations that are reinforced by doctrines suggesting women's
innate unsuitability for participating in these spaces.

Several effects arise from the stress on women's reproductive role in the three cases analyzed here. They include the imposition of rigorous standards of modesty and comportment in dress and behavior, restricted contact with the larger society outside the home, the stringent division of labor by sex, the kind and degree of women's education, women's economic contribution to the household (or lack thereof), and women's very limited participation in the political and religious institutions of the societies in which they live.

Just what are the specific commonalities in all three groups when it comes to women? Perhaps the most striking similarity among them, and the one from which all other parallels arise, is the emphasis all three place on reproduction. Women are essentially broodmares who are expected to give birth to as many children as they are able, preferably male children. There is also a very strong prohibition on the use of birth control even where it is available as well as on any form of family planning.

Associated with this stress on women's reproductive capacity is the separation of adult women from unrelated men. It is important—at all costs—to avoid questions concerning paternity. In every instance, the social father and the biological father must be one and the same with no questions asked. This insistence, in turn, is linked to the strict dress codes imposed on women in all three cases. They are meant to ensure that unrelated males are not "tempted" by immodest attire.

This concern with paternity is also linked to another feature common to all three communities. This is the segregation of males and females, especially the separation of adult men and women from each other. The interaction of unrelated men and women is highly restricted, which limits women's movements and associations. In all three cases women are largely confined to the domestic realm. This means that their legitimate "place" is hearth and home and movements outside its confines are carefully monitored and controlled.

In these communities arranged marriages of young girls are the norm, and in the case of fundamentalist Mormons and Pashtun Muslims such marriages are often polygamous. In all three examples, as a result of early marriage, girls and women move from being controlled by their fathers to being under the control of their husbands. In a very real sense, girls and women are viewed as commodities to be kept in check by their male relatives.

Why is this control so important? Females of all ages are subject to male authority because proper female behavior is considered vital to their family's status and prestige. Blood atonement among members of the Fundamentalist Church of Jesus Christ of Latter-Day Saints is reminiscent of the "honor killings" of women who stray from Pashtun norms and "dishonor" their families. While such violent forms of control are absent among the Satmar Hasidim, any questionable behavior by a family's female members can seriously jeopardize the marital prospects of all unmarried members of the family.

Because the obedient submission of girls and women is seen as the sine qua non of proper female behavior, it is important that females not receive too much schooling. In all three cases educated women are seen as dangerous because of their potential to disrupt the status quo. Among adherents of the Fundamentalist Church of Jesus Christ of Latter Day-Saints, girls only attend school until age thirteen or not beyond middle school. Satmar girls are prohibited from being educated beyond high school or to about age seventeen and the education of Pashtun girls and women is also highly restricted. There is a high rate of illiteracy among the Pashtun, in general, but it is particularly high among girls and women. And many Pashtun fathers simply will not permit their daughters to be educated past the age of ten or twelve.

What girls and women actually learn is similarly restricted. Religion is the focal point of the education of Satmar boys and girls. College, university, and professional training in medicine, science, or law is abjured for both sexes and visiting public libraries is also prohibited. In Hasidic areas of Williamsburg, Brooklyn, there are few newsstands or places to buy newspapers or magazines in English. Women, in particular, are prohibited from reading secular material, watching television, or going to the movies. A psychologist was even asked by the patient's family to treat a young Satmar woman who was thought to be disturbed because of her desire to attend college.

Complained one Orthodox Jewish woman about this Hasidic sect: "In Satmar they don't believe a woman has to learn. That it's basically what they learn in school and then it's finished. Then it's into baking and cooking without learning" (quoted in Mintz 1992:175). Similarly, schoolgirls in the Fundamentalist Church of Jesus Christ of Latter-Day Saints are primarily instructed on how to be good mothers, keep house, cook, comfort their husbands, and raise loyal and obedient children.

Of course, other religious extremists target educated girls as well. Examples include Boko Haram's abduction of over two hundred schoolgirls in 2014 and 2018 in Nigeria and the shooting of Malala Yousafzai in 2015, a Pashtun girl who championed education for girls in Pakistan. "Why are fanatics so terrified of girls' education?" asks *New York Times* columnist Nicholas Kristof (2014). "Because there's no force more powerful to transform a society. The greatest threat to extremism isn't drones firing missiles, but girls reading books."

One way to limit female learning is restricting access to sources of information outside formal schooling. The Satmar, for example, prohibit all contact with secular books, films, radio, and television. While boys and men are also subject to these restrictions, the exposure of girls and women to secular material is seen as a greater threat to the well-being of the family. Likewise, most television shows along with radio, movies, and books are prohibited to members of the FLDS.

Ignorance of all things sexual is another hallmark of all three groups. Young women and men receive absolutely no information about sex and when they marry are generally stunned by the sexual activity expected of them. "There is no such thing as sex education within the FLDS culture . . . sex was and is never discussed with FLDS children," writes one observer (Brower 2012:89, 56). The same has been said of the Satmar. "About sexuality, their minds have been kept free of information and infused with fear," notes a psychotherapist who treats Hasidic women (Bergner 2015:24). Similarly, sexuality is hidden among the Pashtun and sex for women does not exist until marriage and then is only for procreation.

All three communities maintain an identity separate from the larger religious groups from which they arose. The FLDS are distinct from contemporary Mormonism and Christianity; the Pashtun are separate from other variants of Islam and the Satmar Hasidim from mainstream Judaism. This general isolation from the larger, surrounding community is a hallmark of many such fundamentalist religious sects. They usually disdain any sort of cultural interaction that might put them at risk, wanting to protect themselves against "false knowledge." The result is a separatism that involves a constant struggle against the outside world. There is a distinct, bounded group of insiders; all others are outsiders, or "gentiles" in the linguistic construction of Mormon fundamentalists.

What are the ideologies concerning women's true nature and proper place shared by these fundamentalist communities? During certain times of the month Satmar Hasidim consider females a source of pollution. Menstruating women are said to be unclean and must avoid all physical contact with their husbands, making sure not to so much as hand them a plate of food, pour them a glass of water, sit next to them in a car, or sleep in the same bed. And there is no question about their proper place, to wit: "The essence and purpose of a Jewish woman is to be able to lead a Jewish home and to prepare a good . . . kugel[1] for the Holy Shabbos [Sabbath]" (*Der Blatt*, Satmar newspaper, May 9, 2014). To the Pashtun a newborn daughter is said to be "stupid at birth," a being lacking in wisdom because of an inferior brain. Similarly, for the FLDS women do not have men's intellect, which is why, men insist, the study of scripture is a male preserve.

Another commonality, at least between the Satmar and the fundamentalist Mormons, is that because of the high premium placed on fecundity and the fact that women are expected to bear as many children as possible, both groups rely heavily on government programs like food stamps to support their growing broods of children. Over a one-year period in the early 2000s, for example, FLDS families living in the adjacent towns of Hildale, Utah (with a poverty rate of 44 percent) and Colorado City, Arizona (with a poverty rate of nearly 55 percent), collected an estimated three million dollars in food stamps and cash assistance. Similarly, no place in the United States uses food stamps at a higher rate than the Satmar living in the village of Kiryas Joel in New York State. Moreover, by 2014, 93 percent of its residents were on Medicaid (Samaha 2014; Grumet and Caher 2016).

Finally, in the last few decades all three groups have become even more extreme in terms of their strictures on women. The Taliban, a religio-political movement that emerged among the Pashtun after the defeat of the Soviet Union in Afghanistan in the early 1990s, prohibit girls from attending school after age eight and prohibit women from working outside the home.

Likewise, as a rift arose between two brothers for control of the Satmar Hasidim—both are sons of the deceased rabbi who led the sect—the constraints on women have increased. Proclaimed the brother whose bailiwick is Kiryas Joel: "If a woman must go on the street, she should walk quickly and not stroll . . . not talk loudly, not laugh" (quoted in *Failed Messiah* 2015). This faction of the Satmar has now officially prohibited girls and women from wearing makeup even at weddings or other festive occasions, and any girl who violates this ban faces dismissal from school .

Finally, in the early 2000s Warren Jeffs, the so-called "Prophet" of the FLDS in the twin towns of Arizona City and Hildale, who then had unbounded authority, began marrying off girls as young as eleven to sixty-year-old men. If an FLDS man displeased the Prophet in any way, he would have

---

1. Kugel is a traditional baked pudding made from egg noodles or potatoes.

his wives and children taken away from him and "reassigned" to another man.

Despite the striking commonalities that these three communities exhibit in terms of their treatment of and beliefs about women, each has its own idiosyncratic practices that have no equivalent in the other communities under consideration. There is, for example, the custom of *baad* among the Pashtun in which serious disputes between families can be settled by providing a marriageable girl from the perpetrator's family to the victim's family. Among the Satmar there is the practice of *niddah* in which menstruating women are considered polluting and must strenuously avoid all physical contact with their husbands. And among the FLDS there is "placement marriage" in which the sect's Prophet communicates with God to determine the appropriate husbands for the group's female devotees. Though such idiosyncrasies exist, the primary focus here is on the similarities in these populations' behavior towards and conceptions of women.

All of these cases are examples of extreme religious fundamentalism even though they arose from three distinct religious traditions. But what exactly is fundamentalism? What are the underlying tenets of fundamentalist beliefs that we see expressed so vividly among the FLDS, the Satmar, and the Pashtun? This is a question to which we now turn.

FUNDAMENTALISMS

When it comes to issues like LGBT rights, the role of women in society, secular education, acceptance of modern science, human sexuality and so on, fundamentalists tend to be interchangeable across denominational lines.

—Rob Boston, Director of Communications, Americans United
for Separation of Church and State (quoted in Berkowitz 2015)

Whether Christian, Jewish, or Muslim, fundamentalists seek to remake the world by selectively retrieving doctrines and practices from what they regard as a pristine religious past. With a foreboding sense that their collective identity is deeply threatened in the modern era, members of these groups reinforce their distinctiveness by such selective recoveries. As part of this effort fundamentalists require "enemies" or "demonic" opponents with which to contrast themselves. The alleged existence of such adversaries is used as a strategy through which believers attempt to strengthen and preserve their personal identity as a solitary unit. As such, their traditions not only tell them who they are but, more importantly, who they are *not* (Ammerman 1994).

While writing about ethnicity rather than religion the analysis of noted anthropologist Frederick Barth (1998) is pertinent here. Barth defined ethnic groups as a form of "social organization," as a way of arranging and classifying differences among social entities. The boundaries that mark such differences are ascribed to the group both from within—by members of the group itself—and by others, by outsiders. Barth's relevant point in the current discussion is that it is not the shared culture that defines the group as much as the *differences* between that group and other groups.

It is differences in belief and behavior between adherents of these fundamentalist communities and followers of the larger world religions from which they arose that sets the fundamentalists apart and highlights their singular identity. They relentlessly maintain their distance from and powerfully censure what they view as ideas and practices that are opposed to the fundamental truths of their own belief systems. Fundamentalists see themselves as a bulwark against spreading secular contamination, a buttress against the intrusion of outsiders, and as a last stand against irreligious skeptics who would entice believers into a syncretistic, ungodly life. Modern secular culture is antithetical to these groups. Hence, pluralism does not and cannot exist in such communities.

The religion of fundamentalists is inflexible in regard to what its believers see as the true tenets of the faith. They embrace tradition and view even small deviations from it, especially those demanded by modern life, as intolerable. After all, it is only believers who have a correct understanding of the historical past. From this conviction arises the belief that the group's religion, as currently practiced by its adherents, is part of a timeless tradition that began with the earliest practitioners of the faith. Simply put, fundamentalists see themselves as "the true heirs of the ancients" (Heilman 1994:173).

These movements generally require authoritarian, charismatic leadership along with a core of devotees who promote a hard-edged social and moral code among their followers. The rules of these sects are complex and rigid and must be vigilantly followed by everyone. Barriers are continually erected against a common external threat, most often countless features of contemporary life. It is in this sense that adherents of fundamentalist sects feel themselves to be besieged, to be in exile from the modern world. As a result, their followers are deeply alienated from contemporary society.

Believers separate themselves from outsiders as they seek an orderly universe based on strict adherence to what they perceive as traditional values and practices. This separation "reflects the belief that the founding principles on which the larger religion is based have been corrupted, neglected, compromised, forgotten or replaced with other principles. Fundamentalists advocate strict fidelity to the 'true' religious principles of the larger religion" (Kottak and Kozaitis 2012:103).

The core beliefs of fundamentalists are concerned not only with doctrinal truths but also with the ways in which adherents should live their lives. Here fundamentalists make moral claims and insist that not only must believers separate themselves from non-believers, but that certain standards of behavior should apply to all within the religious community. Fundamentalists vilify the secular order, viewing it as polluted and dangerous and an unfit place in which to live. This is the reason reading material is censored and listening and viewing practices are closely monitored. In sum, fundamentalists define themselves in polar opposition to modernity, negating secular society while portraying themselves as a "utopian alternative" to it (Wuthnow and Lawson 1994:41).

One means fundamentalist sects have of ensuring that their members continue to obey their stringent rules is through the threat of ostracism or even expulsion. The stances of these sects vis-à-vis the larger societies in which they are embedded limit adherents' contacts with the world outside their own insular communities. Accordingly, members are well aware that any break with their sect's canons and demands for upright behavior may thrust them into the unknown and force them to live "out there" amongst the "wicked." Living under the threat of expulsion, thus making them "unworthy," while also risking the loss of everyone and everything they have known, is a powerful means for ensuring conformity (Stott 2017).

Two of the religious communities considered here, the Satmar and the FLDS, belong to a particular subset of fundamentalist sects: those that are classified as world renouncing. These are communities that "seek purity and self-preservation more than hegemony over fallen outsiders" (Almond, Sivan, and Appleby 1995b:429). World renouncers, whose large families of proliferating children focus on domestic life and religious ritual, are of necessity multigenerational since they make no attempt to bring in new recruits. In short, they do not seek to transform outsiders who are living what they view as sinful lives.

Such groups typically have charismatic leaders that contrast their movement with the "tepid, compromising, liberalizing religious leadership that has
jeopardized the integrity of the religious tradition" (Almond, Sivan, and Appleby 1995a:476). Though world-renouncing sects are as ideologically doctrinaire as other fundamentalists, all of their energy is inner directed, that is,
devoted to the creation of their own religious world in contrast to the hostile
outside. Since they view the high walls of their religious enclave as the only
hope for maintaining their lifestyles and values, they are, in essence, extreme
separatists.

To these and virtually all other fundamentalists, the realm of domestic
relations—perhaps more than any other—is the one in which antipathy towards what are seen as the moral failings of contemporary social life is most
powerfully felt. It is within the familial domain that sanctions are severely
enforced and that boundaries are highly developed. Here we see identifiable
patterns across religious traditions in the way fundamentalists view gender
roles, relations between the sexes, sexuality, and the nature of the family.
They generally view expressions of sexuality as a critical index of modernity
that must be tightly regulated, taking extreme measures to protect believers
from the enticement of the sensual and erotic. Fundamentalists typically
oppose abortion, contraception, homosexuality, and non-reproductive sex of
any kind while placing a high premium on fertility, with female adherents
expected to bear as many children as possible.

A typical stance among devotees of these sects is that female sexuality is
a hindrance to male spirituality and therefore must be kept in check. This is
why women are often seen as dangerous, as creatures with the power to
undermine male dignity and well-being. Among many fundamentalists the
twin concepts of honor and shame translate into an extreme fixation on a
woman's chastity because so much of a man's honor depends on it. "In this
struggle against spiritual emasculation, woman is cast as the immediate and
proximate 'other' over and against whom men must define themselves"
(Hardacre 1993:144–45).

A pillar of the fundamentalist worldview in terms of gender roles is a
"fierce patriarchalism" that is transformed into a "patriarchal protest movement" against certain aspects of modernity (Marty and Appleby 1993:10;
Hardacre 1993:130). This "patriarchal protest movement" typically attempts
to restore "traditional" family structures and "traditional" relationships between the sexes. It is here that fundamentalists generally have the most

success in instilling customary norms and patterns of behavior. This is, in fact, often their agenda's highest priority.

From the fundamentalist point of view the "traditional family" functions within a divinely ordained and sanctioned social order that insists on a hierarchical relationship between men and women with women submerging their wants and needs to the service of others, especially family members. Men are leaders and women and children are followers. Wives are to be subservient to their husbands and children to their fathers, a subservience that often applies to sisters in relation to their brothers as well.

Because women are in charge of the home and responsible for the well-being and contentment of family members, women's education—aside from the basics—is limited to instilling prevailing gender norms in which their interests are restricted to the domestic realm. Fundamentalists deeply distrust women's engagement in independent political and intellectual activities. As a consequence, women are strongly discouraged from seeking experiences outside the home along with the skills that might allow them to make it on their own in the wider world. For this reason, women must relinquish the benefits of modernity in terms of education, political participation, and rewarding employment. Due to their restricted education and lack of outside experience, women in these fundamentalist creeds are kept from discovering and exploring diverse ways of living. Because of their limited mobility beyond the household, they lack extensive contacts with others who might expose them to novel ideas and alternative lifestyles.

The spiritual and moral training of children is a high priority among fundamentalists and child-rearing tends to be strict, with children expected to closely follow the rules set down by their parents, especially their fathers. Moreover, in order to avoid any misunderstanding, the children of fundamentalists must be confined to an environment consisting of like-minded adherents of the religious sect in question. This is particularly important when it comes to schooling and it is why so many children of fundamentalist parents in the United States are homeschooled or attend sect-affiliated religious schools. Isolation prevents them from being subject to the polluting influences of the wider society, including influences emanating from the written word and the mass media.

Finally, the word "fundamentalism," which originated in evangelical Christianity, refers to the literal interpretation of scripture. But even the most conservative variants of Judaism, including the Hasidic Satmar, do not take the entire Bible literally, so in that sense there is no such thing as "Jewish fundamentalism." Yet the term is also used to refer to rigid traditionalism, to the strict adherence to what followers see as the original and authentic—the fundamental—form of the faith. In this sense Hasidism has a great deal in common with evangelical Christianity, including the FLDS sect we are focusing on here and certain variants of Islam, like the Wahabism in Saudi Arabia as well as Islam as practiced by the Pashtun (Biale et al. 2018).

The three religious communities that are the primary focus of this book are certainly not the only groups that adhere to such stringent doctrines when it comes to girls and women. A number of studies have concluded that, regardless of the religion, fundamentalist beliefs and practices have several commonalities. In this fundamentalists appear to have more in common with each other across religious traditions than they do with their non-fundamentalist co-religionists (American Academy of Arts and Sciences 2000; Marty and Appleby 1993).

UNDERLYING COMMONALITIES

Fundamentalism is primarily a radical patriarchalism.
—Helen Hardacre, *Fundamentalisms and Society*, 1993

What are the shared underlying conditions that give rise to the extreme forms of belief and behavior toward women and girls found among the Jewish Satmar, the Christian Mormon Fundamentalists, and the Muslim Pashtun? One clue is their intense stance regarding procreation. The more children the merrier, with the expectation that every woman will bear as many children as she possibly can. This can best be accomplished without the interference of any form of family planning or birth control.

Nevertheless, the paths taken by the three populations in terms of their increasing numbers have differed. Both the Satmar and the FLDS, but not the Pashtun, have cohered and achieved success by waging social and economic combat against the larger societies in which they are embedded. The two groups receive benefits in the form of welfare payments, food stamps, Medicaid, special education, and other funds by convincing authorities of their inability to support the large broods of children they willfully produce. It has been said that without government funding, for example, the Satmar community "would have expired a long time ago." In fact, government assistance makes much of the Satmar lifestyle possible for the poor, given the high cost of kosher food, private school tuition, and rising rents in gentrifying Williamsburg, Brooklyn, the locale of the main branch of the sect (Bronstein 2015).

The larger the number of offspring the more successful the groups effectively become, success being measured by their ability to overwhelm local governments with their numbers. Moreover, such stances are possible in the United States, where both the Satmar and the FLDS are a tiny minority relative to the nation's population. As such, the costs of the many benefits they siphon off from local, state, and federal sources are spread widely.

One powerful tool to accomplish these goals is the delivery of block votes numbering in the thousands to favored politicians. Both the Satmar and the FLDS do indeed vote in large blocs for candidates based on directives from their religious leaders. Said one member of an ultra-Orthodox community about such directives: "When they tell us to vote, it is a *mitzvah* (good deed) and not an option. When they tell us not to vote, it is an *issur* (prohibited act) and not an option" (quoted in Selengut 1994:255). Ironically, in the 2016 U.S. presidential election the Satmar voted en masse for Hillary Rodham Clinton under a directive issued by the sect's Rebbes, a command that obviously did not do her very much good!

What about the Muslim Pashtun, a population found mostly in Afghanistan and parts of Pakistan and embedded in vastly different nation states than the U.S.-based Satmar and FLDS? Afghanistan, in particular, has long been divided by ethnic cleavages, and while the Pashtun once formed a majority of that country's population, over the last several decades of war and conflict they have lost what was once their solid political dominance and today account for about 42 percent of the Afghan population. The struggles of other ethnic groups for political power in the country—the Tajiks, Uzbeks, and Hazaras—contest the ascendant role the Pashtuns have played in the nation's past. And so, here again, numbers count. Clearly population growth achieved through the (re)production of many children helps provide an advantage vis-à-vis other ethnic populations with whom one's own group is competing (Skaine 2002; Saleh 2012).

How is the successful rearing of large numbers of progeny by the Pashtun, Satmar, and FLDS related to their treatment of females? Obviously, in order to encourage their ability to bear and rear many children, the potential and actual reproductive capacity of girls and women must be subject to control. First and foremost, their physical movements must be limited. Keeping them reined in by placing boundaries on where they go and with whom is the sine qua non of ensuring that females have contact with a very limited number of males, largely close male relatives. Then, too, whom they may (and may not) marry is carefully managed. Marital decisions come largely under the purview of the men in the family or the community.

The attempt to control women's reproductive power is also partly achieved by the strict dress codes to which girls and especially adult women are subject. All-embracing coverage of the body and—in the case of the Pashtun, the face—is meant to make women invisible to and "protected" from men, especially those who are not close relatives. This is also accomplished by keeping women's movements confined largely to the domestic realm with more limited access to the world at large. In the case of the Pashtun, especially in rural areas, women rarely leave their households and when they do, they are always accompanied by a close male relative.

To be sure, much of this insistence on "covering up" and on the seclusion of women from men who are not close relatives is meant to ensure that a woman's ability to have children is limited to the man who is socially recognized as her mate. While motherhood is a biological given and is unquestioned, the same cannot be said of fatherhood. In these three cases, as well as countless others, the issue of paternity is a fraught one because, until the development of DNA tests in the late twentieth century, the principle of *pater semper incertus est* (the father is always uncertain) held sway, while *mater certissima est* (the mother is very certain) is a given because of the observable fact of birth (Milanich 2019). A woman impregnated by anyone other than her socially recognized mate was and still is a grave offense in many cultures. In short, what we have are tension-filled, highly embellished efforts to ensure that a woman is shielded from the advances of all males other than her husband.

The stress on women's reproductive capacity impacts other aspects of these societies as well. One obvious example is the division of labor. In all three cases there are well-defined "male" and "female" spheres of work. Men's work commonly takes place outside the home, while women's work is centered around the domestic realm and is mostly devoted to childcare and household tasks. Wherever women are isolated or segregated like this and are expected to devote their lives almost exclusively to the home front, they necessarily rely on men to mediate their dealings with the larger society. Having limited direct access to the public sphere, women's personal autonomy is also curtailed. In essence, extreme task segregation based on sex, as in the three cases under discussion, may lead to distinct male and female worlds with divergent interests.

Then, too, as we have seen, the education of women in these three populations is largely limited to the basics, to what they need to know to carry out their duties as mothers and wives. A higher level of education for females is not only unnecessary but potentially dangerous since with learning is likely to come greater questioning of the status quo. Ensuring that most females remain illiterate, as in the case of the rural Pashtun, obviously limits their exposure to the wider world. Among the FLDS and the Satmar we also see severe restrictions placed on women's access to information about the surrounding society in which they live, whether it is information from books, from other printed material, or from access to local and national media.

All of this impacts women's ability to contribute much of economic worth to their households, be it in subsistence production or something of monetary value. With relatively little education, lack of information about the wider society in which they live, and limited mobility outside of their own households—and while not dismissing the importance of domestic labor—women in these cases are simply not socialized to earn a living or to contribute in any significant way to the economic well-being of their families.

There is a concomitant isolation from the political realm. Since men dominate the public world, the world outside the home, political power and both formal and informal political positions necessarily reside with them. Women have few or no extra-domestic responsibilities because of their isolation from the world at large. As a result, their wants and needs are rarely taken into account when decisions affecting the external society are made. It is men, to use George W. Bush's inimitable phrase, who are the "deciders." In sum, women's personal influence is muted.

This exclusion is found in the realm of religion as well. Religious rituals that center around males and prohibit female participation suggest a gendered hierarchy in terms of the religious sphere. In the case of the FLDS, for example, women are so low on the heavenly scale that they require their husband's postmortem permission to enter the celestial realm. Likewise, it is only men who can constitute the quorum of twelve necessary for daily prayers among the Satmar and other Hasidic sects. And the Pashtun believe that women lack the intellectual heft to engage in discussions of religious doctrine.

Regulating women's reproductive potential in these populations is also linked to powerful ideologies. One example is the pervasive notion of "shame" as a means of social control. Women who do not conform to the strict limits on dress and behavior demanded of them humiliate their families, especially their male relatives who, it is said, are "weak" and unable to control the females in their households. Another example is the Satmar woman who does not exhibit sufficient modesty and thus brings shame on her family and hinders her own and her siblings' marital prospects.

Belief systems help sustain this control. Ideologies that view separate roles for males and females as divinely ordained not only enhance the sexual division of labor but make it appear both natural and inevitable as well. Similarly, the widely held view that women are innately suited to certain roles and not others shores up the gendered status quo. Moreover, the very notion that males and females have very different innate capacities, that the female brain, for example, is ill-equipped to engage in intellectual pursuits such as the deep study of the Talmud or the Koran, also reinforces these divisions.

These hypothetical differences are also reflected in the valuation these societies place on males and females, in general, both as children and as adults. The birth of a boy is greeted with joy and celebrated by the Pashtun and the Satmar, while the arrival of a baby girl is often met with dismay, especially if the family already has several daughters. Women who bear many sons are fêted, while those who produce only daughters are pitied, even maligned. And among the FLDS the *only* real value women have is achieved by the number of children to whom they give birth, especially male children.

Another powerful belief common in these communities is the notion of female impurity or pollution, the view that women pose a threat to men. The idea that women can be dangerous to men elicits behaviors that separate women and/or their belongings from men, especially their male relatives, as witness the enormous efforts a menstruating Satmar woman must make to avoid any and all contact with her husband until she is ritually purified. Beliefs and behaviors associated with female pollution and avoidance maximize differences between the sexes and are found in societies, such as the three under consideration, in which such distinctions are important organizing principles.

Beliefs about women's "true nature" and "natural place" are not free-floating and random but are grounded in women's actual roles in society. For example, the ideology that depicts women as immature and requiring male protection and supervision is associated with the domestic isolation of women. As such, both material and ideological factors come into play when accounting for cross-cultural variations in gender status and sexual hierarchies.

And, to be sure, it is not only men who impose these ideologies. Women who are born and reared in these societies come under the sway of these ideas and help reinforce them. And it is often adult women as well as men who support the idea of strictly separate gendered spheres of life and insist on "proper" female behavior. After all, questioning such values and patterns would have to overcome a lifetime of socialization in them. Moreover, as anthropologist Sarah B. Hrdy has pointed out, "When the social status of their families and especially that of their offspring, depends on their 'virtue,' women have an obvious stake in complying as well as in advertising their compliance" (quoted in Edsall 2019).

Finally, one theme running through the views of women in these three communities is what might be called a cesspool of misogyny. Time and again females are treated as the second, lesser or inferior sex. Much of the vitriol about what "women are like" and what they are capable of drips with misogyny. The notion in all three communities that females present some sort of hidden danger to males makes for a sense of unease in their presence, especially when a man and a woman who are not close relatives come into contact. Misogynistic attitudes also help smooth the way by justifying actions that subject girls and women to ill-treatment by men. In short, misogyny is an underlying theme that strongly impacts the lives of girls and women spotlighted in this book.

These, then, are the underlying commonalities we see in the three fundamentalist communities. We now look at each of them more closely with brief histories of each as well as their locations in the contemporary world. Then we turn to a more in-depth look at the lives of girls and women in these highly gendered societies.

Chapter Two

Who Are They?

Fundamentalists are boundary-setters; they excel at marking themselves off from others by distinctive dress, customs and conduct.
—Martin E. Marty and R. Scott Appleby, *Fundamentalisms and Society*, 1993

Before delving into the treatment of girls and women in these three fundamentalist religious communities, I want to contextualize who the three groups are by highlighting the history and contemporary circumstances of each one. All three are embedded in larger nation states: in the United States, the Satmar Hasidim and the Fundamentalist Church of Jesus Christ of Latter Day-Saints, and in Afghanistan and to a lesser extent Pakistan, the Pashtun.

As we know from chapter 1, the U.S.-based sects' ability to grow and flourish has been heavily dependent on their access to and use of government aid on the local, state, and federal levels. The Pashtun, however—who are the largest ethnic group in Afghanistan—lack such support. The physical environments in which each of these populations reside are vastly different as well. The Satmar live primarily in an urban neighborhood in New York, one of the world's most cosmopolitan cities, as well as in a village in upstate New York, while the Mormon fundamentalists largely reside in two small isolated towns in parched corners of Arizona and Utah far from the bright lights of a major urban center. The vast majority of Pashtun live in the traditional Pashtun homeland, an area south of the Amu Darya River in Afghanistan and west of the Indus River in Pakistan. Because of geography and topography, this is a region that is somewhat isolated from the outside world.

Despite their vastly different cultures, histories, and geographies, what is truly remarkable about these three groups is the similarities in the fundamen-

19

talist tenets that they hold dear. Out of these doctrines spring their ideologies about and treatment of girls and women, a topic to which we will return after providing some background about each community.

HASIDISM: JEWISH FUNDAMENTALISTS

The less they know about the outside world the better.

—Hasidic rabbi, 2018

Hasidism, of which the Satmar are one faction or "court," arose during the 1700s as a Jewish spiritual revival movement in what is today western Ukraine. The movement then spread rapidly throughout eastern Europe. The founding father of Hasidism was Rabbi Israel Baal Shem Tov (1700–1760)—a title meaning "Master of the Good Name"—who was considered a great scholar and mystic of his day.

The movement was, in many ways, a response to the void felt by many ordinary religious Jews of the era. The Baal Shem Tov and his followers fostered a mode of Jewish life that stressed the ability of *all* Jews to become closer to God through their thoughts and behavior. This contrasted with the scholarly perspective of the Jewish religious leaders of the period who emphasized the primacy of the study of Torah. The early Hasidic movement encouraged the poor and oppressed Jews of pogrom-ravaged eastern Europe to be less bookish and more emotional, to be less ascetic and more joyous, while focusing less on the exact substance of rituals and focusing more on the deep feelings that rituals can impart. Consequently, the movement adopted a somewhat populist stance in the positive way it viewed simple, unschooled Jews as distinct from the elite intellectual religious authorities of that period.

Here is the way one writer expressed the appeal of this new take on Orthodox Judaism to the unlettered Jews of the era: "Caught up in the fervor and magic of a collective spiritual experience, the Hasid could forget the daily grind of eking out a living. He could forget, too, his nagging sense of inadequacy in the face of the abstruse and convoluted Talmudic texts" (Landau 1993:28–29).

The trait perhaps most associated with Hasidism is the singular value of joy and ecstatic prayer as an integral part of worship and religious life in general. Singing, dancing, and clapping hands are among the most pronounced elements of Hasidic rituals. Hasids observe God's commandments as expressed in heartfelt prayer and infinite love of the Deity and the world he created. Many Hasidic ideas are, in fact, derived from Jewish mysticism (*kabbalah*), the ancient Jewish tradition of the mystical interpretation of the Bible.

The adherents of Hasidism are organized in independent sects known as "courts" or "dynasties," each headed by its own hereditary leader or Rebbe. In the early days the followers of a particular Rebbe usually lived in the same town in eastern Europe so that Hasidic courts were referred to by the location of their leader's settlement. Over the years, after moving to the West and to Israel, Hasidic dynasties retained the names of their original towns. Hence, the Belz Hasids originated in the town of Belz in western Ukraine and the Lubavitzer Hasids came from the town of Lubavitsh in Poland, later a part of Russia.

A defining doctrine of Hasidism is that of the saintly leader who serves as both an inspirational and foundational figure around whom followers are organized. The Rebbe represents the collectivity of his Hasidic community. He is the sect's supreme authority in all matters secular and religious. Reverence for and submission to the court's Rebbe is a hallmark of Hasidism; he is viewed as the spiritual authority with whom followers must bond and obey in order to become close to God. The Rebbe's followers are also expected to consult with him on all important matters and seek his advice and blessing. As such, it is nearly impossible for a Hasid to have no specific affiliation; almost all Hasids are followers of a particular Rebbe.

Aside from his spiritual status, the Rebbe is also the administrative head of the community. Each Hasidic court typically has its own synagogues, study halls, ritual bathhouses, and charitable organizations, and larger courts maintain their own school systems. The various courts share basic precepts but function independently, and each possesses unique traits and customs.

Slight differences in headgear and dress distinguish the members of one court from another. And garb does play an important role in differentiating one Hasidic sect from another. Even the way men wear their sidelocks (*payos*), whether loose or curled around the ears, or how they maintain their beards, either long and scraggly or short and neat, is a mark of identity for those in the know. Similarly, the length and color of a woman's skirt, the density of the stockings she wears, and her type of head covering are all clues as to which Hasidic court she belongs (Biale et al. 2018).

Affiliation with a court is often maintained in families for generations. Hence, being Hasidic is as much a sociological role as a purely religious one since it entails being born into a specific faith community that is allied with a dynasty of Rebbes.

JUDAISM ON STEROIDS: THE SATMAR OF WILLIAMSBURG AND KIRYAS JOEL

What Pat Buchanan is to the Republican Party is what the Satmar are to Hasidim.

—Amy Verdon, "Rebbe to Wear," 2005

The Satmar Hasidim first emerged in the early years of the twentieth century as one offshoot of the larger Hasidic movement in Satu-Mare (Satmar), a town in Transylvania, a region of Hungary outside the central orbit of Hasidism. The sect, led by its founding Rebbe Yo'el (Joel) Teitelbaum (1886–1979), fiercely fought assimilation and religious reform, both of which were more pervasive in Hungary than in other Hasidic areas such as Poland and the Ukraine. Rebbe Yo'el took an uncompromisingly conservative stance against modernization and any relaxation of religious tradition. Or as noted religion scholar Samuel Heilman (2017) put it, the Rebbe "embraced a defiant insular Jewish Orthodoxy." Among other issues, he was a fierce opponent of Zionism and the founding of the State of Israel, insisting that such a Jewish homeland should not be established before the arrival of the Messiah (Rubin 1972, 1997).

The sect grew in the years following World War II after the Rebbe's rescue from Hungary in 1944. He subsequently emigrated to the Williamsburg section of Brooklyn, New York. After the war this neighborhood and the Satmar rabbinical court became a center to which large numbers of ultra-Orthodox Hungarian Jews fled, many having escaped the Holocaust only because Hungary was the last country to come under Nazi control. Today an estimated 65,000 Satmar live in Williamsburg with another 24,000 in Kiryas Joel ("Joel's Village") in Orange County, about fifty miles north of New York City. The Satmar are now the largest Hasidic sect in the United States and the one that is widely considered the most traditional and conservative of Hasidic courts (Berger 2012; Weiss, Neumeister, and Mintz 1995).

The Satmar's founding Rebbe subsequently became a controversial figure. Many scholars have noted that Rabbi Yo'el's position regarding the Holocaust and the State of Israel in the postwar years was extreme compared to the views of other rabbis and leaders of the Orthodox community. Yet the

Rebbe Yo'el Teitelbaum
Source: **Wikimedia Commons**

worldview he cultivated, coupled with his theological explanations of the
Holocaust, drew a growing number of followers who believed he defended

the last remnant of a traditional Orthodox ideology and way of life. As his public stature grew, criticism from within the Satmar community moderated, while criticism from without was disregarded and dismissed as slander perpetrated by Zionists (Keren-Kratz 2014a).

Just what is the specific controversy surrounding the Rebbe? In the early 1940s, through his connections with various government and religious authorities, he became privy to reports on the extermination of Jewish communities in Poland. Yet he refrained from calling on his followers in Hungary to prepare themselves for the coming onslaught. To the contrary, he warned his supporters that emigration to what was then Palestine or to other countries including the United States would endanger their Hasidic way of life. At the same time, he thwarted all attempts at cooperation between the leaders of other Orthodox communities and Zionist organizations that might have helped save many of his followers from the Holocaust. When the danger of war became imminent, Rabbi Yo'el did his best to secure for himself and his closest allies visas that would facilitate their escape to Palestine or the United States. His attempts to leave Hungary were part of a broader effort by rabbis and other public figures to flee the country. At the same time there were many other religious leaders, among them Rabbi Yo'el's own relatives, who refused to save themselves and abandon their congregations to whatever fate awaited them (Keren-Kratz 2014a).

Many sources describe the rescue activities of the Orthodox community during the Holocaust and suggest that compared to other rabbis who survived the "final solution," Rabbi Yo'el's attempts to save his followers were negligible at best. Criticism concerning his conduct pursued Rabbi Yo'el during the war years and persisted after the war ended. As a result, the Rebbe felt compelled to explain his flight from Hungary, his objection to emigration to Palestine and the United States—despite his own brief sojourn in the former and settlement in the latter—and his use of a Zionist-sponsored transport that enabled him and his close associates to escape from Hungary (Keren-Kratz 2014b).

He responded to his critics in a series of exhortations that sought to justify his own behavior, including his fierce anti-Zionism. "The Holocaust," he proclaimed, "is God's punishment of the Jewish people for its sins, and primarily for the sin of Zionism." He went on: "The Zionists bear the blame for the Holocaust not only because of their ideological concept, but also because of their actions, which included provoking Hitler and causing him to take revenge upon the people of Israel, obstructing emigration to other countries so as to force Jews to settle in Palestine, and the closure of their borders to immigrants following the demand to establish a Jewish state" (quoted in Keren-Kratz 2014b).

Here Teitelbaum was adopting an extreme form of theodicy, the belief that suffering must be the punishment for sin. As such, the Holocaust was divine punishment for the migration of Jews to the Holy Land before the arrival of the Messiah and, even worse, for the establishment of the State of Israel. It was in this sense that he believed the Nazis were the instruments through which God punished the Jews (Biale et al. 2018).

In more recent years one of Rebbe Yo'el's most controversial rulings was a prohibition against visiting, let alone praying at, Jerusalem's newly liberated Western Wall following the 1967 war. Curses, not blessings, were all that could be incurred by treading on ground contaminated by the evil Zionist army, he declared (Nadler 2011a). Then, too, his anti-Zionism led him to prohibit his followers from speaking modern Hebrew, the language of Israel.

Over time the Rebbe became well known for his ultra-conservative, anti-modern, and anti-Zionist views. Like some other rabbis, Rabbi Yo'el believed that Zionism was bound to intensify the desecration of Orthodox Jewish tradition, especially after the establishment of the State of Israel. He railed against Zionism along with the assimilationist tendencies of many Jews, describing both as catalysts for the Holocaust.

These extreme ideological stances helped consolidate his followers around a singular, albeit controversial, identity. The Rebbe was very successful in attracting non-Hasidic and non-Satmar ultra-Orthodox Jews to his court in the years after he arrived in the United States, resulting in the Satmar becoming, as we have seen, the largest Hasidic sect in North America.

The Rebbe's Satmar became known for their reclusive lifestyle and zealous religious views. From the first days of its presence in Brooklyn there was a belligerent quality to the Satmar court that stemmed from its unique sense of pious virtue that was largely directed against fellow Jews. The Rebbe proclaimed that "the very act of declaring separateness from the wicked strengthens the commitment of the righteous." In endorsing passive resistance and cultural isolation, the Rebbe was determined to wage an unremitting struggle against Jews who acted—even in the most minor way—like gentiles (quoted in Heilman 2017:172; Biale et al. 2018).

Today the Satmar have the reputation of being the most rigorous of the Hasidic courts in building protective ideological, social, and physical boundaries around their communities. They are not just insular but also are engaged in an ongoing culture war against modernity. As a consequence, it has been said of the Satmar that in "the orthodox Jewish world, it does not get any more conservative" (Davidman 2015; Verdon 2005).

One scathing critic, a former Hasid himself, has decried the rigidity of the brand of Judaism as practiced by the Satmar. Calling it "radical Jewish fundamentalism," he asserted that "the only difference between the Satmar and the most radical Islamic fundamentalists is that so far, the Satmar have not wired their children with explosive devices " (Lost Messiah 2018).

Satmar are unusual in another way. Unlike Lubavitchers, a Hasidic court also based in Brooklyn that proselytizes to secular Jews and urges them to return to traditional religious practices, the Satmar are very fastidious about their bloodlines and are highly insular and unwelcoming to outsiders. They have a strong preference for marrying within the sect or marrying other Hasidim of Hungarian origin; they will not marry a Lubavitcher. From the Satmar point of view, "Lubavitchers are damaged goods" (Verdon 2005).

Under the purview of Rebbe Yo'el Teitelbaum, the Jewish life of prewar Hungary was recreated nearly unchanged in Brooklyn. Today Satmar dress would fit right in with that of a nineteenth-century *shtetl*[1] in Hungary. This is particularly true of Satmar men, who, on ceremonial occasions, wear large round fur hats and white knee-stockings tucked into their dark calf-length trousers. "Joel turned his back on secular education," according to a reference librarian at Yeshiva University in New York City. He viewed it as a dangerous tool of acculturation and only the bare minimum would be permitted. "He wanted [to maintain] the folkways, the food, the clothing, even the humor of Eastern Europe" (quoted in Powell 2006a).

The contemporary Satmar are probably the most separatist and bellicose of Hasidic sects. They are resistant to almost all behaviors, activities, styles, and contacts that would lead them to even the slightest accommodation with mainstream American culture. They seek instead to create their own world. For women it is a world that is devoted to the upkeep of a strictly kosher home. For men it is one that is given over to the study of sacred religious texts.

The Rebbe was famous (or infamous) in large part because of his unswerving and increasingly bitter opposition to Zionism, the State of Israel, and all forms of Judaism, including other Hasidic courts, that differed in any way from his own version of an ultra-Orthodox way of life. His writings,

---

1. A *shtetl* is a small Jewish town or village in eastern Europe.

while reflecting a great deal of rabbinic erudition, are polemical edicts, including the repeated charge that the Holocaust was divine punishment for the evil deeds of Zionists and assimilationist Jews. "It is because of the Zionists," Teitelbaum vehemently asserted, "that six million Jews were killed" (quoted in Powell 2006a).

While Rebbe Yo'el and his Hasidim represent something of a "last stand" for certain traditional Jewish attitudes and practices, he was viewed with hostility by most other Jewish groups—including by other Hasidim—as being exceedingly self-righteous and unrealistically antagonistic to the modern world. In short, as Samuel Heilman, professor of Jewish Studies at Queens College–CUNY, has put it, the Rebbe believed that "it was possible to live in this country in a way that was resistant, in the most scrupulous way, against any kind of assimilation" (Green 2009; quoted in Samaha 2014).

As part of this separatist stance, the principal language of Satmar in Brooklyn and their upstate outpost in Kiryas Joel is Yiddish—over 94 percent of residents speak that language—a practice that ensures the community's ongoing isolation from the larger society in which it is embedded. They speak as little English as possible in their daily lives. Sometime in the 1970s Yiddish replaced English as the language of instruction in Satmar schools. At that time licensed New York City public school teachers were replaced by recent graduates of the Satmar girls' school, Bais Rochel, in Williamsburg. Writes one former Satmar who attended that school: "My classmates and I were taught Judaic studies, starting with the aleph-bet in kindergarten and continuing with the weekly *parsha*, or Torah portion, stories in Yiddish. Our textbooks were highly censored with permanent markers and crayons to block out material perceived as a threat to our sheltered brains" (Goldberger 2014a). In Satmar schools young people learn there is no such thing as biological evolution or the State of Israel. And, as one observer put it, "science is an unwelcome term in Satmar" (Rubin 1997:179).

The graduates of Satmar schools, especially boys, are barely literate in English and the schools award neither high school diplomas nor GEDs. Boys receive even less English-language instruction than girls since most of the boys' time in school is devoted to the study of Jewish texts. As a result, if you are a Satmar male, you are either a Torah scholar or a businessman, or you have a blue-collar job. There are very few accountants and no lawyers, doctors, or other professionals among them.

Evidence of limited literacy in English among yeshiva boys is recounted by Shulem Deen in his recollections of growing up Hasidic. A common sight in high school study halls in Hasidic yeshivas, Deen notes, was students learning to sign their names in English, practicing it for their marriage license. For many, it was the first time writing their names in anything but Yiddish or Hebrew. Moreover, he remarks, his own teenage sons—who remain in the Hasidic sect in which he was raised—cannot speak, read, or write English beyond a second grade level (Vizel 2018). Similarly, a woman who works as a physician at a hospital in a Hasidic neighborhood in Brooklyn says she often sees adult male patients who can barely communicate to her what their medical problem is. "It's not just that they're like immigrants, barely able to speak the language," she said. "It's also a lack of knowledge of basic physiology. They can barely name their own body parts" (quoted in Deen 2018).

According to the New York State Department of Education, nearly one-third of all students in Jewish religious schools are "English language learners," Yiddish being their first language. Moreover, reports suggest that many boys schools do not teach the ABCs until children are seven or eight years old. Boys in elementary and middle school study religious subjects from about eight in the morning to three thirty in the afternoon, followed by about ninety minutes of English and math. But as one graduate of these boys schools puts it, "English, math and science were considered 'profane'" subjects (Miller 2014).

Yet, according to new guidelines issued in 2018 by New York State's Education Department, all yeshiva elementary schools *must* teach a "substantially equivalent education" as is taught in public schools. This means a minimum of six hours of secular studies daily. Satmar yeshivas are clearly in violation of this guideline since, as we have seen, they only have secular classes for ninety minutes at the end of the school day. Not surprisingly, this new directive did not sit well with Satmar Rebbe Aaron Teitelbaum. Shortly after the guidelines were issued the Rebbe gave clear instructions to his followers to defy the Education Department's new orders: "We will *not* obey the Education Commissioner in any way," he averred in a fiery speech in Yiddish before a gathering of thousands of Satmar men in a Williamsburg warehouse (quoted in *Yeshiva World News* 2018).

Women are expected to be more fluent and literate in English and also to know more math because it is they who are more likely than men to interact with the world outside Satmar. Newly married women are also apt to briefly take paid employment to help support the family while their husbands continue studying in *kollels*, schools for full-time advanced study of the Talmud and rabbinic literature (Idov 2010).

In recent years the Satmar have been battling the state of New York over their failure—in disregard of New York State law—to provide a secular education for their children. Parents and other interested parties, both from within Satmar and those who have left the sect, have been insisting that New York authorities enforce the current statute. They claim that Satmar's non-compliance with state law was condemning children to a life of poverty and reliance on public handouts. Without minimal skills in English and lacking a secular curriculum, a new generation of Satmar children will be unable to find employment in all but a small number of jobs, these critics assert (Adlerstein 2016; Taylor 2017).

This is not the only battle between Satmar and outsiders. Some longstanding differences and tensions between the Satmar and certain Hasidic courts have been exacerbated over the last few decades. One such feud is between the Hungarian Satmar and the Russian-Polish Lubavitch, who are divided over the Lubavitch tolerance for some aspects of modern life and secular customs as well as Zionism. As we know, the Satmar vehemently oppose the State of Israel, viewing it as a blasphemous entity, and they teach their young people not only to hate Zionism but to hate Zionists. The Lubavitch, on the other hand, have accommodated themselves to Israel's existence and have become involved in attempts to influence Israeli politics and social policies that would serve to increase strict religious observance (Briggs 1983).

In a certain sense the Satmar's enmity towards the Lubavitchers is a reaction to the latter's success in converting young secular Jews to a Hasidic way of life. The insular, xenophobic Satmar strongly condemn the Lubavitchers' outreach to such Jews and particularly resent attempts to entice Satmar men into joining the Lubavitch community. A leader of the Satmar court said about one young Satmar's dalliance with Lubavitch religious texts: "It's worse than if he was to join the Moonies." Such discord between the two has resulted in several violent outbreaks over the years (quoted in Harris 1985:177).

It also is possible that some of the bad blood that exists between the Satmar and Lubavitchers is based on the fact that Lubavitch women are considerably more worldly than Satmar women. Lubavitch women, along with their husbands, actively proselytize non-religious Jews, an activity that often takes them to far-flung corners of the globe (Morris 1995).

A far more serious feud arose within the Satmar court itself. The dispute dates back to 1999 when Rabbi Moses Teitelbaum—the nephew of Yo'el Teitelbaum, who had no sons of his own—appointed his youngest son, Zalman, to lead the Williamsburg congregation. Aaron, Moses's oldest son, was already head of the congregation in Kiryas Joel, the Satmar village in upstate New York. This appointment was viewed as a signal from Rabbi Moses that after his death Zalman was to become chief rabbi of the Satmar, an unexpected turn of events since Aaron Teitelbaum not only had trained to become the Grand Rebbe, but also had represented his father in community affairs. Moreover, according to Hasidic tradition the chief rabbi position generally goes to the older son.

As a result, Aaron and his followers viewed the power split as an attempt to make Zalman the Grand Rebbe of *all* Satmar. But Zalman actually saw his father's decision as a way to deal with the fact that the congregation had grown too large to be handled by one man. Satmar is not only the largest Hasidic community in New York City, but Hasids consult frequently with their Rebbe. They seek his advice on every major and some minor issues, from business deals to family matters to the decision of whom to marry. Zalman asked, How could one man counsel some 65,000 Satmar in Williamsburg and another 24,000 in Kiryas Joel? (Clevstrom 2005)

By the time Rebbe Moses died in 2006, the court was sharply divided into factions organized around each of the Rebbe's two heirs. As if to emphasize the point, both brothers emerged from mourning their father wearing the white socks and silver-topped canes that are the traditional symbols of a Grand Rebbe. This conflict was fueled, in part, by a legion of Hasidic court bureaucrats and their hangers-on. The dispute also resulted in several rounds of litigation. In the end, many jobs and other benefits depend on which son is in charge (Popper 2006; Brostoff 2007).

The Satmar congregation has control over a wide array of educational, religious, and charitable institutions and facilities valued at well over $500 million. For all the putative poverty among its congregants—and there is a lot of evidence for it—the Satmar as a religious organization is an economic powerhouse. It operates its own welfare network, insurance and pension plans, ambulance and security services, and burial society. It has a sizeable organization, Bikur Cholim, that arranges visits to sick co-religionists, especially those in hospitals, and provides patients with kosher food. The Satmar also run the largest Jewish school system in the country. In addition, the sect owns a matzo factory, a kosher meat market, a pharmacy, an employment agency, a loan company, and real estate holdings worth tens of millions of dollars. And this does not include what has been called "a social-service empire" with access to millions of public dollars for health care, welfare, food stamps, special education, and public housing. In short, at stake is control of a nearly 90,000-member congregation along with its myriad assets (Belcove-Shalin 1995; Heilman 2017).[2]

While Aaron occasionally bows to the imperatives of the modern world, Zalman, in contrast, is a proud *kanoi*—a zealot. Nevertheless, as one of Aaron's followers averred, "We're the most ultra-, ultra-, ultra-orthodox in the world." And today thousands of Satmar define themselves as either "Zalis" or "Aaronis," that is, followers of Zalman Teitelbaum or Aaron Teitelbaum (quoted in Powell 2006b).

The long-term split is felt in a number of ways. It has hurt matchmaking, for example, because families from one faction say they do not want a son or daughter to marry someone from the other faction. The rift has also been impacting Satmar political power. In Kiryas Joel, for example, the fracture in the community diminished the town's political clout in state elections. In 2012 Kiryas Joel split its vote between the Republican candidate for state office, who received just under 70 percent of the vote, and the Democrat, who received about 30 percent. The number of votes that went to the Democrat was particularly striking because he is openly gay, an attribute that would presumably be anathema to socially conservative Satmar voters (Wakin 2002; *Crain's New York Business* 2012).

A number of these followers are more than willing to brawl in service of their chosen Rebbe. Since early in the new millennium there have been fights, torched cars, and fire-bombed homes. These divisions took a particularly ugly turn in 2005 when police broke up a melee of hundreds of members from the two opposing factions outside a Williamsburg synagogue. The brawl reportedly erupted when Aaron's followers, accompanied by hired nightclub bouncers, forced their way into Zalman's *shul* (synagogue). As a result, twenty-six Satmar were arrested. With some of Rabbi Aaron's followers from Kiryas Joel moving back to the old Satmar neighborhood in Brooklyn and with Aaron still determined to become the Grand Rebbe of all Satmar, the community is steeling itself for more violence. Still, the enmity between the two has "added a vitality to Satmar, as each side has garnered

---

2. In the mid-1980s Rebbe Moses convinced government authorities to officially designate the Satmar as a "disadvantaged minority," which allowed them to receive a wide array of welfare benefits including food stamps (Heilman 2017).

intense loyalty among its members while trying to outdo the other" (Popper 2006; Biale et al. 2018:691).

Yet another problem confronting the Satmar in both camps is the changing nature of their Brooklyn neighborhood itself as the "artists" (*artisen* in Yiddish)—the Satmar term of derision that encompasses hipsters, Rastafarians, and yuppies—move into the newly "hip" Williamsburg section of Brooklyn. Public notices posted in the neighborhood portray the recent arrival of artists as an ominous threat. One included a drawing of the World Trade Center in a state of collapse and read in Yiddish, "How long did it take the Twin Towers to fall? Eight seconds. How long will it take for Williamsburg??? God Forbid" (cited in Idov 2010). Another asked the "Master of the Universe" to "please remove from upon us the plague of the artists, so that we shall not drown in evil waters, and so that they shall not come to our residence to ruin it" (cited in Bahrampour 2004).

As Rebbe Zalman has said about the invasion of artists in Williamsburg: "You must close your curtains and pray and remember what it is to be Satmar. This is our *shtetl*, and our walls must go high." Then, too, there were many complaints from the Satmar about "scantily clad" female riders on a newly constructed bike lane that ran through the neighborhood. Parenthetically, a Hasidic modesty squad in the neighborhood warned Satmar to stay inside during the "dirty" New York Marathon so they would not see "impure, immodestly dressed, dirty runners" (quoted in Powell 2006; *Failed Messiah* 2014b).

One issue that does not divide the two Satmar heirs is Israel. In keeping with the strident anti-Zionism of his great-uncle, his father, and his brother, Rabbi Zalman Teitelbaum called on his followers to protest Israeli prime minister Benjamin Netanyahu's 2015 visit to the United States, saying that the prime minister's assertion that he speaks on behalf of all Jews was "an unparalleled desecration of God, a serious provocation against the nations" (quoted in Nachshoni 2015). As part of these protests several dozen Satmar boys ran down the street shouting slogans like "A Jew is not a Zionist" and "Israeli government, shame on you," all the while hurling eggs at a vehicle the boys were led to believe carried Netanyahu. These protests coincided with large anti-Zionist demonstrations by Satmar men in front of the Israeli Consulate in New York City (Adlerstein 2016).

Before turning to the Christian and Muslim fundamentalist communities discussed in this book, a closing word about the Satmar. Because of their rigorously religious lifestyle, employment for Satmar men and women can be highly problematic. Some have jobs in Satmar-owned businesses in Williamsburg like kosher butchers, grocery stores, and shops selling religious articles, and both men and women teach in Satmar schools. Others are employed in their own religiously approved businesses such as firms in Manhattan's diamond district on West Forty-Seventh Street and B&H Electronics on Ninth Avenue in Manhattan. Through such employment many Satmar are able to maintain a middle-class standard of living, which for them invariably includes religious school tuition for their large broods of children.

B&H and a few similar businesses provide a work environment that is completely controlled by the ultra-Orthodox community. What is very unusual about this business—particularly in these days of the round-the-clock Internet—is that B&H's online store shuts down every time B&H closes for religious reasons. No B&H business, either online or in its popular store in Manhattan, is conducted on the Jewish Sabbath—from sundown Friday to sundown Saturday all year round—or on any Jewish holiday. Also reflecting Satmar values is the job segregation of men and women at B&H. Nearly all salespeople are men, as are all store managers, while all the cashiers and store greeters are women (Plante 2015).

While jobs at B&H and several other Satmar-controlled companies pay salaries that provide a decent standard of living for their Satmar employees, poverty is still an important issue for Satmar both in Brooklyn and in Kiryas Joel. By the late 1990s at least one-third of families in Williamsburg were receiving public assistance. A 2011 report on poverty in several New York counties found that 55 percent of Jewish households in Williamsburg were poor and another 17 percent were near-poor. It is indeed true that government assistance makes much of the Satmar lifestyle possible for the poor in Williamsburg, given the high cost of kosher food, private school tuition, and rising rents in the neighborhood (Bronstein 2015).

The residents of Kiryas Joel are also poor. In 2011 the community had the highest proportion of its population living in poverty of any of the nation's 3,700 villages, towns, or cities with at least 10,000 residents. About 70 percent of the village's residents live in households whose income falls below the federal poverty line—a figure 16 percent higher than for any other municipality in the United States. Its median family income of $17,929 and per capita income of $4,494 rank lower than any other comparable place in the country. Nearly half of the village's households reported less than $15,000 in annual income. A majority of its residents receive food stamps and one-third receive Medicaid benefits and rely on federal vouchers to help pay their housing costs. Still, so as not to emphasize differences in wealth among residents of his very poor community, Rebbe Aaron decreed that diamond rings were no longer acceptable as engagement presents and that only one-man bands would be allowed at Satmar weddings (Samaha 2014; Roberts 2011).

The reason why so many Satmar live in poverty is evident. With a high birth rate and so many young to feed, clothe, house, and educate and with little secular training and few English skills, supporting a large family under such conditions is difficult at best. That is why a United Jewish Appeal's report on the Jewish population in Brooklyn noted that over 50 percent of Jewish Williamsburg residents were under eighteen and that without government funding the community "would have expired a long time ago" (quoted in Bronstein 2015).

MORMON FUNDAMENTALISM

The Fundamentalist Church of Jesus Christ of Latter-Day Saints (FLDS) is one of several fundamentalist sects that broke with the mainline Mormon Church—officially known as the Church of Jesus Christ of Latter-day Saints—primarily over the question of polygamy.[3] These fundamentalist sects believe in certain aspects of Mormonism as practiced in the nineteenth century, particularly during the era of Joseph Smith and Brigham Young, the first two presidents of the Mormon Church. In essence, Mormon fundamentalists seek to maintain beliefs and practices no longer held by mainstream Mormons, especially the practice of plural marriage, which is also known as "the Principle" or "Celestial Marriage." Mormon fundamentalists view plural marriage as essential for attaining the highest degree of happiness in the "Celestial Kingdom," the final place of residence for those who have been righteous and who have accepted the teachings of Jesus Christ and lived up to all of the required covenants of Mormonism (Quinn 1998).

In 1878 the U.S. Supreme Court ruled that "polygamy leads to the patriarchal principle . . . which when applied to large communities, fetters the people in stationary despotism, while that principle cannot long exist in connection with monogamy" (cited in Hamilton 2014). This ruling was followed by an 1890 decree by the president of the Mormon Church prohibiting

3. In 2019 leaders of the mainline faith announced a game-changing divine revelation: that God had told the church's president that church members should no longer call themselves "Mormons" (Dias 2019).

plural marriage in the United States. In 1896, before Utah was granted statehood, the federal government required it to include a provision in its state constitution that "polygamous or plural marriages are forever prohibited" (Utah Constitution, Article 03).

With this decree Mormon fundamentalists broke with the mother church, believing that this and other principles were incorrectly forsaken by the Mormon Church in its attempt to be accepted by mainstream American society. Thereafter the practice of polygamy went underground and survived in various isolated communities in the American Southwest and more openly in fundamentalist Mormon colonies in northern Mexico and western Canada. Today an estimated 21,000 men, women, and children are Mormon polygamists affiliated with a number of sects. It is noteworthy that the Mormon Church vigorously rejects the term "Mormon fundamentalists" and prefers the phrase "polygamist sects" to make it abundantly clear that the main body of Mormon believers do not practice polygamy. The contemporary Mormon Church does not recognize any of these breakaway groups (Quinn 1993).

THE FUNDAMENTALIST CHURCH OF JESUS CHRIST OF LATTER-DAY SAINTS

The work of God is a benevolent dictatorship. It is not a democracy.
—Prophet Warren Jeffs (quoted in Hyde 2016)

The Fundamentalist Church of Jesus Christ of Latter-Day Saints (FLDS) has the reputation of being the most unbendingly patriarchal Mormon fundamentalist sect in existence and is sometimes dubbed the "American Taliban" because of its treatment of women. The FLDS broke with the Mormon Church proper in the early twentieth century and today it is the largest polygamist sect in North America. Membership in the FLDS is estimated at somewhere between 10,000 and 15,000, with about two-thirds of those living in the neighboring towns of Hildale, Utah, and Colorado City, Arizona. There are also small FLDS communities in Salt Lake City, Utah; Eldorado and Mancos, Texas; Pringle, South Dakota; Creston and Bountiful, British Columbia; Baja California and Senora, Mexico; and several other scattered locales. Like the Satmar, these Mormon fundamentalists do not proselytize. As a consequence, up to three-quarters of FLDS members were born into fundamentalism and some are members of families that have practiced polygamy for generations (Moore-Emmett 2004; Quinn 1993).

The headquarters of this breakaway sect was established in 1913 in what was then known as Short Creek, an isolated town in Arizona located on the southern border with Utah. The town soon became a gathering place for former members of the Mormon Church who refused to give up the practice of polygamy. In 1935 the Mormon Church officially excommunicated the Mormon residents of Short Creek who refused to sign an oath renouncing the practice. The settlement eventually expanded into Utah and became incorporated as the twin municipalities of Hildale, Utah, and Colorado City, Arizona. Both communities are still the center of FLDS fundamentalism.

Aside from the practice of polygamy, FLDS members differ in another respect from mainstream Mormons. They are allowed to consume coffee and alcohol because the sect split from the Mormon Church before it began its strict adherence to the "Word of Wisdom," that faith's health code, which prohibits alcohol, tobacco, tea, and coffee (*Salt Lake Tribune* 2013).

After its founding the first notable event to take place in what was then Short Creek was the (in)famous 1953 raid, which resulted from a decision by Arizona state authorities to crack down on polygamy. The Short Creek raid was the largest mass arrest of polygamists in American history and it received considerable press coverage at the time, much of it negative. State police officers and National Guard soldiers invaded the FLDS community and arrested all of its residents, including well over two hundred children, two-thirds of whom were not allowed to return to their parents for more than two years; some parents never regained custody (Bradley 1993).

After the raid, which deeply shook the community, FLDS members became increasingly isolated from the outside world. The church's teachings about the sinfulness of "gentiles"—that is, non-FLDS members—increased along with the notion that gentiles are utterly wicked and must be shunned at all costs. FLDS leaders also taught then and still teach that African Americans are the worst of the gentile lot. Moreover, when the Mormon Church started allowing African American men to attain its priesthood in 1978, the FLDS began calling regular Mormons, including Mitt Romney, part of the "abominable church of the devil" (Weyermann 2011).[4]

In short, the world beyond Short Creek was to be feared. Even today access to the Internet, cell phones, newspapers, television, radio, popular music, and movies is strictly forbidden and only books and magazines ap-

---

4. In 2005 the Southern Poverty Law Center added the FLDS Church to its list of hate groups because of the church's racist doctrines, including its fiery condemnation of interracial relationships.

proved by FLDS leaders can be read. All such prohibitions make the sect increasingly insular and effectively cut off its followers from any information about the outside world. And, as if this isolation were not enough, a security force known as the "God Squad" was maintained to chase outsiders from town (Brower 2012; Woods 2018).

A second major event in FLDS history was the establishment and subsequent loss of its new community in Texas. Beginning in 2004 published reports suggested a shift of FLDS headquarters might be taking place from the twin towns in Arizona and Utah to Eldorado, Texas, where a temple was being built by members of the church. Once the new FLDS outpost—called the Yearning for Zion Ranch, or the YFZ Ranch—was established a significant number of the church's "most faithful" members relocated there. At one time as many as seven hundred sect members lived on the YFZ Ranch and its surrounding 1,700 acres of land. Estimates suggest that the property and its structures were worth around $3 million. When the complex was under construction it was mischaracterized as a "corporate hunting retreat" in order to hide its true nature as an FLDS outpost (Lewan 2008).

In March 2008 the hotline in a domestic violence shelter in Texas received a call from a girl claiming to be a sixteen-year-old victim of physical and sexual abuse at the YFZ Ranch. The girl was never located, but the call triggered a large-scale operation at the ranch by Texas law enforcement and child welfare officials. The authorities said that the children living there either had been abused or were at the risk of future abuse. Troopers and child welfare officials searched the ranch and a total of 462 children were eventually removed and taken into temporary custody by the state of Texas. Over one hundred women also left the ranch to accompany their children. In May of that year an appeals court issued a writ finding that there was not sufficient evidence that the children were in enough immediate danger to justify keeping them in state custody. A year after the raid two-thirds of the families were back at the ranch with sect leaders promising to end underage marriages, which had been widely reported to have taken place at the ranch (Pilkington 2008; CNN 2008).

In 2012 the Texas attorney general's office began legal proceedings in an effort to seize the YFZ Ranch, with the authorities arguing that the purchase of the ranch property had taken place in an isolated rural area so that the sexual assault of children would be shielded from the interference of law enforcement authorities. The property, therefore, was contraband and subject to seizure since under state law property that is used to commit or facilitate criminal conduct can be confiscated by the state. In 2014 the state of Texas took physical and legal possession of the YFZ Ranch and its surrounding land (Reavy 2012).

The two cataclysmic events described above took place under the purview of a succession of men who have led the FLDS Church since its founding. These men regarded themselves as "prophets" who were called by God to their leadership positions. The most recent prophets were Rulon Jeffs, who led the group from 1986 to 2002, and his successor and son, Warren Jeffs, who has been the most visible and most controversial of the FLDS leaders.

For nearly two years early in the new millennium, Warren Jeffs was wanted on sex-crimes charges and for several months he was on the FBI's Ten Most Wanted list. In 2007 the state of Utah finally convicted him of being an accomplice to the rape of two young girls along with aggravated sexual assault, and he was sentenced to a minimum of ten years in prison (CNN 2007).

Apparently, not everyone was appalled by Warren Jeffs's behavior. After he was charged with two first-degree felony counts for being an accomplice

FBI TEN MOST WANTED FUGITIVE

UNLAWFUL FLIGHT TO AVOID PROSECUTION - SEXUAL CONDUCT WITH A MINOR, CONSPIRACY TO COMMIT SEXUAL CONDUCT WITH A MINOR; RAPE AS AN ACCOMPLICE

WARREN STEED JEFFS

Prophet Warren Jeffs on the FBI's Most Wanted list
Source: The Federal Bureau of Investigation

to rape by facilitating a marriage between a fourteen-year-old girl and her older cousin, Fox News host Tucker Carlson remarked on a radio program in 2006, "He's not accused of touching anybody; he is accused of facilitating a marriage between a sixteen-year-old girl and a twenty-seven-year-old man. That's the accusation. That's what they're calling felony rape. That's bull-shit. I'm sorry. Now this guy may be a child rapist. I'm just telling you that arranging a marriage between a sixteen-year-old and a twenty-seven-year-old is not the same as pulling a stranger off the street and raping her. That's bullshit" (Malloy 2019).

But this was not the only example of Jeffs sexually abusing young girls. It has long been known that he assaulted girls as young as twelve, sometimes after tying them up on an altar under a large domed structure specifically constructed for the purpose. He then raped them in front of his other wives and favored followers. Jeffs called these gatherings "Witnessings." Jeffs also sexually abused his own daughter Rachel from age eight on (Jeffs 2017).

After his arrest and trial, it was widely reported that Jeffs had resigned from his position as head of the FLDS and in 2007, following his conviction, his attorneys released the following statement: "Mr. Jeffs resigned as President of the Fundamentalist Church of Jesus Christ of Latter-Day Saints, Inc." (cited in Perkins 2007). This statement does *not* address his position as FLDS Prophet, only his resignation from his post as president of the corporation belonging to the church.

In fact, much like the Satmar Rebbes, Prophet Jeffs—even from prison—controls the daily lives of every man, woman, and child in the twin cities. In 2011 Jeffs reasserted his control over the church and FLDS leaders still have not clarified who is considered the church's Prophet. The issue of succession has become even more murky because there is very credible evidence that Warren Jeffs still leads the church from his prison cell through frequent phone calls and encrypted letters sent to several of his wives, who then pass on his orders to the faithful living in the twin towns. His wives also are said to wear watches equipped with recording devices when visiting him, thus taping his commands. And when all else fails, he relays instructions through his battery of well-paid defense attorneys (Hyde 2016).

Jeffs's status as a convicted and imprisoned sex offender seems to have done little to loosen his hold on many of his followers. They still await his revelations and follow his often strange commands. "Anybody who thinks that Warren Jeffs' incarceration ended his rule in this community has no idea what they're talking about. He is in many ways more powerful because now he's martyred," according to a journalist who has followed the FLDS for many years (Brower 2012).

In 2011 Jeffs was convicted and sentenced to life in prison plus twenty years for the sexual assaults of two of his underage brides. Within a month or so, the Prophet began issuing still more bizarre rules to his flock based on his "divine revelations." Now it was required that when getting dressed the FLDS faithful put on their clothes from right to left—right sleeve, right sock, right shoe first before putting on the left. There was also a long list of newly forbidden food items including potatoes, milk, beans, peas, onions, and garlic, a list that was later expanded to include chocolate, cocoa, corn, cabbage, cottage cheese, and cold cereal (Jeffs 2017).

Nonetheless, in several ways Jeffs's imprisonment has seriously weakened his traditional role as Prophet. Just as the Satmar look to their Rebbes for advice on most decisions, so too members of the FLDS rely on their Prophet for such counsel. In both cases their followers have been convinced that these religious figures have special knowledge, a talent or a gift that gives them extraordinary insight on all matters great and small. In the FLDS, as among the Satmar, all marriages must be approved by the Prophet and upon death he has to give his consent for a follower to enter heaven. Obviously, an imprisoned Jeffs is not available to serve the Prophet's role of counselor and conciliator.

Yet, it is Jeffs's responsibility as educator that has been most seriously hampered by his confinement in prison. In 1976, well before his elevation as Prophet, Jeffs became the principal of the private Alta Academy in Salt Lake City—despite having only a high school diploma—a role he maintained for the next twenty-two years. This was the FLDS school in which he trained an entire generation of the sect's children.

Each school day began with an hour-long devotional that included hymns, scripture reading, and sermons with the children repeating the school's motto that "perfect obedience produces perfect faith." Jeffs taught a number of subjects—math, history, accounting, home economics, geography, chorus—but it was his "destruction lectures" that, years later, were most memorable to his former pupils. He described in gruesome detail what would happen to the wicked gentiles in the days to come, telling his class that "this will be our last school year" because the destruction of the world was going to happen very soon (*FLDS 101* 2009d).

Jeffs began taping many of his lectures so that students who missed class could still learn from them. As the collection of tapes grew, he began selling copies to FLDS members, who listened to them for hours on end. Some of the content of his teaching was—and still is—highly problematic. Jeffs would relate a tale from the Bible and then put an FLDS spin on it by saying that it meant that followers were to obey the Prophet, that they were to embrace plural marriage, that boys were not to touch girls, that African Americans were evil people, and that the world would be destroyed with only the obedient FLDS faithful lifted up to the Celestial Kingdom. He also claimed that man had never walked on the moon because the Lord would never permit such an event to take place and that pictures of the moon landing were staged by the U.S. government. Like the Satmar, Jeffs called the theory of evolution a fraud that was not to be taught in school. Indeed, he considered the fossil record "a government hoax" and science itself suspect (*FLDS 101* 2009d).

The school, said one former student, was an effort by Jeffs to "mis-educate" FLDS believers (quoted in Carlisle 2014). The Alta Academy in Salt Lake City eventually closed in 1998 after FLDS members living in Salt Lake fled to Colorado City once the Prophet pronounced that the end of the world was nigh.

Aside from those in the Alta Academy, FLDS children living in the twin towns attended public schools that had long been operated and staffed by members of the sect. Then, early in the new millennium, enrollment at the local elementary school plummeted from four hundred students to fewer than a dozen after Jeffs became ever more reclusive and paranoid about outside influences and repeatedly told his followers to abandon the public school system. The school closed and, as a result, residents of the two towns were without public education for well over a decade (Associated Press 2015a).

A form of centralized homeschooling was set up in its place. With the establishment of homeschooling, FLDS children grew up learning scripture and Jeffs's religious pronouncements, but received little or no instruction in geography, math, history, and other basic subjects. Jeffs ordered pupils be taught at home by women who tended their own large flocks of children and who often had little schooling themselves. The curriculum was heavy on Mormon history and the glorification of Jeffs. The children also were taught that Earth was flat and that odd-shaped mountains had been dropped by God onto evil cities (Woods 2018).

Even after a public school reopened in Hildale, Utah, in 2015, the fewer than 200 pupils initially in attendance were only a fraction of the town's estimated 1,200 school-aged children. Many sect members were still follow-ing Jeffs's edict not to send their children to class (Associated Press 2015a).

Education in the twin towns was all part of the lifelong, relentless, and pervasive re-enforcement of FLDS teachings.[5] For people born and raised in the insular FLDS, it is the only world they know. If they break with the church, even when continuing to follow some of its dictates, they will be cut off from family members still within the FLDS who are ordered to shun them as "apostates." Apostates were to be "left alone severely," demanded Jeffs, a line that comes from nineteenth-century Mormon prophet Brigham Young. Jeffs even ordered families whose relatives had been sent away to burn their family photos.

What is more, very few people who live in the FLDS community own their own homes because the FLDS-created trust, the United Effort Plan, owns most of the property in the two towns. If members leave the church, they will not only become homeless, they will lose everyone and everything they know, including their eternal salvation. This is why most FLDS mem-bers, when faced with a choice between family and church, often choose the latter. In this respect they are very reminiscent of the Satmar. Isolation from and ignorance of the larger world, aversion to contact with outsiders, and loss of family following loss of faith are characteristic of both fundamentalist communities (Heaton and Jacobson 2011; Lovett 2015).

One segment of the community that has been forced to live in the secular world after being thrown out of the FLDS and abandoned by their own families are the so-called "lost boys." These are teenage boys who were members of the FLDS Church but who have been excommunicated by church leaders for minor infractions of church rules. While some boys leave the FLDS of their own free will, many more are banished for such transgres-sions as watching a movie or a television show, listening to rock music, playing football, or talking to a girl. Somewhere between four hundred and one thousand boys have been expelled from the sect over the last two decades for such offenses (Borger 2005).

For boys who are raised to distrust the world outside and taught that leaving the FLDS community is a sinful act, their exile from everything familiar is earth-shattering. The FLDS also instructs its devotees from the time they are small children that because non-believers are not privy to any of the sect's religious directives, they are so evil that even talking to a gentile

---

5. Within this environment it is not surprising that fewer than 5 percent of FLDS members hold bachelor's degrees.

imperils one's salvation. These are also boys with very modest secular educations and few skills appropriate to life outside the community. At the same time, they have to deal with the profound anguish of being shunned by their own families along with the belief that having been forced to abandon the FLDS, they are beyond spiritual redemption.

And yet the real reason behind the exile of so many teenage boys is not difficult to fathom. As one observer notes, the "ruthless sexual arithmetic of a polygamist sect" is to blame. Since at birth the ratio of males to females is roughly equivalent in the United States and since relatively few women from outside the community join the FLDS, there are simply not enough women in the community for all the men living there to have at least three wives—the number required to reach the Celestial Kingdom. The systematic excommunication of young men in this polygamous society, which makes it easier for older men to achieve their marital goals, is clearly an attempt to reduce the competition for wives. Teenage boys were not the only ones expelled from the FLDS for this reason. In 2004 more than twenty FLDS men were excommunicated and stripped of their wives and children, who were then "reassigned" to other men (Bennion 2011b; Borger 2005).

While the FLDS has remained isolated from the surrounding society, this has not meant being cut off from government aid. In fact, one of the hallmarks of the sect is its adherents' abundant use of federal social programs. Church leaders have encouraged believers to make the most of government assistance in the form of welfare payments; the Women, Infants, and Children (WIC) program; and the Supplemental Nutrition Assistance Program (SNAP)—once referred to as "food stamps." Since the federal government recognizes only one woman as the legal wife of a man, his other wives are regarded as single mothers and are, therefore, eligible to receive government assistance. The more wives and children a man has, the more welfare checks and food stamps he can receive. Census data for the twin towns show that two-thirds of the population living in them is age nineteen or younger, which translates into a lot of mouths to feed that require government support. As one observer of the FLDS has written, "Fundamentalists call defrauding the government 'bleeding the beast' and regard it as a virtuous act" (Krakauer 2004:15).

In recent years, however, both the federal and state governments have been looking into the internal workings of the FLDS community and its often fraudulent use of government assistance. These inquiries coincided with the departure from the FLDS of several disgruntled members who began talking to the FBI, thus disobeying the Prophet's longstanding order to avoid all contact with law enforcement and to "answer them nothing" (Hyde 2016).

Fear had long silenced the apostates who at first were few in number. They knew they would be separated from their families and shunned and harassed if they spoke out. But a growing band of outcasts now included former cooks and drivers for the Jeffs family, along with ex-wives and others who had hovered around church leaders and their power center. Over time those deserting the FLDS numbered in the hundreds, with several entire families abandoning the sect but still refusing to leave town. Tensions continued to rise between the FLDS faithful and these apostates as their sworn testimony began filling page after page of newly filed federal court documents. Some locals have suggested that these divisions have brought the twin towns to the brink of civil war (Hyde 2016; O'Neill 2016).

Following statements made by FLDS apostates, federal prosecutors allege that while families entitled to food stamps went hungry, sect leaders directed food bought with federal funds to their own private larders or exchanged food stamps for cash—which is illegal—to subsidize church projects. They further allege that the families of church leaders had exclusive access to food bought from stores like Costco, while other FLDS members were left to scavenge at a warehouse of pooled resources. At times there was not enough in the storehouse for everyone so that those at the bottom of the FLDS pecking order had to make do with whatever was left (O'Neill 2016).

A related case was filed in Salt Lake City with criminal charges accusing eleven FLDS members, including Lyle Jeffs, Warren's brother, of engaging in a food stamp swindle and money-laundering scheme. "This indictment is not about religion. This indictment is about fraud," the U.S. attorney declared (quoted in the Associated Press 2016).

Soon other investigations got underway. The federal government alleged that the towns had been operating as a de facto "theocracy" after an inquiry found that public servants like the police chief and the mayor were not just members of the church, but also did the bidding of FLDS leaders. Then the U.S. Department of Justice began looking into allegations that the two towns had been violating residents' civil rights by allowing public officials to try to run members—who had left the faith—out of town by denying them access to housing, water hookups, and other utilities, as well as police protection. A federal court verdict in 2016 found that the FLDS harassed non-believers, while a federal jury in Phoenix agreed that the local governments of the two towns were so corrupted by the FLDS that they illegally discriminated against non-members. "Their plan was to deny basic rights and freedoms to those non-FLDS families so they pack up and move away," a federal prosecutor charged (Associated Press 2016; quoted in Walters 2016a).

Thus, it has become apparent that, as with the Satmar, the lifestyle of the FLDS is undergirded by abundant support from the public trough. Given recent investigations into the shenanigans of FLDS leaders in their often dicey, if not fraudulent, use of funds from various state and federal social programs, along with the testimony of FLDS apostates cited above, the question remains: What would become of the FLDS if these streams of support were to cease? How could the FLDS with their many dependents continue to provide for their followers? With so much depending on the outcome of the myriad investigations underway into these activities, only time will tell.

ISLAMIC FUNDAMENTALISM

Islamic fundamentalism has been called a "subset" of Islam, its most conservative element. It can be more precisely defined as a movement in which believers view the earliest days of Islam in idealistic terms and seek to return to them by living lives similar to that of the Prophet Muhammad and his early followers. Islamic fundamentalists are originalists in that they favor a literal interpretation of the primary texts of Islam, including the Koran, without the corrupting influences of the West. Such harmful influences are deemed to be all forms of Western media, Western greetings like shaking hands, and Western dress—neckties are prohibited. They also discourage activities strongly associated with the West like playing sports. Regarding gender, fundamentalists urge women's return to the home and while in public women are to be kept strictly segregated from men. In short, Islamic fundamentalists aver that all worldly problems stem from secular sources (Fuller 2003; Roy 1994).

One example of a strict variant of Muslim fundamentalism is the Wahhabi movement that is dominant in Saudi Arabia and responsible for spreading this highly austere form of Islam to many other Muslim countries. Wealthy Saudis have contributed billions of dollars to religious institutions abroad, funding the construction of mosques, religious publications, *madrassas* (Islamic religious schools), and scholarships. Another Islamic fundamentalist group are the Taliban, a political movement in Afghanistan that is waging a contemporary insurgency there. The Taliban, who first arose in Afghanistan in the mid-1990s, were educated in many Saudi-funded *madrassas* in Pakistan (Guidère 2012).

As Islamic fundamentalists the Taliban returned to Afghanistan and fought to rid the country of the Soviet invaders. And, as we have seen, they are themselves an offshoot of the country's Pashtun population. The Taliban have been condemned internationally for the harsh enforcement of their interpretation of Islamic Sharia law, the implementation of which has resulted in the brutal treatment of many Afghans, most especially women (Giustozzi 2009).

THE PASHTUN OF AFGHANISTAN

Men's honor lies in women's shame and modesty.
—Benedicte Grima, *Performance of Emotion among Paxtun Women*, 1992

The Pashtun are an ethnic group rather than a religious one and, unlike the Satmar and the Fundamentalist Church of Jesus Christ of Latter-Day Saints, both relatively small religious sects, the Pashtun are the largest ethnic community in Afghanistan. They number close to fourteen million, or about 40 percent of a nation of approximately thirty-three million.

Since its founding in 1747 Afghanistan has been dominated by the Pashtun, who prior to 1978 constituted just over 50 percent of the country's population. The following year the Soviet invasion altered the ethnic composition of Afghanistan because, as a result of the invasion and the war that ensued, over six million Afghan refugees fled, mainly to Pakistan and Iran. The Pashtun comprised about 85 percent of those who left the country. For a time this not only decreased the percentage of Pashtun inside Afghanistan, it increased the proportion of the country's other ethnic groups. By the mid-1990s, however, many of the refugees had returned home, thus restoring the Pashtun to their status as the nation's largest ethnic group (BBC News 2013).

The Pashtun speak Pashto, which is one of the two dominant languages in Afghanistan—the other is Dari—and they are Sunni Muslims. They reside primarily in the east and south of Afghanistan although enclaves of Pashtun are also scattered among other ethnic groups in several regions of the country. Many of the non-Pashtun communities in Afghanistan have adopted some aspects of Pashtun culture and speak Pashto as a second language.

While a large Pashtun population, including Afghan refugees, also lives in Pakistan, primarily in the northeastern region bordering Afghanistan, many Pashtun living there have adopted non-Pashtun cultural practices and speak languages other than Pashto, such as Urdu and Balochi. For this reason, the discussion here is limited to the Pashtun in Afghanistan, their historic homeland. Moreover, Afghanistan remains at the core of the Pashtun sense of identity, which dates back to the city of Kandahar, the seat of an empire once ruled by united Pashtun tribes (*National Geographic* 2011; Saleh 2012).

The Pashtun compose the world's largest tribal society, a society that is organized around what anthropologists call "segmentary lineages." This is an arrangement in which descendants of close relatives unite together against more distant relatives. For example, descendants of brothers are allied against descendants of cousins, cousins against second cousins, and so on. Even quite distant relatives will routinely put aside any conflicts among themselves and unite against a common threat from outsiders who are not kin.

On a higher level of organization, the Pashtun are divided into sub-tribal and tribal groups to which they remain loyal. These tribal divisions have been the source of conflict among Pashtun throughout their history and even now the Pashtun are divided along tribal lines. Nevertheless, despite specific tribal affiliations, Pashtun believe that they are all patrilineal descendants—descendants through the male line—of one founding male ancestor whose sons and grandsons, in turn, were the founding fathers of the Pashtun clans and sub-clans. To be a Pashtun, one must have a Pashtun father (Glatzer and Casimir 1983).

Today a majority of Pashtun in rural areas are farmers and live in settled villages although in times past many were pastoral nomads, herders who moved frequently to find grazing land for their animals. Anthropologists believe that their segmentary lineage organization was advantageous in that it provided the flexibility necessary to unite in the face of outside threats or to divide and scatter in order to move effortlessly with their animals to new pastures.

While the Pashtun remain a predominantly rural tribal people, an urbanizing trend has begun changing Pashtun society as cities such as Kabul and Kandahar in Afghanistan have grown rapidly due to an influx of Pashtun from the countryside. Kabul and Ghazni, for example, are home to around 25 percent of the Pashtun population in the country while another 20 percent live in the cities of Herat and Mazar-i-Sharif. As we will see in the chapters to follow, the rural-urban divide of Pashtun society is significant at times for Pashtun women, whose experiences vary to some degree depending on where they live—in conservative rural areas or in slightly more progressive urban centers (*National Geographic* 2011; Azami 2006).

Although most Pashtun women remain tribal and illiterate, others, particularly those in urban areas, tend to have more schooling, some are gainfully employed, and a handful have had notable success in their fields of endeavor. Nevertheless, the ravages of the Soviet occupation of Afghanistan and the Afghan civil wars, which led to the rise and fall of the Taliban, caused substantial hardship among Pashtun women in *all* parts of the country as many of their rights were curtailed by the Taliban's rigid interpretation of Islamic law that prohibited girls and women from leaving home to work or to attend school.

Also, the suggestion that the lives of rural and urban Pashtun women vary markedly can exaggerate such differences. The Danish journalist Asne Seierstad (2003), who lived with an upper-middle-class Afghan family in Kabul for several months after the departure of the Taliban, found the strictures on the women of the household—including two of its female members who had received relatively good educations—as stark as in more traditional regions of the country.

THE TRIBAL IDEOLOGY OF PASHTUNWALI

Surely the most distinctive feature of Pashtun society is *Pashtunwali*—literally "the way of the Pashtun"—and it is the cultural attribute that provides the clearest insight into Pashtun behavior and ideology in regard to gender roles and the position of women in Pashtun society. Pashtunwali is the customary tribal law that regulates life throughout Pashtun territory in the eastern and southern half of Afghanistan. It is older than Islam and its codes often supersede Islamic canons.

Pashtunwali is based on the values of honor, sanctuary, solidarity, shame, and revenge. It provides a charter for living and its rules are complex. They cover both public and private behavior and its requirements are well known to all Pashtun, including children. Parents see to it that Pashtunwali is internalized by girls as much as by boys. A rural Afghan villager will define himself and his culture to outsiders by reference to this code. In other words, it is by adherence to Pashtunwali that a man makes his claim to a position of dignity and respect in Pashtun society (Rubin 2005; Lindholm 1982).

What does the code entail? Pashtunwali is sometimes called "Pashto" and refers not only to the Pashtun language and ethnic identity but also to a principled way of life. Although not a religion but a sacred code of conduct, the Pashtun are so partial to its customs that it has all but achieved the status of a religious faith. According to the code, one's identity is intimately bound to being a member of a particular tribe so that individual honor and shame are closely tied to the honor and shame of the larger tribal group to which one belongs (Khattak, Fida, and Lee 2009).

Pashtunwali, then, governs and regulates large areas of Pashtun life ranging from tribal affairs to an individual's honor and many Pashtun, especially those living in the rural areas of Afghanistan, continue to follow its basic precepts closely. In short, only individuals who can live a life according to the laws and rules of Pashtunwali are fit to call themselves "Pashtun" (Kahn 2015).

Anthropologists believe that Pashtunwali originated in pre-Islamic times and has since fused with many Islamic traditions. Its relationship with Islamic law is complicated and, especially with respect to women, often contradictory. Most Pashtun simply assume their practices conform with Islamic law because they identify as Muslims. But in reality Pashtunwali codes sometimes contradict the Koran. They often fail to enforce those tenets of the religion that could potentially obstruct the continuity of the ethnic group's patriarchal system, and the steps they take to preserve their traditions may be in clear violation of Islam. This is true, for example, of the Pashtun practice of dividing inheritance equally *only* among sons since in Pashtun society only males have the right to inherit and own property. The Koran, however, plainly states that daughters are to inherit property as well. Also, unlike the prescriptions of Islamic law, familial revenge among the Pashtun can be taken by killing any male member of an opponent's family rather than by doing harm to a specific individual. In practice, the provisions of Islamic law are often disregarded in favor of customary tribal law, that is, Pashtunwali (Kakar 2005; Saleh 2012).

A fundamental concept in Pashtunwali is *izzat*. This term may be translated loosely as "honor," but it more precisely signifies having a good name or being respected by people who matter. It is well to have financial resources, but to the Pashtun wealth is useful primarily as a means of increasing one's *izzat*. The currency that matters most is honor. Pashtun are usually judged as honorable based on their behavior as gauged by their fellow Pashtun. Certain actions help to build one's honor, while others negate honor and cause shame. Only men can accrue honor, although both men and women can negate it. These beliefs impose a set of norms that are aimed at preventing a loss of honor. Yet, because it is not codified, honor can only be established through various social practices such as hospitality, preserving community cohesion, and observing strict boundaries between males and females (Blank 2013; Kahn 2015).

A related notion is *nang*, which also translates as "honor" but implies dignity, courage, and bravery as well. *Nang* is considered a central pillar of Pashtun culture and it touches several spheres of life: oneself, one's family, and one's clan. Maintaining the honor of his immediate family is the most important duty of every upstanding Pashtun male. The very strong emphasis on *personally* defending one's status and honor within Pashtunwali makes it difficult for followers of the code to delegate enforcement to other persons or institutions, including the state (Khattak, Fida, and Lee 2009; Kahn 2015).

Conversely, to be called *benanga* (shameless) is a terrible insult to the Pashtun and a mortal threat to the social position of the person so insulted. This pejorative has three meanings: someone who is lazy and weak, someone who has lost his land, and someone who has no control over his women. To a proud Pashtun the loss of honor is said to be worse than death because it makes him unworthy of the name "Pashtun" (Lindholm and Lindholm 1979).

The term "shame" in this context is culturally bound and its meaning is not the exact equivalent of the term in English. Within the Pashtun code modesty is a requisite for avoiding shame. But while modesty is an expected characteristic of all Pashtun, the attribute is especially vital for Pashtun women. Respect for this quality in a woman is an absolute necessity; dishonoring any woman is an unpardonable offense. If modesty, which also encapsulates notions of propriety, decorum, and discretion, is violated then an individual is disgraced (Blank 2013).

In societies with a strict code of honor—such as Pashtun—the ostracism suffered by a man who fails to avenge an offense to his honor can be crushing. Aside from other people's disdain, norms are also upheld by the shamed individual's own strong sense of embarrassment and guilt. A man who does not care about his honor is not qualified to wear a turban—the external symbol of male chivalry and Pashtunness (Khattak, Fida, and Lee 2009).

Another principle of the code is that perceived wrongs or injustices demand *badal* (vengeance, revenge), which compels a forceful, often violent, reaction to a death, injury, or insult. A Pashtun proverb says that "*Badal* ends with *Badal*," which is best translated as "tit for tat" because it means that an action demands an equivalent response. Such a response is evidence of manliness. To be a Pashtun male one must display such courage at all times so

Pashtun man in turban
Source: **Shutterstock.com, Emroo Photos**

that if retaliation is not forthcoming, the man who was the target of the affront, along with his family, are said to have lost their honor (Banting 2003; Khattak, Fida, and Lee 2009).

Numerous other tenets of Pashtunwali shape Pashtun social behavior. Perhaps Pashtunwali's best-known canon is *melmastia* (hospitality). This requires that any person be afforded the protection of his host regardless of any prior relationship between host and guest. Hence, even an enemy who arrives seeking refuge must have it granted, and while in the care of a host a guest can neither be harmed nor handed over to a foe. Hospitality and protection have to be offered to all who arrive at one's doorstep without expectation of favor or return (Glatzer 1998).

The code also requires men to protect their *zan*, *zar*, and *zameen* (women, wealth, and land). An action against any one of these is the most common offense that requires revenge. The only adequate defense of one's honor is vengeance, which is to be equal to but not exceed the original offense. Also subsumed under this part of the code is the stalwart protection of one's land and other property (Ali 2013).

The concept of *namus*, the sexual honor or virtue of women (*zan*), is a crucial element in a man's honor. The insistence on *namus* focuses on those individuals for whom a Pashtun man is accountable in very specific ways: his wife (or wives) and daughters as well as his unmarried or widowed sisters and any other female member of his household. In the Pashtunwali world-view, the honor of a Pashtun man and the honor of all females for whom he is responsible are tightly intertwined. Defending a female's honor entails pro-viding her with care and shelter, and a Pashtun man who does so accrues honor and maintains his reputation within his own community (Kahn 2015).

At the same time, a woman's character and behavior reflect the status and honor of her family as a whole. It is said that Pashtun men routinely see women as encompassing the "essence" of the family. If a woman gets a bad reputation, her entire family, including its males, is dishonored. Again, the focus is on the word "honor." Male honor is proactive and expressed through aggressive and sometimes violent actions. Female honor is, by definition, passive, submissive, and centered around avoidance of shame. It is generally believed among Pashtun that women are stricter in their adherence to Pash-tunwali than men and are less ready to compromise when matters of honor and shame are at stake (Glatzer 1998; Saleh 2012).

A vital element in maintaining female honor and virtue is *purdah*[6] or seclusion, that is, a woman's limited access to the world outside her own household. Such a severe measure stems from the importance ascribed by Pashtunwali to the way in which other Pashtun evaluate an individual's be-havior. A woman who remains in the home and is nearly invisible to outsid-ers cannot dishonor herself or her male relatives.

Both *purdah* and patrilineal descent and inheritance—traditions consid-ered vital for ensuring female honor—relegate women to a lower social status than men. Women may not own property because the norms of Pash-tunwali obligate males to provide for the well-being of their close female relatives. Then, too, because of patrilineal descent and patrilineal inheritance, a woman cannot inherit from her father or her husband, nor can any of her daughters inherit from their father or other male forbearers. They, like their mother, remain completely dependent for support on men within the family.

---

6. *Purdah* is a religious and social practice of female seclusion prevalent among some Muslim communities in Afghanistan and elsewhere in South Asia and some Hindu commu-nities in India.

As a consequence, a woman who can only receive protection from a Pashtun male simply lacks the means to protect herself on her own initiative (Kahn 2015).

Avenging any insult to a woman's sexual purity is especially crucial. A male Pashtun must defend the sexual integrity and chastity of all the women in his household. Or, as a common Pashtun proverb has it, "He who cannot protect the integrity of his family cannot protect anything, anyone is free to snatch away from him what he wants, his possessions, his land" (cited in Glatzer 1998). In a broader sense the sexual purity of females also involves the privacy and protection of the sanctity of the home. More pointedly, it refers to the integrity, modesty, and respectability of the household's women and to the absolute duty of men to protect them at all costs (Kahn 2015).

The institution of marriage or *wadah* follows the canons of Pashtunwali. Marriage is usually arranged by the parents of the couple, who themselves play no role in the negotiations. This reflects the strict segregation of the sexes in Pashtun society, making it impossible for a would-be suitor to propose to a woman of his own choosing. An important element in the marriage negotiations set at the time of the engagement is *walwar* (head money), what anthropologists term "bride price." Under *walwar* the suitor's parents agree to pay a certain amount of money, usually in cash, to their future in-laws. Many Pashtun aver that *walwar* is not the "selling" of the bride. Rather it is meant to compensate her parents financially for the cost of buying the gold and silver jewelry, clothes, and household effects—in essence, the trousseau—that she brings into the marriage (Afridi 2010).

Providing *walwar*, moreover, is viewed as a matter of honor. The higher the bride's "price" the greater the respect she commands from her husband's family. A bride's price is determined by her age, her beauty, and her skills as well as by the status of her family. Even prosperous parents who have no need for the money must accept it in order to ensure that their daughter is honored by her in-laws (Afridi 2010).

There is a strong preference among the Pashtun for consanguineous marriage, that is, marriage between blood relatives, since most parents are reluctant to have their daughters marry outside the extended family or kin group. This is evident in Afghan marriage customs, which include marriage between first cousins. Other preferred forms of marriage are what anthropologists call the "sororate" and the "levirate." These are marriages in which a man weds the widowed sister of his wife and a woman marries the brother of her deceased husband. Pashtun society considers it the absolute duty of brothers to marry their brothers' widows—and leaves those widows with little choice but to go along, or else risk losing their children and their homes (Nordland 2018b).

All these forms of marriage ensure that property and children remain within the protection and control of a particular patrilineal kin group. In these marital arrangements the motives of male relatives and of the larger community take precedence over the wishes of the would-be bride and groom (Kahn 2015; Afridi 2010).

The Pashtun are patrilocal, meaning that after marriage a Pashtun man remains in the household in which he was born and his wife moves there to live with him along with any children they may eventually have. The wives of married sons join the paternal household and married women no longer reside with their families of birth. After marriage a young woman not only goes to live in her husband's household, but also is expected to transfer her loyalty to her husband's kin group.

All family members, including married sons and unmarried daughters, live jointly in a house large enough to separately accommodate each married couple under the authority of the father who, as head of the family, has a great deal of influence in household affairs. All males in the family, married as well as unmarried sons, contribute their share of income to a common pool. Then all expenses for food, clothing, education, and health care as well as the costs associated with births, marriages, and deaths are paid out of this common fund. After the father dies or when old age no longer allows him to discharge his duties, authority falls to his eldest son.

Anthropologists have long recognized that certain features of social organization, specifically post-marital residence rules (where a couple lives after they marry) and descent rules (from whom an individual traces descent and may receive an inheritance) influence the relative status and power of the sexes. In fact, some researchers suggest that the strongest association with equality or inequality between men and women in different cultures around the world are these post-marital residence and descent rules. They argue that such kinship variables may exert an effect on women's status independent of the specific economic and political institutions that are found in a given society (Johnson and Hendrix 1982).

Why is this so? In patrilocal societies, such as the Pashtun, the woman is the outsider. She leaves her kin behind and moves to her husband's place of residence, where she is unlikely to have her own relatives nearby to provide aid and comfort in time of need. Moreover, she is faced with the scrutiny of strangers, her husband's relatives, who may make life difficult for her if she does not live up to their expectations. Then, too, a woman's autonomy is reduced because of her isolation from her own close kin. In case of divorce she must return to her natal household (Margolis 2004).

Because of the patrilocal residence rule, once married, a young Pashtun woman literally vanishes from her family of birth. Writes one observer of Pashtun life: "A wedding is like a small death. The bride's family mourns in the days following the wedding, as though it was a funeral. A daughter is lost—sold or given away. The mother especially grieves. . . . After the wedding the daughter disappears, completely; she goes from one family to the other. She cannot visit when she wants, only when her husband allows her. Her family cannot drop in on her without an invitation" (Seierstad 2003:106).

Before concluding this chapter I want to emphasize that all of the customs and ideologies of the Satmar, FLDS, and Pashtun described here—including the canons that comprise Pashtunwali—are normative, that is, they are ideal models of behavior and are based on what is considered to be the correct way of doing things. Nonetheless, such customs and beliefs are often breached through ignorance, negligence, or personal choice. And so, it is important to stress that I very much doubt that these norms are adhered to precisely as described in this chapter. In the Pashtun case, for example, evidence suggests that some of the tenets of their code of conduct, including respect for women, are frequently violated. This is also true of the FLDS, where polygamous marriage is the ideal because it is deemed essential to achieve entry into the Celestial Kingdom. Yet many FLDS men, possibly a majority, have only one wife. Then, too, among the Satmar where the only acceptable use of the Internet is to conduct business, many Satmar, both men and women, go on the Internet to learn about the world outside of their own insular community. This use of the Internet, in fact, appears to be one of the main catalysts for questioning some of the group's basic doctrines and sometimes leads to leaving the community entirely.

After this introduction to the three fundamentalist communities that are the focus of this book, we now turn to the striking parallels in how women are viewed and treated in each of them. In chapters 3 and 4 the extreme forms of modesty required of women are described as well as the iron control that males exercise over marriage and other aspects of female behavior. Chapter 5 analyzes the critical role such constraints play in women's unrestrained pro-

creation. The ideologies concerning women's true nature and proper place—
a means of rationalizing their subordinate position in each of these cases—
are also discussed in this chapter. In chapter 6 we look at the contemporary
scene among the Satmar, FLDS, and Pashtun, all of which appear to have
become even more rigid in regard to gender roles than they were in the past.
Finally, in the last chapter we ponder what the future may hold for each of
these communities.

Chapter Three

Modesty Above All

Modesty is invisibility. To be seen—to be seen—is to be . . . penetrated.
—Margaret Atwood, *The Handmaid's Tale*, 1985

All over the world are women whose bodies are covered, not by their own decision but by one of the patriarchal religions that, by definition, rule their wombs.

—Gloria Steinem (quoted in Lax 2015)

The demand for female modesty is one of the hallmarks of the Satmar, the Fundamentalist Church of Jesus Christ of Latter-Day Saints, and the Pashtun. The insistence on modesty is twofold. First, it involves appropriate female dress. This usually means covering most of the body, especially in public, and, in some cases, the hair and face as well. Modesty also requires diffident behavior on the part of women, particularly in their contacts with men who are not close relatives. In all three cases women are told that modesty is essential because they are responsible for managing men's sexual desires. In essence, codes of modesty call on women to adjust their clothing and their self-presentation so as to avoid enticing men and inflaming their libidos.

This command is perhaps most apparent among the Satmar. Ultra-Orthodox ideology places most of the burden for thwarting male sexual desire on women and it is they who are to blame if male desire is aroused. The command to be modest is an obligation of all Satmar girls and women. It is meant to protect Satmar men—who devote most of their time to the study of Torah and other religious texts—from being distracted by lustful thoughts. Because of the power of the human sexual drive, modesty's aim is to keep it in check so as to diminish the possibility of improper enticements that could lead to sinful behavior. In effect, Hasidic ideology places an immense burden on women to thwart male sexual temptation (Angel 2012).

Of the three groups under consideration, the Satmar have far and away the most detailed views on the issue of modesty, especially when it comes to female dress. From time immemorial rabbinic sages have discussed and elaborated on the concept, adding all manner of prohibitions to it. What constitutes modest dressing has been interpreted with slight variations—and a good deal of creativity—by each Hasidic court's Grand Rebbe. These men dictate details like skirt and sleeve length and appropriate head covering. The demand for modesty in dress and behavior—called *tznius* in Hebrew—is traced to the Biblical injunction in Psalm 45: "The whole glory of the king's daughter is within." Likewise, a Hasidic woman recalls, "They taught in 7th grade, again and again, *bas melech, kol kvoda pnima*, a princess's honor is all inside, a divine jewel to be kept hidden." A young male Hasid strongly concurred with this sentiment: "Don't you agree . . . that if you have the most precious diamond in the world, you keep it wrapped up? You don't take it to the streets to show the entire world!" (Fader 2009; Chizhik-Goldschmidt 2015).

The various rabbinic interpretations of this Biblical command have all concluded that the Almighty meant for women to be modest in all things. "*Tznius* is expected to be the dominant religious obligation of the female population (and that of their male overseers)," according to one reading of the rule, which is said to be an elemental attribute of all Satmar females. Modest behavior is a woman's responsibility, but judgments about modesty are not hers to make. Satmar girls and women are told that they should be discreet and that they should never call attention to themselves through their dress. But modesty here refers not only to what women wear, their outward appearance, but also to their inner thoughts and external behavior. *Tznius* requires a woman to be modest in how she presents herself to the world. She should speak in a quiet voice and not draw attention to herself by laughing loudly or by appearing to enjoy herself too much in public (Sable 2013; Davidman 2015).

The take on modesty and its role in controlling sexuality is somewhat different among the Pashtun. Here modesty is demanded, in part, to protect the reputation of a woman's male relatives. Men's honor rests on women's modesty and sense of shame. Safeguarding male honor, in fact, is said to take precedence over everything else in the life of a Pashtun female. This is why a

Pashtun woman's status and social purpose is determined by her degree of modesty (Grima 1992).

To the Pashtun, modesty is essential to female life because women are thought to be less able than men to reason and to act rationally. They are said to have less self-control and so to be more prone to sexual misconduct. In short, all women are believed to be easy prey to a world filled with would-be male seducers. Thus, men feel a strong obligation to keep their female relatives under tight control in order to protect them from their own frailty. Only by doing so can a man maintain his honor. But, here again, the way women dress and behave is also responsible for how men act. As with Satmar males, Pashtun men are assumed to have uncontrollable sexual impulses and it is women's duty to tame them (Glatzer 1998).

Like the Satmar, the honor of Pashtun women is tied to their restraint and timidity in both language and behavior. The quality of *sharm*, meaning a unique blend of modesty, timidity, shame, and subservience, is said to be a fundamental attribute of Pashtun womanhood. That is why a woman laughing in public and appearing to enjoy herself is anathema; it is seen as an attempt to attract male attention. In the presence of men Pashtun women are expected to be silent, docile, and obedient. They are not to ask men questions; they are to keep their eyes lowered in the presence of men and to eat only after a man has finished his meal (Billaud 2015; Grima 1992, 2004).

For the FLDS, women's conservative prairie-style dress is meant to set them apart from the outside world, a world filled with Satanic enticements, a world that is utterly evil. The late FLDS Prophet Leroy Johnson, who preceded the two Jeffs, father and son, declared that he was disgusted that "the daughters of Zion would walk the streets of our great and glorious city of Salt Lake as harlots; and you will not be able to tell the face of a Saint from a Gentile"—as noted earlier, FLDS members refer to all non-members as "gentiles" (quoted in Driggs 2011:80). Women are told not to wear form-fitting clothes or bright colors because they might provoke men's lustful thoughts. Beware of immodesty, women are warned, because dress and comportment will be the deciding factors that God's armies will use on Judgment Day to differentiate between the righteous and the damned (Jessop 2007).

KEEPING THEM APART:
THE SATMAR, THE PASHTUN, AND THE FLDS

The sine qua non of modesty in the three cases we are considering is the separation of the sexes. Among the Satmar the norm of strict sexual segregation comes from the Code of Jewish Law, which states that "a man must very much distance himself from women." This is referred to as *yichud*, the Orthodox rule forbidding a man and a woman who are not related from being alone together.

The Torah demands the greatest degree of separation possible between men and women, the essential argument being that any intermingling of the sexes will inevitably lead to sinful thoughts and, perhaps, sinful actions. Because the male libido is uncontrollable the genders must be kept apart. Even if a man feels no attraction to a woman sitting next to him in a bus or on a train, he is obliged to follow his community's collective standard of strict gender segregation and move away from her. This explains why there have been a number of media reports concerning incendiary incidents involving Hasidic men who simply refused to sit next to unrelated women on airplanes (Kershner 2017).

To a Hasidic male this prohibition on any physical contact—however innocent—with an unrelated female is not just a communal idiosyncrasy; it is Torah law dictated by the Almighty. And since it is women, not men, who are seen as the "enticers," it is up to women to dress and act modestly at all times. This doctrine of gender separation, in fact, is found in nearly all domains of Hasidic life (Heilman 2006).

Hasidic norms prohibit unrelated males and females from being alone without a chaperone. Among the Satmar the commandment that forbids any contact between unmarried boys and girls is taken very seriously because even a slight violation has negative repercussions for the family's standing in the community and may impact family members' marriage prospects (Davidman 2015).

All Satmar schools are segregated by sex. Girls over age twelve are prohibited from being alone with boys over age nine and when a boy reaches thirteen, he can only be alone with girls under age three. After a boy's *bar mitzvah*, he is warned not to even greet someone of the opposite sex, even a first cousin. In short, the only girls a boy is allowed to play with throughout his childhood are his own sisters. All of these prohibitions grew out of the deeply held belief that terrible things happen when girls and boys intermingle, even when they are relatives (Berger 2014b; Brown 2015).

This systematic separation of the sexes throughout the school years has additional implications, especially for boys. They live in a world that is virtually devoid of females other than those who are very close relatives. From an early age boys spend long days in classes that may last from early morning to eight or nine at night. Going to school only with boys, being taught exclusively by male teachers, and having virtually no contact with girls and women when not in school means that boys know almost nothing about the opposite sex and are awkward and uncertain about how to act when in the presence of this rare breed. While this insecurity is likely true for all Satmar boys, it is a particular conundrum for those without sisters who, while growing up, have little or no contact with young girls.

Satmar males typically marry by around age twenty and have met their intended spouses only a handful of times before being wed. As a consequence, their new brides are necessarily viewed as alien and exotic beings who bewilder them. What this means for the course of marriage is certainly an open question.

The constraints on behavior demanded by the Hasidic code of modesty fall most heavily on girls and women, who must always monitor their conduct lest they provoke unwanted male attention. One example: a man is not supposed to hear a woman singing, especially if she has a beautiful voice, because it may distract him from thinking about the Almighty. A woman's singing is considered "nakedness" among the Satmar and other Hasidic courts.

For this reason, listening to the radio is considered *treyf* (not kosher) among the Satmar. A radio may transmit "the voices of singing women to which men are not supposed to listen." As a result, when the Lubavitchers began using radio broadcasts for lessons on the *Tanya*, that court's sacred text, the Satmar Rebbe was scathing in his denunciation of using such an offensive vehicle, calling it "an act of Satan," once again expressing his aversion to modernity (Ravitzky 1994).

Some say that the streets belong to men, so that a woman must make certain that a Satmar male is not distracted by her presence there by hearing the sound of her heels as she goes by. "The very click-clacking of a woman's heels on the pavement may be provocative to a sheltered Torah scholar," writes one researcher. Similarly, modesty also entails limiting photos and drawings of girls and women so as not to distract boys and men from their immersive study of religious texts and give rise to fleeting sexual twinges. The upshot is that drawings of little girls—but not little boys—are blacked out in the elementary texts used in Satmar schools. Billboards in Hasidic communities almost never display partially clothed female figures. And the Satmar newspaper *Der Yid* blacked out the image of Hillary Clinton from the widely viewed photo of the White House War Room during the 2011 raid in Pakistan on Osama Bin Laden's compound (Fader 2009:150).

Meeting a powerful woman in person can also present problems for the modesty-obsessed Satmar. A 2006 meeting between Hillary Clinton and the Satmar Rebbe almost did not take place because the then-senator was wearing pants. The situation was resolved after Clinton agreed to wear a long raincoat over her clothes.

In keeping with these directives, the Satmar Rebbe warns females not to talk loudly or laugh in public. "If a woman must go on the street, she should walk quickly and not stroll," he instructs, "and if she walks with her husband and there's contact . . . with each other, it's a disgusting act." In the same way, if a woman meets a female friend on the street and talks to her while her husband is present, this is also deemed a "disgusting act." A couple "pushing a baby carriage together is disgusting," as well (quoted in *Failed Messiah* 2015).

When a Satmar girl is found to have violated community norms, retaliation is swift. This is why the case of one twelve-year-old Satmar girl received widespread media attention. The girl, who was described as a "free spirit," was found to have breached Satmar customs by reading the magazine *People* and arguing about the length of her skirt. Her parents were required to send her to an unlicensed religious "counselor" and were told that their failure to do so would result in her expulsion from Bais Rochel, the Satmar girls school. The counselor was later accused of sexually abusing the girl and he was subsequently tried and convicted in a court in Brooklyn. But this did not sit well with the Satmar Rebbe, who was furious about the trial and blamed the victim for its outcome: "A Jewish daughter has descended so low. There hasn't been such a disgusting saga in (the history of religious) Jewry" (Otterman 2012a, 2012b; quoted in Weichselbaum 2012).

It will come as no surprise that gender segregation, along with the demand for proper dress, is ubiquitous in the all-Satmar village of Kiryas Joel in upstate New York. The most telling aspect of this in the village is the segregation of males and females in all public spaces. A sign written in Yiddish in the local park warns men and women to stay on their respective sides of a low wall that separates male from female areas of the park and not to mingle or stop to talk with the opposite sex at the park's divider. Signs further direct women and girls to use only those areas in the park with red and pink benches, slides, and jungle gyms, while boys and men are confined to areas with blue park benches and playground equipment. A sign in English notifies non-residents that the park is private and that they are not welcome to use it. Failure to leave could result in an arrest for trespassing, the sign warns. Although the New York Civil Liberties Union announced an out-of-court settlement with Kiryas Joel over this issue, the settlement has been largely ignored and the park remains segregated by sex, as does the local playground (Grumet and Caher 2016).

It is not only parks and playgrounds that are gender segregated in Kiryas Joel. "Please stay on the designated sides of the street, especially on *Shabbos*," read signs in Yiddish posted on electric poles and streetlights. The red sign indicates the women's side of the street, the blue sign the men's. In the local supermarket there are designated checkout lanes, one for women, the other for men.

Such gender segregation is not limited to the village itself. In buses transporting men and women from Kiryas Joel to New York City—where many are employed in the diamond district on West Forty-Seventh Street—the men

Sign at the entrance of Kiryas Joel
Source: Maxine L. Margolis

and women sit on opposite sides of the bus and a curtain is hung down the center aisle, ensuring that the segregation of the sexes is maintained among bus passengers (Weiss, Neumeister, and Mintz 1995).

This practice led to what might be dubbed "The Curious Case of the Female Bus Drivers": In the mid-1980s female bus drivers with seniority over male drivers in Kiryas Joel's school district won a grievance they filed charging that they were not being allowed to drive the longer and higher-paying routes because of sex discrimination. But in order to maintain the strict separation of the sexes, Satmar schoolboys refused to ride in buses driven by women.

After the female drivers won the right to drive the longer routes, the Kiryas Joel community chose to give up the free county bus service and arranged their own private transportation to school. The case also hinged on the fact that not only were the Satmar intent on the segregation of the sexes but women in Kiryas Joel may not drive cars. "None of our children can ride in a bus driven by a woman," said a community leader. "Women do not drive in our community. At all. We do not want our children to think it is all right or even possible for women to drive machines like that" (quoted in Grumet and Caher 2016:34).

As noted in the tale above, Satmar women in Kiryas Joel are not allowed to drive. A village woman who drives a car would face serious consequences; she would be shunned by relatives, friends, and neighbors, and her children would be expelled from the Satmar school. One former resident of Kiryas Joel who was born and raised there eventually got her driver's license at age twenty-three. Her parents, who still live in the village, were horrified. When her father heard about the license, he said to her mother, "She will kill herself and her children." The fundamental reason for the ban on women driving appears to be to remove any modicum of independence they may have and ensure that they are dependent on their husbands or other male relatives to get around town. Then, too, because modesty is best enforced at home, the idea that a woman could travel on her own anywhere she desires is unacceptable (Goldberger 2015).

The behavior of Satmar men also requires care in order to preserve female modesty and avoid temptation. As part of their "modesty training" Hasidic males are raised from childhood to believe that non-Hasidic woman are "loose." "As a young teenager I knew that on the outside—the non-Orthodox world—every woman is promiscuous," said one Satmar man (quoted in Berger 2014b:114). What is more, modesty training for such men means that they will not accept a traffic ticket or a summons from a female police officer because "they have internalized to a radical extent Hasidic scruples about engaging in conversation with unfamiliar women," according to one student of the community (Berger 2014b:324). Satmar and other Hasidic men shield their eyes when walking down the street, keeping their gaze focused on the sidewalk so as to avoid looking at any passing female. And the Satmar Rebbe will not shake the hand or even look directly at a woman who accompanies her husband on a visit to his office or his home (Davidman 2015; Mintz 1992).

Even married couples may not hold hands, touch each other, or show any sign of mutual affection in public. Touch is considered an intimate gesture, making it entirely inappropriate for public display. A woman, in fact, usually walks a few steps behind her husband when they are out together on the street. In one wedding photo the bride's hand rests lightly on her new husband's shoulder. This had to be blacked out because the gesture was considered inappropriately intimate by the norms of the Satmar community (Winston 2005).

> The essence of their Islamic jurisprudence is to make women melt away. To make them invisible.
>
> —Rasha Al Aqeedi (quoted in Callimachi 2016)

> If women are going outside with fashionable, ornamental, tight and charming clothes to show themselves, they will be cursed by the Islamic Sharia and should never expect to go to heaven.
>
> —Decree by Taliban Religious Police (quoted in Tristam 2019)

What about the separation of the sexes among the Pashtun? According to one observer, "gender segregation in Afghanistan is among the strictest in the world." The situation, in fact, is so extreme that it has been hailed as an example of "gender apartheid." One key to this segregation is the institution of *purdah*, which, as noted earlier, is the practice of female seclusion found in some Muslim and Hindu communities including the Pashtun (Nordberg 2014:18; Chesler 2014).

When Pashtun families are living among strangers rather than within their own close kinship networks, the pressure to adhere to *purdah* is powerful. "Men and women who do not belong to the same family may not sit together in the same room. They must not talk to one another or eat together," notes one observer. Shopping both in the Afghan countryside and in cities is done almost exclusively by men and elderly women. It is unacceptable for a young woman to go out and bargain with shopkeepers, all of whom are male (Seierstad 2003:51).

A Pashtun woman must not be seen by men who are not close family members and she must avoid being heard beyond the four walls of her house. This is the reason Pashtun women fear men hearing them sing. "We only sing in the remote valleys when no men are about at all to see us," one Pashtun woman explained (quoted in Grima 2004:24). If word gets out that a woman has danced or sang before spectators outside her immediate family, her family's honor would be harmed and her male relatives would have to take extreme measures like ostracizing her or even killing her to regain their honor. Also, as a consequence of gender segregation, women make few casual visits and have almost no access to public spaces like cafes or parks. Or as one Pashtun saying goes, "Women's place is either in the *kor* (home) or the *gor* (grave)" (Jamal 2014).

One ethnographer of Pashtun culture notes the minimal interaction of males and females. "Women . . . were at eternal play with each other, teasing, entertaining, flirting. Once in mixed company—actually it took only a single male presence—the behavior vanished instantly. Outside the bedroom, men were rarely a part of women's everyday existence." Another observer provides a similar analysis: "According to [Pashtun] tribal logic, the important thing is the ownership of a woman's body. The body of a woman belongs to a man, and other people should not even use her body indirectly, such as by looking at her. Based on this logic, the body, face, and name of the woman belong to the man" (Grima 2004:41; Mashal 2017).

Just as with Satmar and FLDS women, the spatial mobility of Pashtun women is strictly limited. While driving cars is forbidden to Satmar women and FLDS women drive unregistered cars without license plates, preventing them from leaving the twin towns, Pashtun women are not permitted to ride horses. Driving a car—or riding a horse—implies freedom of movement and independence, which might lead to immodest behavior. Since modesty is best enforced in the home, the idea that a woman could travel on her own anywhere she wants is shocking.

The mobility of Pashtun women is further limited by their male relatives because they are not supposed to leave the household without the explicit permission of their husband, father, or brother and then only when accompanied by a close male relative. And here, too, honor is involved. A Pashtun woman must never leave her husband's walled compound without his permission because by remaining a virtual prisoner in it, she upholds his honor. After all, she is a part of all he possesses and her behavior directly reflects his power and control (Grima 1992).

This is why a Pashtun woman who must work outside the home destroys her reputation. Such a woman is forced to labor in the public domain, away from the all-encompassing safety of her household and her male relatives. Then, too, she becomes vulnerable to abuse because she is unlikely to be accompanied by a father, husband, brother, or grown son who will protect her. As one Afghan woman commenting on the frequency of sexual harassment of females in Afghan society notes: "Everyone thinks that those women who work outside the home are whores and Afghan men can say and do anything they want with them" (quoted in Nordland and Faizi 2017).

In rural Pashtun areas male visitors do not loiter about when a woman is out fetching water or gathering firewood. They do not speak to her and it is considered indecent for her to speak to them. In fact, a girl over the age of ten is forbidden to address men other than those who are close relatives. Strangers are to be avoided and when a girl or woman crosses the path of one when she is outside doing chores, she covers her face and stands with her back turned towards him until he passes. Similarly, a male stranger will lower his eyes, stare at the ground, and step away from the path when he encounters a woman.

What is more, Pashtun men are reluctant to say the names of their female relatives in public. Women are not addressed or referred to by their names. Even on wedding invitations and tombstones, women are typically referred to as the daughter, wife, or mother of their father, husband, or eldest son, respectively. Many say that uttering a woman's name in public dishonors her, but at the same time it makes her invisible, a non-person. When men have to provide their female relatives' names in government offices or hospitals for purposes of identification, they will first look around to make sure no other Pashtun man is within hearing range before they whisper the name of their wife or daughter or sister (Jamal 2014; Sorush 2019).

Treat the girls in your acquaintance as though they were snakes. Hands off!
—Prophet Warren Jeffs (quoted in Musser 2013)

Then there is the Fundamentalist Church of Jesus Christ of Latter-Day Saints. In some sense the separation of the sexes among FLDS members is akin to that of the Satmar. While FLDS schools are not segregated by sex, any kind of physical contact between boys and girls is strictly forbidden. Prophet Warren Jeffs was obsessed by boy-girl interactions. He was always asking: Did he pass you a note? Did he touch your body? He told his flock that the sexes should treat each other as if they were "snakes." Said one former student, "We started treating males as if they were, indeed, foreign, scaly and reptilian in nature. We avoided even our brothers and cousins. We ran from them, refused to sit by them, and were careful not to converse with them" (quoted in Musser 2013:22).

Boys received the same message. Said one boy of Jeffs's constant lectures on the subject, "I hated the boy-girl sermons he would give. They made you never ever want to look at, or even talk to a girl until you were married. So girlfriends were definitely out of the question" (*FLDS 101* 2009d).

Yet another student recalled being called to Jeffs's office when she was in first grade. "Warren had been told that I was holding the hand of my seven-year-old male cousin while playing outside earlier in the day. This was true, but I had no idea why he was bringing it up. As he explained, what I had done was absolutely not to be tolerated. I was never to touch boys. I was to treat them as poisonous reptiles." One steadfast rule stated that girls were never to talk to boys. If you looked at or smiled at a boy, you were a Jezebel—a scorned woman (cited in *FLDS 101* 2009d).

In all of these examples the insistence on gender separation in public spaces reflects a worldview that is fixated on sex and has a jaundiced notion of male and female relations. Also, while most of these conventions deal with control of women's bodies and their mobility, they also imply that "immodest" women have the power to dishonor not only their male relatives, but the entire community as well (Winston 2006–2007).

To be sure, gender separatism is not limited to the Satmar, Pashtun, and FLDS. Similar segregation of the sexes has appeared in other societies. There is also the current example of the vice president of the United States, Mike Pence, who, in following the so-called "Billy Graham rule," will not have a meal alone with a woman who is not his wife. As with the three communities discussed above, Mr. Pence's tacit assumption is that extramarital contact—no matter how innocent—with an unrelated woman is perilous. To him as well as to the Satmar, the Pashtun, and the FLDS, there is the abiding sense that women are sources of sexual danger, which is why they must be kept in check (Angel 2016; Tolentino 2017).

WHAT'S A WOMAN TO WEAR?
THE CASE OF THE SATMAR

Orthodox is you don't want to look at a girl in a bathing suit. Ultra-Orthodox is
you want to close down a beach.
　　　　　　　　　—Michael Idov, "Clash of the Bearded Ones," 2010

What does modesty in women's dress entail in these three communities?
Once again, among the Satmar, more than in the other two cases, dress codes
for women are laid out in excruciating rabbinic detail. Viewed positively, as
one Satmar adherent does, *tznius* (modest) attire "liberates a woman from the
dictates of fashion and allows her to externalize the standards that suit her
soul." Whatever one may think of this statement, it is certainly true that
tznius governs Hasidic fashion. For females the word incorporates not only
the idea of modesty in dress but sanctity and purity in appearance.

According to the dictates of Hasidic law, each style and article of clothing
must be gender specific. The Torah commands that women not wear men's
clothes and vice versa: "The woman shall not wear that which pertains to a
man. . . . All who do so are an abomination to the Lord." This is the reason
girls and women can never wear jeans, slacks, or any sort of leg covering
associated with men. This is also the rule among modern Orthodox women,
who are not supposed to wear slacks or blue jeans. But in real life this
prohibition is not always followed. I live near the women's college of Yeshiva University in New York City and occasionally see students there quickly
change out of pants or jeans and into skirts before entering their dorms
(Zakutinsky and Gottlieb 2001:86; Deuteronomy 22:5).

The Satmar dress code for girls and women specifies the portions of the
body that must be concealed, that is, the parts that are considered indecent to
display. The Satmar believe that a woman's thighs, knees, and legs, her
upper arms and elbows, and her collarbone are *ervah* (sensual) and so are
never to be exposed in public. A store in Williamsburg, Brooklyn, carries a
line of accessories that ensure such modest coverage. A woman might buy a
dress at Lord & Taylor or Macy's but then alter it by buying a "neckline kit"
to sew in to make sure her collarbone is hidden. Or she might purchase a full
slip to wear under a dress that she deems too sheer to wear. She can also buy
a set of sleeves to sew on to a short-sleeve blouse or dress that reveals her
elbows or too much of her upper arms. Through these additions store-bought
clothes can be made to conform to Satmar norms of modesty (Berger 2014b).

Informal "modesty committees" in the community make sure that all such rules are carefully followed. They may warn a shop owner that her daughter's skirts are too short or that the mannequin in the store window is indecent and should be removed lest one's business be affected. Given these strictures, it is not surprising that in Satmar Williamsburg "no shops selling women's garments are in evidence . . . the flagrant display of female garments would be an affront to the Orthodox male" (Gersh 1959).

There also once were dress codes for customers entering Satmar-owned businesses. Several small stores in Williamsburg—a bakery, a grocer, a butcher, and a store selling Hasidic attire—each posted a sign in their windows saying "No shorts, no barefoot, no sleeveless, no low-cut neckline allowed in this store." The city of New York sued the stores, arguing that they discriminated against women and non-Orthodox men, and the signs were eventually removed (Berger 2014a).

Sometimes these dress requirements can restrict a woman's ability to move freely. Since there are no gym classes in Satmar schools, if a girl wants to exercise to stay in shape or to lose weight, she may walk briskly. Running is considered immodest. Because of the demand for modesty Satmar girls who do exercise perspire through their thick stockings, their heavy skirts, and their long-sleeve shirts. Another example of Satmar women being constrained by their required dress is at the public pool in Williamsburg. They swim there when it is segregated by sex—i.e., all female—for a few hours each week. The "bathing costumes" of these women were described as follows in the *New York Times* :

> Their swim outfits would have been considered prudish even by the standards of 1922, when the pool opened. They swim in dresses, some with long sleeves. One paddled in thick black tights. Inside the locker room, wigs sat upside down on window ledges and benches while their owners swam with heads under ruffled swimming caps or knotted silk scarves. (Nir 2016)

One Hasidic woman describes her smoldering resentment against these compulsory clothing requirements: "I basically do as little as possible—because I honestly don't believe in all of the *tznius* minutia that has been created by men for women and turned into law. Women are made to wear uncomfortable clothing that restricts movement in order to control our behavior and our ability to do various activities" (Anonymous 2017).

The rules of *tznius* apply to all females over the age of six. Girls under six can wear short skirts as long as they wear high socks or tights that cover the rest of the leg. However, Aaron Teitelbaum, the Rebbe of Kiryas Joel, subsequently decried "a lapse in standards by some people [in] that girls from the age three are going dressed with short socks." He then warned that "households who do not take care of this issue . . . their children will not be accepted into our schools, which have been established to educate our children to behave themselves according to the Torah" (quoted in *Failed Messiah* 2014a).

Skirt lengths and fabrics are also a concern. The skirts of Satmar women must be four inches below the knee. In the mid-1990s, floor-length skirts became popular among secular and modern Orthodox women, but the Satmar Rebbe forbade such skirts to his followers. He felt the apparel of his female acolytes was beginning to blend in too much with the clothes worn by women in secular society, hence the ban. Likewise, most Satmar parents do not allow their daughters to wear denim skirts because denim is considered "a modern, immodest material unbecoming of a Jewish girl" (Brown 2015:48).

As the modesty dicta became ever more elaborate, some principals of Hasidic girls schools started sending home meticulous lists of colors, brand names, accessories, and garment types that their students were not allowed to wear. A recent rule at the Satmar girls school, Bais Rochel, decreed that students were not permitted to wear knitted clothes that cling to the body, revealing its shape, and that as the girls mature they must avoid fabrics like wool sweaters that show off their budding figures. Instead, they were told to always put on a long-sleeve blouse *under* a sweater or other knit fabric that hugs the body so that its contours remain hidden. A modesty sheet about this requirement was sent home with girls in first grade (Feldman 2011).

This new directive was also part of the daily modesty lecture at the Satmar school. Girls are warned that those who do not follow the rules of modesty risk making others sin since every time a man glimpses a part of a woman's body that the Torah says should be covered, he is sinning. In other words, immodesty can cause others to transgress (Feldman 2011).

The following story is a popular one at Bais Rochel girls school:

> A tale often taught to Haredi [ultra-Orthodox] school girls is about a Jewish woman who is about to be to be roped to a horse by Cossacks and dragged through the streets until she dies. But before this takes place, she pins or sews her skirt to her lower legs, stitching fabric to flesh so that, during her torturous execution, the garment won't reveal anything that would infect the thoughts of Jewish men. (Bergner 2015:24)

Satmar women in New York City
Source: Alamy stock photo, Alamy.com

The legs of Satmar girls and women are also the focus of unending rabbinic attention. Satmar girls begin wearing long stockings between the ages of three and six—depending on the piety of the family. Once in high school, girls must wear opaque tights or stockings with seams up the back so it is clear that their legs are not bare. In other words, people should only see fabric and not the "horror of exposed skin" (Shein 2006; Feldman 2011:94).

At one time it was acceptable for Satmar teens and women to wear sheerer nylon stockings, but the Rebbe came to believe that such stockings were too provocative. In fact, he ruled that "the redemption of the Jewish people depended on the opacity of women's stockings." As a consequence, he began taking a keen interest in the density of the fabric—the technical term is denier count—of the stockings worn by women in the Satmar community. "The rebbe taught that even 70-denier stockings should not be worn" because this density "is also transparent," according to one of his followers. With the assistance of a Brooklyn businessman the Rebbe developed an exclusive line of fully opaque women's hosiery. The businessman visited several hosiery manufacturers, collected fabric samples from each one, and brought them to the Rebbe to inspect. The Rebbe tested each sample by pulling it over his own arm. If the hair on his arm showed through, the fabric was too transparent, and therefore insufficiently modest. The new dense stockings were given the brand name "Palm," the English translation of the Rebbe's surname—Teitelbaum—which means "date palm" in Yiddish. The palm tree is now used as a logo by members of the Satmar court. Today almost every Satmar woman and girl wears Palm stockings (Heilman 2017:176; Nadler 2011b).

Word of this new stricture quickly spread throughout the Satmar community. An article in *New York Magazine* recounted the reasons why one woman had abandoned Kiryas Joel along with its Satmar restrictions. She specifically cited the horror she felt when her four-year-old daughter proclaimed that "if G-d sees you with your legs uncovered, you go to hell." There is also the sign at the entrance of the Kiryas Joel cemetery: "It is strictly forbidden for women to enter with transparent stockings less than 70 denier. Also, their heads should be completely covered. Respect the holiness of this place!" (Jacobson 2008; Weiss, Neumeister, and Mintz 1995).

The legwear of Satmar females must not only be opaque but also have seams up the back to make plain that no bare skin is exposed. In her novel, Pearl Abraham (1996), herself raised in an ultra-Orthodox family, describes her protagonist's struggle with the Satmar dress code: "The *shadchan* [matchmaker] calls back and tells Father people inform him I do not wear seams. That I've never worn seams. Father says, 'I see her every morning and evening. She's wearing seams. I bought them for her myself.' Ma walks behind Father and beckons me. 'Tell me the truth, once and for all. What you are wearing?' I don't answer."

The Satmar Rebbe continued with his prohibitions. Wearing makeup, he proclaimed, causes cancer: "We are not in heaven, and we can't necessarily point fingers at what precisely is the cause [of breast cancer], but when we see things by women [who apply makeup], and then we see them suffer [from cancer], they must do tshuva—repent!" The author of this report on the

Rebbe's new ban (a former Satmar herself) remarks with tongue in cheek that the Rebbe has received "a doctorate in Causative Holistic Medicine from the Institute of Blame Women." And she continues:

> Actually, the "spiritual" theory that all ills—from hurricanes to cancer—arise from women's un-tznius (immodest) dress is not novel; it has been around for as long as I can remember—intensifying any time there is a tragedy. We were conditioned to believe that mascara, uncovered wigs and other breaches of extreme modesty are to blame for everything. And I mean everything! Hashem [God] keeps close tabs on all his Hasidic ladies, wields a powerful stick, and brings swift punishment onto his people. For eyeliner, cancer; for a skirt that's above four inches below the knee, a hurricane; for stockings that are not bulletproof, a car accident; and so on and so forth. (Goldberger 2014b)

The Rebbe also forbade Satmar girls and women from wearing the color red, a color associated with "loose" morals. This decree was in accord with the stance taken by the famed Talmudic commentator Rashi, who wrote, "Bright red clothing is considered immodest because the clothes are the color of wine and are worn by women to entice" (quoted in Kaye 1987:161).

In case Satmar women are not fully apprised of all such injunctions, a poster on a wall in Williamsburg publicized a forthcoming lecture on female modesty and encouraged all women to "bring a friend" since modesty is of great concern to the community and women need to be "fortified" so they take this teaching seriously. And, indeed, many do. Before the Day of Judgment on Rosh Hashanah, notes one lapsed Satmar, "it wasn't unusual for girls to make tznius-related vows . . . to wear thicker stockings, to never, ever (!) wear eye makeup, to lengthen their skirts and tighten their collars" (Heilman 2006:253; Goldberger 2014e).

All of these directives are overseen by so-called "modesty squads" that operate in Williamsburg and Kiryas Joel. These are groups of Satmar men who seek to enforce "standards of modesty" in their respective communities. One shop owner in Williamsburg, for example, was warned that the female mannequins in her store window "might inadvertently arouse passing men and boys." "Do the neighborhood a favor," she was told, and "take it out of the window. We're trying to safeguard our community." Their power is evident in the fact that of the half dozen or so women's clothing stores on Lee Avenue, the main shopping street in Satmar Williamsburg, only one has mannequins, and those have shapeless, completely clothed torsos (Berger 2013).

Here is one man's account of the modesty police in Williamsburg: "They walk into a store and say it would be a shame if your window was broken or you lost your clientele." Or "they might tell the father of a girl who wears a skirt that's too short and he's, say, a store owner. Then they will say: 'If you ever want to sell a pair of shoes, speak to your daughter.'" Some Satmar concur with this description, saying they are aware of a shadowy group of men who pressure parents to rein in their daughters whose dresses are too short or whose stockings are too sheer, or who talk to boys on their cell phones. One family reported being harassed because the wife had stepped outside her house wearing a housecoat rather than a mandatory, knee-concealing, skirt (quoted in Berger 2013).

One former resident refers to Kiryas Joel's "moral police," the Vaad Hatznius, as "those stupid Taliban." The Vaad write down the car license plates of people who drive on the Sabbath and note which women enter the local supermarket with their legs insufficiently covered. And if they hear a rumor about someone ignoring Satmar directives, the Vaad have been known to show up at the person's house to see if illicit movies are being watched on a computer or a small television set is hidden under the bed (Jacobson 2008).

Another former resident of Kiryas Joel notes a further action by the Vaad. Fitness classes for women were offered a few days a week at a gym in the village. A number of women enrolled and arrived wearing terry cloth turbans, black skirts, and thick Palm stockings to do strength training for the first time in their lives. Some became quite proficient doing push-ups and other exercises. But it did not take long for the Vaad to close the gym down, calling the classes "immodest" even though no men attended them and everyone was dressed in the same modest fashion they wore in public. Wearing leggings or shorts or other gym clothes, of course, was simply inconceivable (Goldberger 2014c).

These self-appointed modesty police also use social and economic pressure to enforce conformity in women's dress. Those who do not conform are often dealt with harshly. In one instance, a woman's home in Kiryas Joel was broken into and her cell phone was confiscated by the Vaad. Similar home invasions have taken place in Williamsburg, where iPads and computers, deemed inappropriate for children, were seized. Some members of these groups consider themselves *Gut's polizei* (God's police). They are self-appointed but they could not operate without at least the tacit consent of the Satmar Rebbes (Berger 2013).

The dress of Satmar women in Williamsburg and Kiryas Joel is quite uniform and contrasts with that of slightly less conservative Hasidic sects in Boro Park, Brooklyn, and elsewhere. While Satmar women in Williamsburg are almost uniformly dressed in navy blue, dark brown, or black suits or coats, opaque seamed stockings, and head scarves or turbans, women in Boro Park wear more colorful and diverse clothing—long-sleeve sweaters, denim skirts, brightly colored suits, and sneakers on some young girls, as well as the occasional luxuriant wig made of real human hair. The elaborate clothing constraints placed on Satmar women are seen by other conservative Hasidic courts like the Bobov, also in Brooklyn, as the most *frum*, the most religiously extreme, and Satmar women's self-presentation is considered *nebby*—nerdy. In short, the Satmar are widely viewed even by other conservative Orthodox Jews as the most zealous in their demand for female modesty (Winston 2005; Benor 2012).

WHAT'S A WOMAN TO WEAR?
THE FLDS AND THE PASHTUN

> The Pashtun are so jealous of the modesty and sanctity of their women that they cannot tolerate even appreciation of the beauty of their women by an outsider.
>
> —*Pashtun Culture and History* blog, 2010

> In a country where women are still kept hidden . . . a naked face is almost the same as the fully bared breasts of a prostitute.
>
> —Phyllis Chesler, *An American Bride in Kabul*, 2014

The dress codes that ensure female modesty for members of the Fundamentalist Church of Jesus Christ of Latter-Day Saints and the Pashtun are decidedly less elaborate than those of the Satmar. After all, they have not been the subject of centuries of rabbinic debate and embellishment. Nevertheless, in these two groups, as with the Satmar, the single most compelling command for women is to cover up! Women belonging to the FLDS sect are clothed from neck to ankles in their highly distinctive long-sleeve, floor-length "prairie-style" dresses, while when Pashtun women appear in public, they are swathed from head to toe in yards of billowing fabric.

The FLDS practice of wearing prairie dresses and covering nearly every inch of flesh did not begin until after the infamous 1953 raid at Short Creek, today the twin southwestern towns of Colorado City and Hildale. As we know, the shock of that raid led members of the FLDS to further withdraw from American society. One way to distinguish themselves from the surrounding "gentiles" was to require all female adherents to dress like the women of yore heading west on a wagon train.

The modesty code for FLDS women is not limited to these old-fashioned dresses. Every day they must also don four or five layers of clothing beneath their frocks—Prophet-mandated long underwear, bras, leggings, and long slips. Recall that the two towns in Arizona and Utah, the home to a majority of FLDS adherents, are breathtakingly hot during several months of the year. Thus, the mandate to wear such attire in all kinds of weather is not unlike the

FLDS women in prairie dresses
Source: Alamy stock photo, Alamy.com

Satmar Rebbe's insistence that women wear thick stockings and long sleeves all year round (Jessop 2007).

The color of the FLDS prairie dresses is limited to pastel shades because "the spirit of God cannot reside in anything colorful." Apart from this, "the spirit of God" cannot reside in anything that is black, or is printed, or in any item of clothing that is red because "red is reserved for Christ." Another reason for banning bright colors is because "such vibrancy bespeaks a proud and arrogant woman." Of note is that when Warren Jeffs led the sect the color rules laid down were always changing. "Wearing certain colors was evil one week but perfectly OK the next," said one former FLDS member (*FLDS 101* 2009d; Musser 2013:67).

How to explain this dress code? In order to conform to FLDS beliefs, women have to be covered from neck to toe because, they are told, their bodies are considered "sacred temples" that must be concealed from the world at large. This is why girls and women should always be covered in public—showing bare arms or legs or feet is considered offensive to God. Others suggest a more practical reason for this uniformity: it discourages co-wives from becoming jealous of one another since all wear nearly identical outfits. After all, as an observer of FLDS dress has remarked, "One consequence of the strict hair and dress uniform prescribed to all FLDS women is that they lose their individuality, resembling thousands of versions of the same ideal" (Oswaks 2016).

But more fundamentally, the unique prairie dresses of FLDS women also serve to distinguish them not only from secular American society but also from members of other Mormon polygamist sects. As one former devotee of the FLDS notes: "Every [Mormon] fundamentalist group has its own particular rules and mode of dress . . . every group is convinced that they are a 'peculiar people'" (Singular 2008; Spencer 2009:7).

What I find fascinating in all of this are the striking parallels between the FLDS and the Satmar in some of the dicta surrounding modest female dress. Both prohibit women from wearing pants, both forbid them from wearing red articles of clothing as well as face makeup, both insist they be clothed year-round in outfits that are at times inappropriate for the weather, and both use differences in dress to distinguish themselves from other related sects, for the Satmar from the dress codes of other Hasidic courts and for the FLDS from other Mormon polygamist communities.

The Satmar and FLDS are also alike in the emphasis they place on the defense of modesty at all times. A sign outside the lone restaurant in Colorado City decrees the following: "Cover your elbows, knees, shoulders and toes, or out this door you goes" (cited in Quinn 1993:269). This, of course, is reminiscent of the sign at the entrance of Kiryas Joel stating the dress code for all female visitors to the village.

In Pashtun society the command for women to "cover up" is taken to an even greater extreme than in the other two cases we are examining. The broad separation of males and females in Pashtun society is reflected in the clothes that women are required to wear. "Pashtun culture," writes one observer, "cannot respect a woman unless she is covered from head to toe." Anyone who has seen the *burqa*, the blue billowing outer garment that Pashtun women are required to wear in public, will realize the accuracy of this statement. Not only is the entire body covered but the head and face are completely veiled, with a semi-transparent piece of fabric covering the eyes. So complete is the coverage of the *burqa* that it has been called a "sensory deprivation chamber, a moving prison shroud that renders women socially invisible" (Orbala 2013; Chesler 2014:184).

For Pashtun women to leave home without an all-encompassing *burqa* is the equivalent of Western women running naked through the streets. And a

Pashtun women in *burqas*
Source: Alamy stock photo, Alamy.com

man lifting the *burqa* of a woman is akin to undressing her in public (Pessala 2012; Rubin 2015a).

And, once again, we have the prohibition on wearing the color red. Women are not to wear bright colors, especially red, that will attract attention to themselves. "The color of fire is considered to be overtly sexual, meant to arrest the eyes of men. It is for someone who means to be flamboyant," writes a student of Pashtun culture. As a consequence, no respectable Pashtun woman will wear red in public (Nordberg 2014:28).

One might ask: Was the all-enshrouding *burqa* and the other dictates about female modesty mandated by the Taliban, a Sunni Islamic fundamentalist political movement whose members are largely Pashtun? Or are they requirements imposed on women in Afghanistan before the Taliban came to power in the late 1990s? Clearly, the latter is the case. A few years *before* the Taliban took over, a ruling in Islamic law (a *fatwa*) was issued that stated:

> Women were not to wear perfume, noisy bangles or Western clothes. Veils had to cover the body at all times and clothes were not to be made of material which was soft or which rustled. Women were not to walk in the middle of the street, or swing their hips, they were not to talk, laugh or joke with strangers or foreigners. (cited in Billaud 2015:53)

Then, once the Taliban regime was in control, many of these restrictions were formalized:

> Women, you should not step outside of your residence. If you go outside the house you should not be like women who used to go with fashionable clothes wearing cosmetics and appearing in front of every man before the coming of Islam. (cited in Billaud 2015:57)

Although the Taliban are no longer in complete control of Afghanistan, dress codes for women have not changed. From early puberty through old age what women wear is subject to strict social control. Many "freelance enforcers," including young boys, take on the role of the religious police and harass grown women if they deem them inappropriately dressed (Nordberg 2014).

WHAT IS IT ABOUT WOMEN'S HAIR?

Just as with clothing, FLDS and Pashtun directives concerning women's hair and hair covering are less elaborate than those of the Satmar, although all three groups have something to say about a woman's "crowning glory." The Hasidic preoccupation with women's hair is based on the Talmud's suggestion that a woman's uncovered hair is equivalent to physical nudity. *Sair B'Isha Erva:* literally translated, "the hair of a woman is [considered] nakedness" according to the Talmud and therefore must be covered. Says one former Hasid: "A woman showing her hair is akin to showing her private parts." The result is that the Torah forbids married women from appearing in public with their heads uncovered[1] (Goldberger and Steinmetz 2014; Deen 2015:68).

Just as what is deemed modest attire for women differs among Hasidic courts, so do customary hair coverings vary depending on how *frum* (devout) the court's adherents are. "A woman wearing a wig is fairly liberal. A woman in a wig and a hat is a bit more religious. A scarf indicates extreme piety. The term here might be 'a hat family,'" remarks one observer. "The *shadchen* (matchmaker) would say, 'I have a great girl from a 'hat family,' or from a 'scarf family,'" indicating the family's level of piety (Turkewitz 2014:23).

In Hasidic communities the head coverings used by the mothers of the bride and groom are often the first consideration in arranging a *shidduch*, a match. Except for the occasional bride who challenges maternal tradition and covers her hair with a less, or sometimes more, stringent head covering, a woman's headgear indicates her family's level of religiosity and, more importantly, the piousness of the traditions that her mother follows. Fundamentally, the type of head covering worn by the females in a family is of key importance when a match is being considered (Goldberger 2014d; Vizel 2014).

One example of this variation is found among the Lubavitchers, the proselytizing Hasidic sect mentioned in chapter 2. Uncovered wigs are approved for married women in this court because the late Lubavitcher Rebbe said that if a woman wore a hat or a scarf, she might be tempted to remove it, but no one would ever remove a *sheitel* (wig) in public. However, wearing *only* a wig is considered impious among the Satmar and women are told not to enter

---

1. Unmarried girls are not required to wear a head covering.

a synagogue in Williamsburg with an uncovered wig (Goldberger and Steinmetz 2014; Vizel 2014).

While most Hasidic women wear wigs, many also cover the wig with a kerchief or a hat, which is considered more pious. Moreover, some Rebbes insist on an additional covering over a woman's wig to ensure that no one mistakes it for natural hair (Mintz 1992).

Contrast the Lubvitchers' stance with that of the Satmar who, once again, are at the extreme end of the piety continuum. As we have seen, for Satmar and other Hasidim the nature of one's head covering bespeaks one's religiosity. As such, notes a Satmar woman, "In our world, it's not acceptable to wear *just* a *sheitel* (wig)." Indeed, married Satmar women are expected to shave their entire heads and wear a kerchief or hat along with or instead of the more common wig. Many of the most pious Satmar women do not even wear wigs. Instead they shave their heads and cover them with a solid or floral scarf (a *tichel*) or with a round woven piece of silk (a *shpitzel*) that is then topped with a hat. Writes one former Satmar woman about this practice: "To me, shaving embodies the enormous power the community has to make its rebellious women naked, humiliated, powerless and defenseless" (Shein 2006:48; Goldberger 2014d; Vizel 2012).

The Satmar Rebbe feels so strongly that married women's hair is *ervah* (nakedness) that he prohibits them from taking a chance that a single strand of hair will be exposed. The safest, and according to the Satmar Rebbe, the *only* way to assure that is for women to completely shave their heads (Goldberger 2013a).

In Pearl Abraham's novel *The Romance Reader* (1996, 254–55), character Rachel Benjamin describes the first time she shaved her head shortly after her marriage. "I'm not shaving my hair," she tells her mother. "Think of the scandal," her mother replies. "Rabbi Benjamin's first married daughter with a full head of hair!' . . . I sit on the edge of the chair . . . I hear the drone of the razor begin. It vibrates on my scalp, and a chunk of long hair falls in my lap. . . . I run into the bathroom. . . . In the mirror above the sink, my eyes are wide open. I'm different now. There's a big hole where my hair is missing."

The late Rebbe of the Satmar, Yo'el Teitelbaum, once gave an emotional speech decrying married women who did not shave their heads:

> Jewish daughters, our mothers and fathers gave up their lives to our Father in Heaven for the sanctity of His name, but you, their daughters, don't want to give up even a few hairs? What does (God) ask of us? A few hairs! Because of

a few hairs you are making yourselves lose both worlds. Jewish daughters,
shave your hair and give honor to the Torah. (quoted in Goldberger 2013a)

Following this admonition, one lapsed Satmar woman recalled how difficult it was for a woman living in Kiryas Joel to hide any growth of hair. A
lone lock of hair sticking out of a turban might be noticed by a neighbor or by
the *"mikvah* lady"[2] (attendant in a *mikvah*), who was then sent to inspect the
offending growth:

> "I was sent to go down to your house and check if your head is completely
> shaven," she said in Hungarian Yiddish, "so we can know that your son can be
> in religious school. We cannot accept your son in school until you've done
> what every holy Jewish woman should do, so I'd like to come to your house as
> soon as possible." Then she told me about the many blessings that will come to
> me for this great *mitzvah* [good deed], and she reminded me of the illnesses
> and accidents that come from women like me who cannot resist their feminine
> *yetzer horah* [evil inclinations]. She talked about cancer and recent tragedies
> and said that I [may] never know if God had not sent them because of my sins.
> (Vizel 2012)

As with other matters concerning female modesty, the customs of the
FLDS and the Pashtun in regard to women's hair are less elaborate than those
of the Satmar. For FLDS women there is one simple command: Never cut
your hair. Many have internalized this directive and agree that for a woman
to cut her hair is a truly shameful act. According to FLDS teachings, the
reason for this prohibition is that during the Second Coming of Christ when
all true believers rise up to Heaven, women will need their waist-length hair
to wash the feet of Christ. The hair of FLDS women is their "crowning
glory," they are told, and they must wear it swept up in a towering, sculpted
hairstyle with a Gibson girl wave in front that requires cloud upon cloud of
hairspray to stay in place. These hairstyles, which are "rigidly monitored,"
are facetiously dubbed "plyg-dos" (polygamous hairdos) by gentiles (Bennion 2011a).

Finally, what do the Pashtun have to say about women's hair? There does
not seem to be much discussion about it other than that it should always be
completely covered when a woman is in the presence of men who are not
close relatives. As one visiting ethnographer reports, she was constantly told

---

2. A *mikvah* is a ritual bath that Orthodox Jewish women must submerge themselves in after
completing a menstrual cycle. This is discussed in chapter 5.

by Pashtun women to "cover your head" and that "it's a sin to go bare-headed. It's not doing Pashto." As we know, Pashto refers not only to the Pashtun language but also to a person's ethnic identity and an honorable way of life. Suffice it to say that it is simply unthinkable for a Pashtun woman to appear in public with her hair uncovered (Grima 2004:27).

We now turn to the issue of marriage and male control in these three communities, a topic that is essential for understanding each group's subsequent insistence on unlimited procreation. We will also see the ways in which, because of early marriage, girls and young women pass from being under the control of their fathers to being controlled by their husbands.

Chapter Four

Marriage and Male Control

Give me a girl at an impressionable age and she is mine for life.
—Muriel Sparks, *The Prime of Miss Jean Brodie*, 1961

What is it about marriage that largely sets in stone the life trajectories of females in each of these three communities? The most striking commonality in marriage in each one is a woman's minimal control over her life as she is passed from the authority of her father to that of her husband. She not only may have little say as to whom she marries, she also usually has little influence on the timing and conditions of her marital union. In each case couples are paired for marriage with little or no regard for mutual attraction or compatibility.

In a real sense, women in these communities have been trained to submit to these marital measures for their entire lives. Because there are very few converts to the FLDS or the Satmar and Pashtun females are taught from an early age to be submissive to the wishes of their male relatives, most women have been lifelong members of these communities whose values and behavioral expectations have been instilled in them from birth. It is simply the only way of life they know.

Take the FLDS, for example, where the paramount goal for all women devotees is—using the local expression—"to keep sweet." In essence, to be totally obedient and passive. "Perfect obedience produces perfect faith," the sect's women are taught from an early age. Or as one FLDS woman put it: "Men were in charge of us. They were the only way we were going to get to Heaven. We had to love them no matter what" (quoted in Bennion 2011a:115).

Recalled another FLDS woman: "Everything was devoted to the father. When girls got married, they were supposed to transfer all ties and loyalties to their husbands and have perfect obedience to them because their husbands were their direct ties to God" (quoted in Daynes 2011:126).

In line with this stance, the Prophet himself stated again and again that "a woman's desires should be to her husband" and that she should "build up her husband by being submissive." In short, this arrangement made it nearly impossible for a woman to make decisions about her own life (Jessop 2007:204).

Similar attitudes are expected of Satmar wives. Once a woman is married, she must be disciplined in her modesty, which requires that she "recognize and submit to new male authority figures, her husband and his *rebbe*" (Fader 2009:207). Likewise, under Pashtun tradition fathers have absolute power over their daughters until they marry, when such power passes to their husbands. Fathers can betroth girls at birth, or at any age, with or without their consent, sometimes making them bartered goods to resolve family disputes.

MARRIAGE: FLDS STYLE

What is involved in "Celestial Marriage" or "the Principle," as the FLDS call polygyny?[1] It is essentially at the core of FLDS beliefs, and adherents not only actively promote plural marriage, but nearly everyone in the community either is living in a polygamous household or was born into one. Recall that members believe that plural marriage is a divine commandment and when it was outlawed by mainstream Mormonism in the late nineteenth century this eventually led to the FLDS break with the mother church (Quinn 1993).

A man requires three or more wives to enter the Celestial Kingdom and these wives are expected to bear and raise a "righteous seed," that is, children, for their husband's kingdom. While not all members of the FLDS are polygamous—some are in monogamous unions—and a man can delay taking a second wife, he will not be considered truly faithful if he rejects the Prophet's command that he marry an additional woman (Bennion 2011a, 2012).

Prophet Warren Jeffs believed that he should marry off girls while they were still young so that they would not have the chance to think of other males in a romantic light. Thus, men would be provided with a "clean girl,"

---

1. Polygyny, one form of polygamy or plural marriage, is defined as the marriage between one man and two or more women such as occurs among the FLDS and the Pashtun. A much rarer form of polygamy is polyandry, in which one woman is married to two or more men.

clean both physically and mentally. Clean girls, he thought, would "imprint" on their older husbands and follow their commands.

As one might imagine, feminism of any kind did not sit well in this patriarchal milieu. Declared Prophet Rulon Jeffs, father of Warren: "We hear a lot in the nation today about the liberation movement of women. I want to tell the world . . . the only true freedom of woman is in submitting herself to her husband and head, and living his law as he lives and abides the law of God" (quoted in Bramham 2009:191).

According to one former FLDS member, the motto for the sect's females was to "keep sweet, never complain, and always, always defer to your husband in every important decision." Women were never to try to lead their husbands. "It was in the very roots of our religion that a woman was bound to follow her husband's instructions and decisions no matter what" (Musser 2013:46). A woman should defer to her husband in all things, including his personal tastes so that if a man does not like shrimp or a certain vegetable then his wife cannot eat them either (Jessop 2007).

Similarly, one plural FLDS wife raised in Colorado City said she believes that the husband "controls the family, controls the wives, controls the income, controls the discipline" and that the wives are "expected to submit themselves to their husband in all things" (quoted in Quinn 1993:263).

Rachel Jeffs, one of Prophet Warren's daughters, highlights this woman's perception when describing the treatment her father received from his many wives. "Father was like a king in his household, and the women bowed to his every command. They stood around, eager for the privilege of handing him his spoon or washing the table after he'd finished eating. It was the highest honor to be the wife chosen to make his meal" (Jeffs 2017:114).

Once of marriageable age, a girl would be "turned into the priesthood" by her father or another male relative, meaning that it was time for the Prophet to find a suitable mate for her. Although the would-be husband and wife were supposed to have the right of refusal, both were under a great deal of pressure to go along with the Prophet's wishes. This form of arranged marriage is called "placement marriage" and it occurs after the Prophet declares that God has revealed the match to him. The only way to avoid the placement system is for a couple to have sex with each other and confess their sin to the Prophet, who then tells them to get married civilly and repent. After a year, if he believes the couple has repented, they will be rebaptized and sealed in an FLDS marriage ceremony (Daynes 2011).

Some of Warren Jeffs's wives posing with his photo
Source: Office of the Attorney General, Texas

As soon as the Prophet announces his divine revelation the couple is informed and the marriage takes place within a matter of days or even hours. Until a young woman is placed, she is supposed to have no relationships with boys or men, and falling in love without the Priesthood's consent is deemed an act of rebellion. If a boy and girl decide to get married and just go ahead and wed, they can never be gods because one must be married by revelation through the Prophet (*FLDS 101* 2009a). As a consequence, it comes as no surprise that dating is strictly forbidden (Driggs 2011; Miles 2011).

Parents cannot object to a marriage ordered by the Prophet. To do so is to be disobedient and to risk losing one's FLDS membership, home, and family. One member explained, "I never wanted to be married to my husband. My parents objected to the marriage, but they never said a word about that until it was over and it was safe to do so. They were afraid of what would happen if they did." After a daughter marries, she is no longer part of her father's family. He no longer has a claim on her since she now belongs to her husband's family (*FLDS 101* 2009a, 2009b).

Following the law of placement, a young girl is sometimes assigned to a much older man, especially if she is not his first wife. On average polygamous husbands are about twelve years older than their young brides, although some teenage girls are wed to men who are twenty or thirty years older than they are. The average age of marriage for girls in the twin towns of the FLDS is sixteen, but marrying at fourteen or fifteen is not uncommon. However, if a woman reaches twenty-one and is still unmarried, she is considered an "old maid" (Bennion 2011a; Daynes 2011).

Boys as well as girls are raised to accept these traditions. In the FLDS community twelve-year-old boys are initiated into the "Aaronic Priesthood," which allows them greater authority over females, including their mothers and sisters. From then they are expected to act superior to, or at least feign indifference towards, the girls and women in their lives. Moreover, boys are encouraged not to be overly devoted to any one woman since "polygamy depends on a man desiring multiple wives and being available emotionally and physically to all of them" (Singular 2008:50).

At the same time, FLDS girls are taught that being married and giving birth is their highest calling, their very reason for being. By age fourteen girls are eager to marry, for that is the only future open to them. Besides, FLDS girls are constantly being groomed for marriage. "Learn how to keep house, behead a chicken and cook it up for your husband," instructed a manual at Alta Academy, the FLDS school in Salt Lake City (*FLDS 101* 2009d).

Said one former FLDS devotee: "I'd been taught that all women needed a man to make it into heaven. A woman's husband was going to be her savior. He would take her hand and lead her through the veil into heaven." This belief established that the husband was indeed the divinely ordained head of the household, or its "Priesthood head," as he was called (Spencer 2009:18–19).

A woman's only path to God and salvation is through her husband. Women cannot directly receive revelations from God, so that anything God wants to communicate to a woman will be transmitted to her only through her husband, her Priesthood head. Indeed, women are so low on the heavenly totem pole that they require their husband's postmortem consent to enter the Celestial Kingdom (Weyermann 2011).

How does a woman deal with the realization that her husband is likely to take on more than one wife? From birth on girls are raised to believe that being married to a man with multiple wives is the highest form of holiness, that being part of such a polygamous union is the only way they are guaranteed their own god-like entry into heaven. Moreover, even if a woman disapproves of her husband taking another wife, the Prophet warns women against running "to their friends or someone they think can give them counsel. You run anywhere else besides your Priesthood head, you could run into trouble . . . don't ever go beyond your bounds and try to rule over him." The price of doing so means being locked out of heaven (quoted in Bennion 2011b:178).

To the FLDS a man's wife is his property and he can do whatever he wants with her. If a woman complains about violence or abuse, most fellow FLDS members will turn on her. In fact, such complaints—like anything else that goes wrong in a woman's life, from a miscarried pregnancy to a child breaking an arm—are viewed as proof that she is unworthy of salvation. Besides, going to outside authorities about the abuse is simply unthinkable. It is also assumed that a woman's disobedience or defiance is the cause of the problem. It is always *her* fault. To admit to being beaten is a great disgrace, so women rarely speak about the abuse they suffer because to do so would be considered disloyal. "As a culture, we're taught to just hold it all inside, put on a face, and raise the kids," said one ex-FLDS woman (Wall 2008; quoted in Havens 2017).

The physical and sexual abuse of women and children is generally ignored by the larger FLDS community. "As a community, the feeling was that the outside world was our enemy. Its laws and rules did not apply to us in any way. There was no way that someone in the FLDS would report abuse that they'd witnessed or suspected to the authorities for investigation. Anyone who did that would be seen as a traitor to the entire community," according to one former FLDS member. This is very reminiscent of the Satmar's failure to report the sexual abuse of minors within their own community along with the ostracism faced by anyone who dared to report such abuse to the authorities (Jessop 2007:37, 92–93).

Physical abuse was not the only means of control. Prior to Warren Jeffs's ascent as Prophet women and children were routinely beaten by the men in their lives. But after he took over from his father Jeffs banned such behavior and said that anyone who strikes a family member again would be expelled from the FLDS. Despite momentary relief, the women of the twin towns soon learned that some punitive actions were even worse than being beaten. Now when a woman failed to obey her husband and he reported this to the Prophet, Jeffs would order the man "to take her kids from her, and move her to the trailer court, or put her in complete isolation from the family. Ban her from the church." Complete control achieved (quoted in Anderson 2018).

To make certain that women continue to go along with these polygamous ideals it is best that they not receive too much education. In a 1998 sermon Prophet Warren Jeffs warned about the perils of an educated woman: "Such a woman will seek to rule over her husband . . . rather she should completely submit [to her husband] where he shall rule over her" (quoted in Bennion 2011b:177).

When the future Prophet was principal of the FLDS school in the 1990s, the main instruction for girls was how to be good wives and mothers. Jeffs taught them how to keep house, cook, comfort their husbands, and raise loyal and obedient children. "Never ever stand up against him. Never say no to your husband," inveighed the Prophet. "Girls and women must never raise their voices, criticize their husbands or question male authority" (quoted in Singular 2008:39–40, 87). In short, they were told to always "keep sweet."

In keeping with these sentiments, here is a questionnaire seventh-grade FLDS girls were required to fill out in class:

> Are you a girl in the FLDS applying for the job of mother?
> Have you acquired heavenly smiles? How about unshakable sweetness?
> Have you learned to put the priesthood first? (Carlisle 2015b)

One element left out of schooling in the FLDS community was any discussion of sex. In fact, the topic of sex was strictly off-limits and a girl's husband was supposed to teach her all she needed to know about this "sacred matter." This is why the chapter on human reproduction was deleted from the fifth-grade health education textbooks in the FLDS school and its science books were doctored so that parts of the human anatomy were covered up. "They would just cut little pieces of paper and stick it over the private areas even if there wasn't a private area there just to make a point" (*FLDS 101* 2009d).

One former FLDS adherent writes that at the time of her marriage at age fourteen, "I knew nothing about sex. Absolutely nothing. I didn't even know that sex existed. It was a word not used in the FLDS culture, and what it described is never discussed before marriage. I didn't know husbands and wives did it. Growing up in the FLDS, I had no concept of where babies really came from" (Wall 2009:168).

The sex act itself is often a formal, mechanical affair in which men and women do not remove their sacred long underwear. One FLDS wife who had been married for seventeen years said she never saw her husband completely undressed. It is sinful for men to derive pleasure from the sex act, the Prophet decreed, and sex with multiple partners—other than wives—or someone of the same sex is strictly forbidden. Then, too, FLDS men are not supposed to have sex with their pregnant wives because of the belief that sex is strictly for procreation; if one's wife is already "with child," then what is the point? (Wall 2009; Singular 2008)

Because of their potential as brides and child-bearers, girls are seen as a valuable and scarce commodity within the FLDS community. But, as we know, plural marriage creates a numerical problem. While in most American communities the male-female ratio is roughly fifty-fifty, in the FLDS community polygyny makes for a mathematical conundrum in terms of gender. Sex ratios in the twin towns are skewed, with only eighty-eight men for every one hundred women aged eighteen to sixty-four, likely the result of the "lost boys" phenomenon. If older men marry multiple young brides, what is to become of young men? If young girls are allowed to choose their own husbands, they most likely will choose someone close to their own age, leaving the good old boys and the aging FLDS male hierarchy to do without an additional wife. One woman, a former FLDS member, claims the placement system originated because of the intense competition for wives between bachelors and married men (Heaton and Jacobson 2011; Brower 2012).

In short, there are simply not enough women to go around to satisfy the demands of plural marriage, resulting in an excess of single young men with few prospects of marriage to even one woman. By 2000 the pool of young girls who could be assigned to older men was running low and the solution was to "get rid of" the glut of young, unmarried males. And, as we have seen, under the orders of the Prophet, hundreds and hundreds of boys—some as young as thirteen—were abandoned by their parents, driven from the community, and left to fend for themselves. These boys were expelled from the FLDS for such minor infractions as listening to music, talking to a girl, or wearing short-sleeve shirts. Quite simply, expelling teenage boys from the sect meant more potential wives for the older men who remained behind (Singular 2008; Weyermann 2011).

What about divorce in this setting? Divorce is uncommon since a couple's marriage is commanded by God as revealed to the Prophet. As such, there is no formal means of divorce in the FLDS. Still, the Prophet sometimes allowed a woman in an unhappy marriage to leave her husband and then be "reassigned" to another man. If a woman and her children had their own house and were rarely or never visited by her husband, she was essentially a divorcée even without a formal decree of any kind. Sometimes wives were "free" to leave their husbands but they would have to leave without their children and with nothing but the clothes on their backs. But there is yet another possibility. Beginning in the late 1990s the Prophet sometimes excommunicated FLDS men who displeased him and expelled them from the community while their wives and children were reassigned to other men (Daynes 2011; Moore-Emmett 2004; Spencer 2007).

In the world outside the FLDS only the first wife has legal standing. She is the legal wife; the others are simply single women. While these other wives might have had a church wedding performed by the Prophet, after children arrive the larger society views them as "unwed mothers." That label, as we know, is very valuable to the FLDS since they help support the large number of children born in the community, a community in which nearly one-third of FLDS families fall below the official poverty line. "Single" mothers and their sons and daughters qualify for public assistance, typically around $1,000 a month, making them highly useful tools for "bleeding the beast," as the FLDS male hierarchy refers to taking money from the United States government (Heaton and Jacobson 2011).

WHAT IS IT ABOUT SATMAR MARRIAGE?

One observer of Satmar life concisely summarizes its marriage customs for girls and women as follows: "There are rules, always have been—that one must be married after eighteen and before twenty. By twenty-one every matchmaker is involved. By twenty-two, special prayers are uttered at holy graves. By twenty-three—by twenty-three. . . . Well, there was no such thing as twenty-three. By twenty-three, you are married. You just are." This is reminiscent of the FLDS dictum that if a woman is unmarried at twenty-one she is "over the hill" (Brown 2015:114).

In the Satmar community men and women must marry soon after reaching physical maturity so as to avoid being tempted by any prurient thoughts or desires. Satmar fathers are instructed by their Rebbe that all of their children should marry at a young age while they are still "holy and pure." Here, too, the Satmar resemble the FLDS with their emphasis on the "purity" of youth, their total ban on dating, and their vigorous warnings against romantic entanglements of any kind before marriage (Poll 1971).

Sex and sexuality are topics to be diligently avoided and Satmar women and men are expected to know little or nothing about the subject before marriage. What is taught in Satmar schools is limited, especially when it comes to anything to do with men, women, and sex. To wit, here is what one school principal says to his teachers: "We don't expect them to talk about boys and girls. Girls have their activities and boys have activities, but not

together. You wouldn't talk about sex or anything that has to do with reproduction. Or boyfriends [or] girlfriends." Similarly, one Satmar school gave
its teachers a short bullet point list of what *not* to teach in class:

> Do not talk about boyfriend-girlfriend parties and so on.
>
> Any discussion or story regarding boy-girl relationships, romance, sexual
> problems, sexual organs, etc. is strictly forbidden.
>
> Certain subjects should never be discussed when in the classroom: the
> theory of evolution; the creation of the world. (quoted in Shaffir
> 1995:44, 46)

Sex and bodily functions appear to be among the most taboo subjects in
the Satmar world. Modesty in women not only entails what they wear and
how they behave but also that they have little knowledge about their own
bodies. Many do not know the names of the parts of the body or have any
information about the physical changes that occur during puberty. One girl
who attended a Satmar school notes that in ninth grade she was taught to use
the bathroom quickly lest her exposed unmentionables lead her to sinful acts
of self-examination (Davidman 2015; Brodesser-Akner 2017).

For ultra-Orthodox women their entire sex education comes right before
their wedding nights in classes or tutorials with a *kallah* or marriage instructor, typically a *rebbetzin*, a rabbi's wife. Here they are taught the sacred rules
of sexuality, including the laws of family purity. Instructs one manual: "The
lights should be off, a sheet should cover the couple, the position should be
missionary—the wife is charged with keeping sex spiritual, keeping it
chaste." One *kallah* instructor told a Satmar teenager about to be married
about the "holy place inside each woman." She described it as a "hallway
leading to a little door," which opens to the womb, the *mekor* or the "source,"
as the instructor called it (Bergner 2015:26; Feldman 2011).

One formerly ultra-Orthodox woman insists that such *kallah* instruction
simply cannot overcome a lifetime of sexual repression. "There is no such
thing as affection or hugging that is not sexual, we are taught. Boys can't
possibly hold our hands without thinking of sex, or listen to us talk without
thinking of sex. Our bodies are a thing to be feared and covered and not
talked about. Our bodies are owned by the collective—by the male-dominated collective—not by ourselves," she explained with bitterness (Sztokman
2014).

There is indeed a great deal of sexual repression in the Hasidic world. As
one observer remarked, Hasidic customs are resolute on holiness and priva-

cy, but they also proclaim that "there's only one kind of sex and it tells you when you can and when you can't. The [Orthodox] Law puts sex and sexuality into a box, just like it does the rest of life." Teenagers are routinely terrorized into avoiding masturbation and taught to treat sexuality as degrading and shameful; casual interaction with the opposite sex is seen as deviant (Lax 2015:313; Sable 2013).

One Satmar woman describes sexuality among her co-religionists in the following terms: "Sleeping with your husband on Friday night is twice as good as any other night. But you can't look at him. The room has to be pitch dark. There's no foreplay. This is totally about reproduction. You're supposed to be thinking about God the whole time" (Jacobson 2008).

Says one sex therapist who treats Satmar women: "About sexuality, their minds have been kept free of information and infused with fear." And she goes on: "They have zero—zero connection to pleasure. And there's no vocabulary to start with them. We have an intake form to fill out, and they get to 'orgasm' and go to the receptionist and ask, 'What is this?' When [I begin] to explore whether they've ever been aroused, they have no understanding of the concept." But, according to the therapist, there is also an erotic ideal that Hasidic cultures share. After a young Satmar woman marries—often to a man she has met and spoken with only once or twice before the wedding—she is supposed to feel that sex is a blessing, not just a painful or repellent reproductive chore (Bergner 2015:24).

The therapist went on to discuss her experience with such women. In order to treat frigidity in one Satmar woman, "the suggestions ranged from the seemingly modest to the more direct, from reading romance novels to kissing with the lights on to wearing a lacy nightgown to his touching her clitoris to the use of a vibrator." The Satmar woman said she was willing to try some of these things if her Rebbe okayed it. The woman then brought the list of suggestions home to her husband, who took it to their Rebbe. He then ruled, one by one, on whether these interventions were allowed. The woman reported back to the therapist that the Rebbe had ruled against all of them. After this woman found out what and where her clitoris is—following the birth of her three children—the sex therapist commented wryly, "Merely having this basic knowledge put her ahead of plenty of [my] orthodox patients, who tend to be from the Satmar sect" (Bergner 2015:24).

Satmar and other Hasidim who appear to break the rigid sexual codes of their respective communities are sometimes sent to one of a handful of accommodating psychiatrists in the New York area where they are prescribed antipsychotics, hormones, or antidepressants. A Satmar man claims to know rabbis who hand out medications to boys who are caught or who confess to masturbating. Such behavior is often interpreted as a sign of mental illness, which is punished where it matters most—in the marriage market. If word gets out that someone is on medication, that could hurt any chance of making a good match. But what are such people guilty of? Other than masturbation, some have been accused of displaying a "too high" sex drive or experimenting with or even fantasizing about same-sex partners (Unger-Sargon 2016).

The omission of any discussion of sex and sexuality should be seen within the larger context of the education of Satmar women, the contours of which were and are still open to question. As one observer of this community remarked, "In countries around the world, a woman with an education is the most powerful instrument of social change that any society can devise. Of course the isolated Satmar wish to keep women uneducated" (Bellafante 2016). Higher education is abjured in Satmar redoubts like Williamsburg, where in 1990 only 4 percent of residents were college graduates, and Kiryas Joel, where in 2000 fewer than 3 percent of the population held higher degrees. In fact, in Kiryas Joel fewer than 40 percent of residents have the equivalent of a high school diploma (Heilman 2006; McAfee 2015).

In 2016 the United Talmudic Academy, the governing body for Satmar girls schools, issued an edict saying it was now forbidden for young women to receive any training beyond the twelfth grade. "It has lately become the new trend that girls and married women are pursuing degrees in special education. And so we'd like to let their parents know that it is against the Torah." The Yiddish-language decree then goes on to say that college education for girls is "dangerous" and that "no girls attending our school are allowed to study and get a degree. We have to keep our school safe and we can't allow any secular influences in our holy environment" (Bellafante 2016).

Prior to the edict a number of Satmar girls pursued education degrees after high school online or at a religious school with the aim of teaching at Bais Rochel, the sect's girls school. Now, however, the edict stated that they "shouldn't, God forbid, take a degree which is according to our sages, dangerous and damaging." The edict went on to say that girls should not learn college subjects and that those who refused to obey would be denied positions as teachers in Satmar schools. After all, it was the responsibility of leaders to protect the religious educational system from outside influences—

and, I would add, to keep women as ignorant as possible (*Times of Israel* 2016).

Said one woman, a lapsed Satmar, about these restrictions: "People think that the girls have it easy because they get a better secular education[2] than the boys but that is not necessarily true. Unfortunately, people don't understand or realize that Satmar girls do not graduate high school with an accredited high school diploma or Regents diploma. Sadly, there is no one advocating for Satmar girls since the guys have a louder voice, so the Satmar girls are being victimized over and over again and that sucks. It is a journey through hell and I wouldn't wish it on my worst enemy" (quoted in Trencher 2016).

The primary reason for the restricted educational opportunities of Satmar women is that, after marriage, they are expected to have limited interests outside of their main responsibilities for home and family with, perhaps, some involvement in charity work. At the same time married men, who, unlike married women, are obligated to engage in religious learning, also hold all positions of leadership and power in the Satmar community. That is the reason why, according to the Satmar newspaper, "it is better and more important for [Hasidic] girls schools to give a test on . . . [kosher] cookbooks than for them to give tests on American history and other secular subjects" (*Der Blatt*, May 9, 2014).

So here we see just how the different responsibilities of women and men result in gender segregation. Because males study sacred texts they are prominent in the public sphere, as religious leaders of the Jewish community, and with significant roles in its yeshivas. Females mediate the secular world and are responsible for most of their family's contacts with it. It is they who deal with doctors and dentists, social service agencies, landlords and utility companies. And, of course, they are also in charge of the domestic realm despite the fact that Hasidic males are officially the heads of household (Fader 2009).

Still, there is no doubt as to which of these spheres is more highly valued. As one Hasidic woman put it, she learned as a young girl that "some activities were deemed dangerously emasculating: clearing the table, food preparation of any kind, dressing a baby, reading a novel, letting a woman finish a sentence without interrupting her. At the same time, a corollary lesson for us girls suggested that while these same activities defined ladylike behavior,

---

2. Here "secular education" refers to the fact that Satmar girls receive more English-language instruction in school than Satmar boys and so are more literate in the language.

they were, in the larger scheme of things, of no great significance" (Deitsch 2015:63).

Finally, what about divorce among the Satmar? Among Hasidim, in general, the "patriarchal underpinnings" of divorce are very stark. A woman can be divorced only if her husband agrees to give her a *get* (a religious document of divorce). Since only her husband can provide such a document, he is the only one who can initiate and finalize religious divorce proceedings. Even if a woman obtains a civil divorce, she is not considered divorced under Jewish law until her husband provides a *get*. Without it, she is an *agunah*, a "chained woman," a woman who cannot date or remarry within the religious community. If she did remarry without a *get* she would be labeled an adulteress and any children she had with a new husband would be deemed illegitimate (Levine 2003:202).

The man, on the other hand, can move on without a religious divorce and date other women with no disapproval from members of his religious community. Some men simply refuse to provide a *get*, while others may try to extort money from their wives or only agree to a religious divorce if they are given custody of the children. This is the ultimate form of power and control the husband has over his wife, which has been labeled a form of domestic abuse. The idea is, "If I can't have her, then no one can" (Jones 2013).

SUFFERING AND PASHTUN MARRIAGE

Cruel people, who see how an old man leads me to his bed
And you ask why I weep and tear out my hair!
> —Pashtun woman's *landay*[3] (quoted in Rubin 2005)

The value of a bride is her maidenhead; the value of a wife, the number of sons she bears.
> —Asne Seierstad, *The Bookseller of Kabul*, 2003

Suffering, especially after marriage, is the crucible of Pashtun women's lives and the searing reality under which they live. "A woman suffers much under her male relatives, whether they are husband, brothers, father-in-law, uncles or brother-in-law," observes a student of Pashtun culture who goes on to opine that "tears and the endurance of hardship exemplify Pashtun womanhood" (Grima 1992:163). Given these circumstances, women "protest with

---

3. The *landay* is a traditional Afghan poetic form consisting of a single couplet.

suicide and song," writes the Afghan poet Sayd Bahodine Majrough, in a collection of Pashtun women's poems (cited in Seierstad 2003:37–38).

In Pashtun society young women are objects to be bartered or sold. They have no right to love or to choose a potential spouse. Falling in love, in fact, is viewed as a serious breach of custom and may result in an honor killing. Thus, the ownership of a Pashtun girl is literally passed from one male to another—her father to her husband. And if the latter so desires, he will be in charge of her life down to the smallest detail. All of this takes place at a young age. In Afghanistan almost 60 percent of girls are married by age sixteen and some 70 to 80 percent of these are in arranged marriages to men who are sometimes considerably older (Seierstad 2003; Bohn 2018).

And, as among the Satmar and the FLDS, a Pashtun woman is considered too old to marry once she reaches the ripe age of twenty-two. Although under Sharia law a woman can refuse to marry a man chosen for her by her family, in Pashtun tribal custom she does not have this right (Nasimi 2014).

When a Pashtun woman arrives at the peak of the female social hierarchy as a result of age and having many married sons, it is not in her self-interest to let women junior to her challenge her or defy her higher status. Basically, what this means is that girls and young women are at the lowest point in their lives in terms of their ability to influence what happens to them. They are controlled first by their fathers and other male relatives and later by their husbands, and their only rise in status comes as they age, bear sons, and eventually come to control the other females in their household, in particular, their daughters-in-law (Nordberg 2014).

In traditional Pashtun culture men take control over a girl's life at birth. They exert authority over everything from her schooling to the choice of a husband. The very notion that women can make decisions for themselves, such as whom to marry, undermines the seamlessness of male control. Then, after she is wed, it is a woman's husband and her in-laws who take charge of her life. They can decide how many children she will bear, what her role in the household and the local community will be, and what, if anything, she is permitted in terms of medical care, education, and employment. Key to all such decisions is the pivotal role of female chastity and honor, which, as we know, are highly sensitive concerns in Pashtun society. Even a slight violation of a woman's honor can bring ruinous costs in a society rooted in tribal bonds (Jamal 2014).

One type of Pashtun marriage that is not found among the FLDS or the Satmar involves a system of dispute resolution called *baad*, which can have

Pashtun couple. The woman in the *burqa* is seventeen years old.
Source: TOLOnews, 2016

serious consequences for a woman's life. In some Pashtun communities, in order to settle a conflict girls and women are exchanged in marriages be-tween families. A standard penalty for a crime such as murder or theft is for the offender's family to give a marriageable female to the victim's family. Some of the most severe cultural practices, like the selling of young girls to pay off debts, are elements of the Pashtun tribal code that would be unaccept-able in most other Muslim societies. This tribal custom, which has no basis in Islam, is officially outlawed in Afghanistan but is still practiced particularly in rural areas, which lack state courts to administer formal decisions and to mete out penalties (Pessala 2012; Ahmed and Zahori 2013).

Another Pashtun marital custom that has no counterpart among the Sat-mar or the FLDS is *ghagh*, which allows a man to force a marriage proposal on a woman. Once invoked, *ghagh*—which means "a call"—can have sever-al outcomes, none of which is likely to benefit the woman involved. She might wind up being married against her will or she might remain single for life, or her family might be drawn into a dangerous and prolonged feud. *Ghagh* typically involves a man firing a gun into the air outside the compound of his intended bride and shouting her name to let her family know that it is he alone whom she will wed. Or "the call" might be made more peacefully by a man informing the family of his intentions through a messenger. But, in either case, it amounts to the same thing—a man publicly declaring his desire for a woman, a pronouncement that is taboo in conservative Pashtun society and is, therefore, considered a challenge to the family's honor (Siddique 2012).

In an unexpected way, given all these patriarchal impediments, what little power a woman does have in marriage stems from her ability to dishonor her husband and his male relatives. This is why women are feared. While her husband's potential physical violence against her is, to be sure, of great concern—a woman has almost certainly been the victim of such violence since early childhood—her personal pride is sometimes more powerful than her fear of being beaten. Although she is captive in her husband's household, her position is in some ways stronger than his for she holds the weapon to bring about his dishonor, whereas he merely holds a stick with which to beat her.

Violence is indeed a fact of life for Pashtun women. Using Pakistan as an example where a survey on the issue was carried out, Pashtun women were found much more likely to be subjected to violence than other women living in that country. A 2008 report by the NGO Global Rights found that nearly 90 percent of Afghan women had experienced domestic violence in their lifetimes. Data from a 2012–13 national survey revealed that 20 percent of Pashtun women aged fifteen to forty-nine experienced physical violence in the year prior to the study and 30 percent of women said they had suffered both emotional and physical abuse from their husbands in the previous twelve months—35 percent of whom reported they had been scarred physically. Of these, 10 percent said they were subjected to violence during pregnancy. Most suffered in silence. The survey found that over half of the women subjected to violence never sought help or shared their plight with others (Haider 2014; Ferris-Rotman and Evans 2015).

Such habitual violence against Pashtun women can lead to something far worse: honor killings. These are executions of girls and women who are accused of bringing shame and dishonor on their families. Honor killings are carried out for various reasons—for example, after a girl or woman runs away from home even if she only does so to escape violence. Or it can be the punishment meted out for refusing an arranged marriage or for being a victim of rape. In Pashtun culture rape is almost uniformly considered the fault of the female victim. Local custom dictates that women are shamed by rape and should kill themselves to restore their family's honor or risk being killed by a family member. Such honor killings in rape cases are common in Afghanistan, and are often more important to the victim's family than vengeance against the attacker. Rape victims, moreover, are seen as unmarriageable and therefore risk becoming lifelong burdens on their families. Human rights groups estimate that about 150 honor killings come to light annually, but many more likely go unreported (Knafo 2015; Nordland and Faizi 2017).

The backdrop to these practices is the following: A woman's fertility and reproductive capacity is "owned" by her family, not by the woman herself. If she is even suspected of being "damaged goods" her natal family will have to care for her for the rest of her life. And such suspicions are often a killing offense. Since a woman's virginity belongs to her family and is a token of their honor, if she is not a virgin, the shame belongs to her family and they must cleanse themselves of it with blood: her blood.

These killings are anchored in Pashtunwali, the age-old tribal code of the Pashtun described in chapter 2, and are not necessarily associated with Islam. As a consequence, very few honor killings result in convictions or other penalties for those who commit these crimes because the practice is often written off as part of tribal custom. In fact, estimates suggest that fewer than half of the cases of honor killings are even formally reported to the authorities (Nordland 2014a).

An often-invoked offense against girls and women, one that does not exist in Afghan law, is running away from home. Even if the runaway girl is eighteen years old, legally an adult, courts still frequently impose a jail term of one year, once again based entirely on tribal law. In fact, more than half of the women in one prison in Kabul are there for "moral crimes," a large category than includes running away from home and intending to commit adultery (Rubin 2015a).

"For a young woman from an Afghan village to go home after running away with a man is tantamount to crossing a busy street blindfolded," writes a journalist in the *New York Times*. "There is a strong likelihood that she will be killed for bringing shame on her family." Women who run away from home are forever tainted and become unmarriageable. Says an imam in Kabul: "Once she leaves the family, she's in the hands of others, and they can do whatever they want with her—sexually abuse her—because she has left the family circle" (Nordland 2014b; quoted in Rubin 2015b:1, 14).

Given these conditions and with no credible means of escape, is it any wonder that 80 percent of all suicides in Afghanistan are committed by women? As it turns out, that country is one of the few places on earth where suicide rates are higher among women than among men (Bohn 2018).

This is the bleak backdrop of marriage in Pashtun tribal society. After marriage, raising children, doing household chores, and entertaining guests are the essential roles of Pashtun women, who live their lives behind high walls where they are seldom alone. Some women, especially for a year or so after they marry, are kept in total seclusion by their husbands. No one comes to visit them nor do they visit anyone. As such, a young bride comes to live in her in-laws' home and her husband's extended family becomes her entire social universe and her sole network of interpersonal relations. And she is expected to work hard to be accepted by these new relatives. A married woman is usually the last to eat, the last to go to sleep at night, and the first to rise in the morning. Her skills in hospitality, along with a diligent work ethic and a submissive bearing, are all important to her husband and her in-laws (Grima 1992).

According to two students of Pashtun culture, its domestic arena, concealed as it is behind the opaque walls of the *purdah* household, is the site of frequent confrontations. Pashtun marriage, they argue, is very much like prolonged combat and is recognized as such by both men and women. On the one hand, the husband is expected to exhibit casual indifference towards his wife in all things and he carries this feigned unconcern for her into the public sphere, never mentioning his wife to his friends. Nor do they inquire about her; to do so would be a breach of etiquette. On the other hand, according to one Pashtun woman, "we cannot ask men anything. We know nothing about their work or their earnings, and if we ask they can beat us. It is not for us to know or be curious about them" (quoted in Grima 1992:87, 2004:40). Still, while Pashtun men "can indulge outwardly in being masters of their households . . . they cannot claim control or even knowledge of the intrigues and connivances that take place in these closed female circles," write the same two students (Lindholm and Lindholm 1979).

As we have seen, mentioning the name of a female relative in public is a grave breach of custom. Instead a man's friends will ask him, "How is your house?" Some of the terms Pashtun men might then use to refer to their wives in public include "mother of children," "my weak one," or even "my goat" and "my chicken"! In public the most common word a man uses to refer to a woman—no matter what her relationship to him—is "aunt." Calling a woman by her real name is considered a serious offense and one that can, in fact, lead to violence. Even young boys sometimes get into fights to defend their honor, having been taught that it is besmirched if someone mentions their mother or sister by name. When Afghan president Ashraf Ghani[4] mentioned his wife, Rula, by name in his inaugural address before the nation, the surprise and shock was so marked that it "was as if no one had ever heard a woman's name before" (Mashal 2017).

It has been said that a Pashtun woman can be made or broken by her husband. If her husband stops supporting her, she is reduced to the role of household drudge. And if her husband takes off and leaves her behind, her in-laws may well refuse to give her any assistance. Writes an ethnographer about her experience with the Pashtun: "I was beginning to understand the impact of what few women had dared to answer when I asked them who a woman's greatest enemy was." One said, "Her husband. He can ruin her as well as make her a queen." Given this—and although some Pashtun women do rail against the severe limitations placed on them as women—they cannot leave the protection of their husband's household. On their own they would never receive support in the wider society. "Women are respected in the house," one Pashtun woman told this same ethnographer. "They have no reason to go out, so if they do stray we no longer have any reason to respect them" (Grima 2004:150, 127).

Given the high premium placed on the isolation of married women, the ideal for a Pashtun man is to have sufficient financial resources so that his wife never has to leave their compound to do her chores. In rural areas this may mean having the resources to dig the compound's own well so his wife does not have to leave to fetch water from a public well, or to have a pickup truck to bring firewood to the compound so that his wife does not have to go out to gather it herself. Therefore, having resources often means putting additional restrictions on women's free movement (Grima 1992).

Even in urban areas women's movements outside the home are strictly limited. Writes one American woman who married an Afghan and lived with him for a time in Kabul: "An Afghan woman who walks or shops alone is seen as proclaiming either her sexual availability or her husband's or father's poverty. A male servant and a female relative are the minimum requirements for any proper Afghan woman who shops in the bazaar" (Chesler 2014:23).

---

4. President Ghani is an anthropologist with a PhD from Columbia University. The author was briefly acquainted with him some years ago.

It is also true that Pashtun women have little economic value in the sense that the vast majority do not work outside the home and are completely reliant for support on their husbands and their in-laws. Only 16 percent of Pashtun women are in the labor force, a figure that helps explain the conditions under which they live. Anthropologists have long known that in most societies female status is linked to the importance of their contribution to the household economy. Accordingly, women's greater role in production can lead to their higher status across several domains of social life. However, in societies in which women contribute relatively little to their households in terms of subsistence or producing anything of monetary value, their status tends to be low, which is certainly the case with Pashtun women (Rubin 2015a; Brown 1970).

Another finding by anthropologists that helps explain the relative powerlessness of Pashtun women within the context of marriage is that wherever women are isolated or segregated from public life and expected to devote themselves exclusively to domestic tasks, they necessarily rely on men to mediate their dealings with the larger society. Having no direct access to the public sphere, women's personal autonomy, sexual freedom, and legal rights are also limited. Hence, wherever the public and private spheres are sharply divided, as is the case in Pashtun society, women's status is likely to be low (Margolis 2004).

Pashtun women, in fact, often have their legal rights in the political realm curtailed by their husbands or other male relatives. In Afghanistan and Pakistan, for example, although women technically have the right to vote many have not been permitted to do so by their male relatives (Bezhan 2013).

Again, like the Satmar and the FLDS and for similar motives, Pashtun males generally limit their female relatives' access to education. Many Pashtun fathers do not allow their daughters to be educated past the age of ten or twelve. Only 40 percent of Afghan girls attend elementary school and a mere one in twenty go to school beyond sixth grade. Many families will only permit their daughters to attend all-girls schools close to home, and in some rural areas few such schools exist. Under the Taliban schools for girls have been burned down, hundreds of teachers educating girls have been threatened or killed, and girls have been physically harmed while attending or walking to or from school, Malala Yousafzai being the best-known example (Nasimi 2014).

Fathers and other male relatives cite issues of security as a way of explaining their resistance to female schooling. But some families simply believe it is unnecessary to educate a girl who will marry and be a mother before too long. Moreover, an educated girl may be less attractive as marriage material. She may want to work outside the home or have opinions of her own. Then, too, if women were educated and wanted to go out into the world to get a job they might be seen as dishonoring their families. As a result of these constraints the literacy rate of Pashtun women has long been considerably lower than that of Pashtun men. A 2014 UNESCO study found that only 18 percent of adult Afghan women could read and write, while 52 percent of men were literate (Nordberg 2014; Ferris-Rotman and Evans 2015).

An occasional feature of Pashtun marriage that is absent among the Satmar and the FLDS is the forensic virginity test—an invasive exam to check whether the hymen is intact in order to "prove" virginity. This is still practiced in Afghanistan even though it was officially banned several years ago. Both researchers and human rights groups have discredited the practice, finding it unsound and tantamount to sexual abuse. Yet, "it is a big deal here in Afghanistan," one woman said. "If your hymen is broken, you are finished—you fall into hell" (Nader and Mashal 2017).

These examinations are still being ordered by officials, a situation that makes the trauma even worse for women who in many cases have been raped or otherwise abused. The main forensic medical center in Kabul, which also processes cases from other provinces, conducted forty-two virginity tests in the first six months of 2016, about the same number as the previous year. The overall number of such tests is almost certainly far higher given that official records across the country, especially in rural areas, are difficult to come by. A study by Afghanistan's human rights commission found the persistence of virginity tests so routine that the justice system was still regularly ordering female victims of domestic abuse who had sought protection in women's shelters to be subjected to the procedure. The commission called these examinations "violence against women" (Nader and Mashal 2017).

Even so, according to doctors at the forensic center in Kabul, newly married couples were still arriving there soon after their weddings because of the husbands' suspicions that their new brides were not virgins. Parents have also brought in their young daughters who may have damaged hymens so that the forensic center can issue a certificate documenting each girl's "purity" to any future husband. Fear of social ruin has also given rise to underground clinics that promise to repair hymens—for as much $1,500, a staggering sum in Afghanistan (Nader and Mashal 2017).

Finally, what about divorce among the Pashtun? Given the conditions under which a majority of Pashtun women live, one might well expect many to seek divorce. But divorce is, in fact, rare. While a divorced man can soon move on by finding another woman to marry, a divorced woman's chances of remarrying are slim. Not only are Pashtun mothers loath to countenance their sons marrying a divorcée, many men are also reluctant to marry someone considered "used goods." Consequently, in most cases the only new husband a divorced woman can find is an older, divorced or widowed man. And these matches are often encouraged by the divorced woman's family because it may well be her only option (Kakar 2014).

Divorce is seen as a disgrace and a divorced woman is often blamed for her failure to stay in her marriage, even if she ended it because of severe abuse. Other married women are encouraged to avoid *talaqi*, divorced women, because it is thought that they have a bad influence. The idea that *talaqi* could convince some married women to divorce their husbands has enough force that, in some cases, even their own female relatives and friends sever ties with a divorced woman. The condemnation of a divorced woman is so intense that it not only destroys her own reputation, it also brings shame on her entire family. That is the reason a woman is strongly encouraged by family members to submissively accept her fate and stay with her husband. For some Pashtun women the stigma of divorce may seem even worse than living miserably in an abusive relationship (Kakar 2014).

Perhaps the biggest impediment to Pashtun divorce is that the custody of children is almost always awarded to the father and he has the power to refuse his ex-wife's access to them. In the rare cases that the mother does gain custody, she lives in fear that her children will be taken away from her with no notice and if she does remarry, she will have to give her children back to her ex-husband's family. Pashtun men will not willingly raise the progeny of another man. As a result, because husbands have a near absolute right to their children many women are reluctant to even consider divorce (Lindholm and Lindholm 1979).

Even if a divorced woman is allowed to keep her children, the challenges she faces raising them are considerable. The children of a divorced mother are often bullied in school and any daughters she may have will not readily find husbands. Many families believe that the dishonor of divorce is passed from a woman to her female offspring (Kakar 2014).

Aside from the stigma, Pashtun divorcées face other major obstacles both in terms of their own support and their personal safety. For one thing any property of the couple remains with the ex-husband. Then, too, in much of Afghanistan it is simply unsafe for a woman to live without a male relative. Besides, because a majority of Pashtun women are not educated and are ill-equipped to work outside the home, their only option after divorce is to return to their parents' household, whether they are welcomed there or not. Their families may be poor and an extra person becomes an economic burden. And if the divorced woman is accompanied by her children, paying for their upkeep can also be difficult for families living in poverty. This is yet another reason Pashtun women remain in their husbands' households, no matter how bad their situation is there (Seierstad 2003; Kakar 2014).

What is more, the Pashtun tribal code has no way of dealing with a woman alone. Because a woman's identity is so completely bound up with that of her husband and other male relatives, there is simply no place in the code for widows, divorcées, or women without sons or brothers or other close male relatives who will protect them (Grima 1992).

Has anything changed in recent years in the marital and associated conditions that confront Pashtun women? Over the last four decades the Soviets and later the Americans as well as other Westerners have sought to alter many of the practices described above—child marriage, violence against women, forced marriage, honor killings, the trading of women and girls to settle family disputes, virginity tests, and the loss of children upon divorce. However, such moves generally have been vehemently resisted by Pashtun men, who fear losing both their power and their resources (Nordberg 2014).

Since 2001, the United States alone has spent an estimated $1.5 billion on improving women's lives in Afghanistan, and while there have been some improvements, the lives of the vast majority of Pashtun women remain bleak, most especially within the context of marriage. Women have been helped in the larger urban areas where conservative Pashtun traditions are somewhat less robust, but in the countryside, nothing has changed and women remain imprisoned in their homes and entirely under the control of their male relatives (Ferris-Rotman and Evans 2015).

Afghanistan has received resources to expand and improve maternal health care as well as to open up schools for girls in both urban and rural areas. But as one observer has remarked about the education of girls in recent years: "That's the reality until the sixth grade, then they get married" (quoted in Ferris-Rotman and Evans 2015).

Critics of these aid programs have pointed out that in some ways they have been misguided from the beginning. Says one such critic: "These women are told, 'Go to school and then anything is possible,' but that is simply not the case. The West should have looked at the politics of women, the domestic violence, the sexual violence, and evaluated how this affects their paths in daily life" (quoted in Ferris-Rotman and Evans 2015). Unfortunately, in this regard, *plus ça change, plus c'est la même chose.*

Next, we turn to the issue of unrestrained procreation in each of these three fundamentalist communities and what it means for women's lives. Here again, we see the remarkable parallels in the fervent insistence on unbridled reproduction and the burden that this places both physically and emotionally on the women who are the broodmares of these communities.

Chapter Five

Women as Broodmares

Power has always been held by those who manage to control the origins of life by controlling women's bodies.

—Jenny Nordberg, *The Underground Girls of Kabul*, 2014

The Satmar, the Fundamentalist Church of Jesus Christ of Latter-Day Saints, and the Pashtun all strongly believe in and act upon the principle that female members of their communities should produce as many offspring as possible. All three are singularly committed to rapid-fire childbearing.

The Satmar and FLDS do not permit birth control or any form of family planning and it is highly likely that were the means of limiting births available to most Pashtun, they, too, would prohibit them. FLDS members believe that a woman who has used contraception to prevent a pregnancy will pay for her transgression in the next life. For all eternity she will labor as a childless servant to her husband's other wives. Then there is the Satmar position on this issue: "We *do* believe in family planning," insisted a resident of Kiryas Joel with tongue in cheek, "we plan to have families of sixteen to eighteen children!" (Jessop 2007; quoted in All Peoples Initiative 2009).

As the title of this chapter suggests, women are the broodmares in all three of these fundamentalist communities. They, however, are not the only ones that laud unbridled reproduction. The Quiverfull movement is another example of the premium some groups place on fecundity. Quiverfull started among Christian fundamentalists in the United States in the late 1980s. Couples in the movement try to have at least six children and some have fourteen or more. They consider all forms of birth control, including natural family planning, sinful. Children are viewed as "unqualified blessings" and women should be willing to have as many as God provides. Not surprisingly—as with the three groups considered here—Quiverfull is a fiercely patriarchal movement in which children are homeschooled, women do not work outside the home, and the male head of household is to be obeyed without question (Joyce 2009).

What, then, are the lives of women like among the Satmar, the FLDS, and the Pashtun as they labor under the dictum "to be fruitful and multiply"?

MOTHERHOOD IN THE FLDS

Women are vessels to be worn out in childbirth.
—Andrea Moore-Emmett, *God's Brothel*, 2004

The entire FLDS structure is supported by how many children can be contributed to the system.
—Sam Brower, *Prophet's Prey*, 2012

It is evident that for the FLDS the command to bear many children undergirds the sect's control of its female members. Prophet Warren Jeffs himself decreed that girls should be impregnated as soon as they are capable of having children. Girls with children "do not daydream of a different future," he opined. With little education, no experience outside the sect, or much hope of any fresh prospects, young girls who have children are more easily taught to obey. According to the Prophet, a girl who has "problems with obedience" should be married off and made pregnant as soon as possible so she will give up her "wicked ways" and conform to the FLDS ideal of womanhood—in other words, she will "keep sweet" (Weyermann 2011). FLDS wives are, indeed, expected to remain pregnant from puberty on and some FLDS women give birth to no fewer than twenty children (Wall 2009).

Quite simply, from the FLDS perspective the best way to control women is to keep them pregnant. And if this does not work and a woman is still rebellious, then she risks being exiled from the community or given mood-altering drugs or being committed to a psychiatric facility—all reprisals which have actually taken place in the twin towns. In fact, a significant number of FLDS women do take Prozac for depression (Bramham 2009).

As one former FLDS member has written: "A 14-year-old girl who'd just had her first baby confided in me that she'd never even had a menstrual period until after the baby was born. Her husband had married her at that young age so she could bear as many children as possible. This was important to him because he wanted to become a god with his own kingdom in heaven, where he and his wives and children could be numberless" (Spencer 2007:41).

To the FLDS motherhood is not only a means of taming girls and women, it is also the single most important obligation that women have because it is the key to heavenly rewards. Everything is ancillary to "the Principle," notes an FLDS woman, which meant that "men were to have as many wives and as many children as they possibly could" (Spencer 2007:8). At the end of these earthly years followers of the Principle will be divinely rewarded. The inability to have children is viewed as a reproach from God. Infertility is a curse placed on a woman and her husband and they will, as a consequence, never be received into the Celestial Kingdom (Bennion 2011a).

One woman who eventually abandoned the FLDS notes the importance of procreation to the sect. She was taught, she says, that "God had created women for one purpose alone—for the enjoyment of men. Women were possessions just like cattle. We had no rights in and of ourselves. God had created the world and the heavens above so that men could reign, and the women were given to the men as wombs to bear their children" (Schmidt 2006:351).

In the FLDS worldview procreation is the principal reason for marriage; love and companionship are ancillary. The two most important duties a polygamous wife has are bearing as many children as she possibly can for her husband and recruiting new wives for her husband to allow him to beget still more children. Since a woman cannot become a god in her own right, her only hope of salvation rests on being a wife—one of her husband's several wives—and a mother of his many children. Such a woman contributes to her husband's future kingdom and will ultimately share in his glory as a goddess, an immortal being who will rule under him and alongside her sister-wives[1] for all eternity (Spencer 2007).

Yet, even though the most important motivation for marriage is procreation, sexual attractiveness is still often the key to a woman's status in a polygamous household. A woman who is favored sexually by her husband generally has more authority than his other wives. A woman's sexual power—or lack thereof—is important in determining how she will be treated by her sister-wives and the degree of respect she will be shown by their children. As a result, the sex lives of household members are a frequent topic of

---

1. This is the term commonly used to refer to co-wives, that is, women married to the same man.

conversation. Everyone knows who is in favor and who is not, that is, who is sleeping regularly with the man of the house and who is left by the wayside in terms of sex. Given the rash of rumors and gossip that pervades many polygamous households and the distress that may ensue, most FLDS members recognize that the motto for women to "keep sweet" is a reminder to them to keep control of their emotions, sound practical advice because they are expected to maintain amiable relationships with several sister-wives and their many children (Jessop 2007).

It comes as no surprise that these conditions can cause a great deal of stress in women. One FLDS wife wrote of her profound disappointment in what her marriage turned out to be. Where was the "excitement and romance" she had anticipated as the wife of a leader of God's church, she asked plaintively. "We were supposed to be an army for the Lord, and yet babies, dirty diapers, backbreaking work, and never enough money to go around, was the lot of a polygamist's wife. All round me were poverty-stricken homes filled with lonely women and children, living for the scattered moments when our husbands could find time for a hurried visit home" (Schmidt 2006:299).

For the children of polygamy these conditions of multiple mothers and numerous siblings are also trying. Each child may be told that he or she is special. But when one has ten or twenty brothers and sisters and three or more sister-mothers, what does "special" really mean? As one FLDS boy noted ruefully: "All told, I have roughly sixty-five aunts and uncles on my dad's side and twenty-two on my mom's—with probably over a thousand cousins. In families as large as mine, even keeping track of your own siblings—let alone cousins and aunts and uncles—is difficult" (quoted in Gross 2009).

Furthermore, many FLDS devotees treat their children as if they are chattel. Girls are valued as would-be brides, as trade items for their fathers to gain power and prestige vis-à-vis other men in the community. Boys are valued as cheap labor that allows FLDS-owned businesses to successfully compete against gentile-owned companies that comply with minimum wage and other labor laws (Bramham 2009).

The practice of polygamy and the power structure it produces both in the larger FLDS community and within individual households causes a constant and exhausting struggle for attention and resources. Men vie with each other for wives and those most successful in this community-wide competition gain status. At the same time, in families as large as the boy's family cited above, it is simply impossible for all the women and children to have their needs met. Just making sure multiple children are fed, clothed, and accounted for is an ongoing struggle; simply keeping dozens of children physically safe is also a challenge.

Nor are these conditions easy for most polygamous fathers. FLDS men with many children and one or more jobs may only spend a few minutes a week with each child. Although the father is the unconditional head of the household, he must frequently disappoint, ignore, or fail to satisfy at least some of his wives and children. He has only so much time and attention to go around. Moreover, providing support for multiple wives and children requires many long hours at work.

One former FLDS member estimates that possibly one in five FLDS families has lost a young child, often from accidents that more adult supervision could have prevented. There are tales of toddlers wandering off by themselves, getting lost, and not being missed because of the multitude of other children in the household, as well as accounts of babies swallowing harmful substances while no one was paying attention to them or of young children being burned in kitchen accidents (Gross 2009).

This estimate of fatalities does not include another source of death related to polygamy. Here I am referring to fumarase deficiency, a genetic disorder that produces profound physical and mental disabilities, unusual facial features, brain malformation, and epileptic seizures. Children with the syndrome often die at a young age. Fumarase deficiency is an extremely rare inherited disorder with only a few dozen cases known to medical science; it occurs in about one in every 400 million births. It is very rare indeed and yet a total of eight cases have been diagnosed in the twin towns of Hildale, Utah, and Colorado City, Arizona. As a consequence, it is sometimes referred to as the "Polygamist's Down's Syndrome." Polygamy, as practiced by the FLDS, is associated with high levels of inbreeding because it reduces the number of males contributing to the gene pool and increases the relatedness of the entire community. In such a homogeneous population a rare genetic mutation is more likely to be passed on from one generation to the next. As a consequence, the number of people carrying the fumarase gene in the twin towns is thought to number in the hundreds, another unforeseen and tragic consequence of polygamy (Gorvett 2017; Szep 2007).

WOMEN AS BROODMARES AMONG
THE SATMAR HASIDIM

I learned that [Satmar] women who become mothers at a young age are essentially powerless, because anything they try to do puts the children in the balance.

— Frieda Vizel, "On Women Shaving All Their Hair," 2012

To the Satmar, like to the FLDS, the sky's the limit when it comes to procreation. The birth rate among this Hasidic sect—now at nine or ten children on average per woman—is one of the highest among any group in the United States today. To have a clear sense of what this means on the local level, there is the example of the Satmar village of Kiryas Joel in New York State, which has the distinction of being one of the fastest-growing communities in the entire country, with an estimated growth rate of 6 percent annually. And the town is destined to grow still more. In 2017 Kiryas Joel officials received final approval for a major development that will increase the village's population by 40 percent over five years. It is expected to bring in nine thousand new residents and when completed the development will have a higher density than Manhattan (Feldman 2017).

In 1980 the U.S. Census recorded its population as a little over 2,000 people; by 2017 it had more than 24,000 inhabitants. And prior to 1975 Kiryas Joel did not exist at all! Said one resident, "We double our population every eight to ten years" (McAfee 2015; Goldman 1990).

This growth is largely due to natural increase. The Satmar town has among the highest birth rates of any municipality, not just in the United States, but in the industrial world. In 2010 an astounding 730 of 1,000 women between the ages of twenty and thirty-four gave birth, a high figure even by the standards of many developing countries. Kiryas Joel also has the youngest median age population—a little over thirteen years—of any municipality in the nation. This is an extreme outlier since no other place in the United States has a median age of under twenty years (McAfee 2015).

As a result of this unbridled growth and the demand for additional land to accommodate its burgeoning population, Kiryas Joel gained its independence from the town of Monroe in late 2017, a move that was overwhelmingly approved by the town's voters. Prior to the vote officials and residents in the town of Monroe clashed repeatedly with representatives of the Satmar in Kiryas Joel over the village's efforts to annex hundreds of acres of land and to build four-story apartment buildings to house its growing numbers in a suburban area of single-family homes. The new Satmar town of Palm Tree was inaugurated on January 1, 2019; its name, like that of the thick-gauge Palm stockings worn by Satmar women, honors Joel Teitelbaum—his surname means "date palm"—the Satmar Rebbe who founded Kiryas Joel in the late 1970s. As many as 3,700 new homes are planned for Palm Tree, which is New York State's first new town in thirty-five years and the first official ultra-Orthodox town in the country (Foderaro 2017; *Times of Israel* 2019).

Moreover, Palm Tree, along with several offshoot communities nearby, is not the only burgeoning Satmar enclave in the vicinity. Some nine miles away in Chester, New York, plans are afoot for a brand new 431-unit housing project that is being developed by several members of the Satmar community (Otterman 2019).

Such unrestrained growth is not limited to Kiryas Joel. The Williamsburg neighborhood in Brooklyn, the principal headquarters of the sect, has been increasingly unable to house its burgeoning population of Satmar. The Jewish population in Williamsburg had increased by a notable 41 percent between 2002 and 2012. The growth, in part, is also a consequence of the contemporary trendiness and gentrification of the area that has led to an influx of what the Rebbe deridingly refers to as "the artists."

But it is also the result of the Satmar's own skyrocketing birth rate. At Bais Rochel, the Satmar school for girls in Williamsburg, for example, the population explosion is palpable. The school, with close to 3,700 students, has ten classes of eighth graders, fifteen of first graders, and sixteen of preschool girls with new classes being added every single year. And the population boom has continued unabated. "People used to talk about [families having] an average of seven children. Now they talk about nine or ten" (Cohen 2012).

As Williamsburg's population exploded it became clear that it could no longer accommodate many more large families. Consequently, in 2012 Zalman Teitelbaum, the Williamsburg-based Rebbe, began planning a new Satmar settlement in the hamlet of Bloomingburg, a half hour north of Kiryas Joel in New York State. This new Satmar enclave is developing an additional five thousand housing units. Despite the vocal protests of locals who argued that the Hasidim were transforming their quiet bucolic community of only several hundred residents, the growth continued unabated largely due to the dubious election of a village council suspiciously sympathetic to the Satmar.[2] In 2014 Rebbe Zalman gave his formal blessing to the new village, naming it Kiryas Yetev Lev, in memory of Yetev Lev, the Rebbe's great-great-grandfather, who was the founder of the sect. The Satmar community now sees the growing Hasidic population there as an official Satmar outpost (Nathan-Kazis 2016a, 2016b; Tannenbaum 2014).

This, then, is the backstory of the Satmar's insistence on unbridled procreation. Yitta Schwartz, a Satmar woman who died at age 103 in Williamsburg in 2010, provides us with the front story. Mrs. Schwartz gave birth to no fewer than fifteen children, all of whom survived to adulthood. She also left behind more than two hundred grandchildren and so many great- and great-great-grandchildren that, by her family's own count, she could claim perhaps two thousand living descendants (Berger 2010)!

This singular focus on producing large numbers of children among the Satmar and other Hasidic sects in the United States, Israel, and elsewhere is "reinforced by a commonly understood need to replace the generation that vanished," according to one scholar of the Hasidic movement (Mintz 1992:68). In essence, multiple offspring are a response to the Nazis' attempt in the 1930s and 1940s to annihilate the Jewish population of Europe. The feeling was that every child was "the best revenge on Hitler."

This is why these communities so intensely immerse their children in the rigorous doctrines and practices of Hasidic life and try to maintain a wall of separation between their offspring and the secular society surrounding them. This intention is also reflected in a Satmar woman's tale of her own grandfather, a Holocaust survivor. He got tears in his eyes, she recounts, every time he looked over his brood of fifteen grandchildren. As a consequence, writes Samuel Heilman, noted professor of Jewish Studies at Queens College–CUNY, "this is a population that sees childbirth as a sign of high status and for women a fulfillment of their divine and socially sanctioned role in life" (quoted in King 2009).

Within this setting it is not surprising that the use of birth control of any kind is considered an "idolatrous" act and a serious "sin," one strictly prohibited by all Hasidic religious authorities. The stated reason for the prohibition is that because birth control impedes the uniting of sperm and egg, it prevents

---

2. Federal agents arrested the enclave's principal developer and his two colleagues for conspiring to corrupt village elections. They were charged with a cash-for-votes scam during Bloomingburg's 2014 mayoral election. The alleged plot arose after the village planning board voted to block the Satmar building projects (Nathan-Kazis 2017).

new souls from being born. A woman who uses it is a dangerous sinner and a damaged vessel. Such a Jew does not deserve a place in heaven, opined one Hasidic sage (Brown 2013).

Suspicions about the use of family planning flourish within this environment. If a Satmar woman does not have another child for two or three years after giving birth, she risks being subject to rumors that she is using an illicit means to control her fertility. After a woman gives birth to four, five, or six children, however, the community may come to believe that, in the words of one student of Hasidism, "she has ceased bearing in the course of nature" (Poll 1971:56). If the children are close in age—an indication that there was no intentional birth spacing—a woman will likely escape nasty gossip about her reproductive proclivities. The only time birth control is ever countenanced is when an additional pregnancy could seriously endanger the life or health of the mother. But even then, contraception is only permissible if a medical expert testifies to the danger of another pregnancy and convinces one of the Satmar Rebbes to sanction its use (Poll 1971).

It is not enough just to have children; a woman is also expected to produce *male* children. Just as we will see among the Pashtun, the Satmar and other Hasidic sects have a decided preference for the birth of boys. This is reflected in the plethora of religious rituals surrounding boys; far fewer rituals honor girls. One of the best-known celebrations for Jewish boys is the *bris*, the Jewish circumcision ceremony that takes place on the eighth day after birth. For the *bris* the boy's parents and other close relatives organize a celebratory feast with a great deal of eating and drinking. After the infant's foreskin is cut by a *mohel*—a religious figure who performs the actual circumcision—his father recites a blessing for fulfilling the commandment to bring his male child into Abraham's covenant. Then three days after the *bris* another observance marking the birth commemorates Abraham's healing from his circumcision wound. If the boy is the couple's first child still another ceremony will take place three weeks later, followed by rituals marking the child's first haircut at age two, a buzz cut that leaves only his sidelocks (*payos*) untouched; first day of *cheder* (religious preschool) at age three; first Bible lesson at age five; and, of course, *bar mitzvah* at age thirteen, celebrating the boy's official entry into adulthood after which he is required to perform all the religious duties that fall on adult men. A boy's *bar mitzvah* is generally the most elaborate of these rites, all of which are celebrated in the company of many friends and relatives (Deen 2015).

Contrast this with the religious rituals for girls and young women. A baby girl receives an apple from the Rebbe on a Friday night soon after her birth. Then she is present for a reading of the Torah in the synagogue on Saturday morning followed by a simple naming ceremony where, following morning prayers, wine and pastries are served. And that is it. These are the two low-key observances marking the birth of a female child and ones that are usually attended only by her parents. There are no further celebrations or rites of any kind in a girl's honor until she is engaged to be married (Deen 2015).

Unlike the *bar mitzvah*, there is no celebration marking puberty for a Hasidic girl and she receives virtually no social recognition until she marries. The Satmar are especially appalled at the idea of having *bat mitzvahs* for girls, as is common among non-Orthodox Jews. Unlike boys in traditional Jewish law, there is no requirement to initiate girls into Judaism, which for boys is the purpose of the *bar mitzvah*. From the Hasidic perspective a girl should not become a *bat mitzvah* (daughter of the commandment) since she is not obligated to perform "positive commandments," only to refrain from "negative" ones (Poll 1971).

This general spiritual and ritual neglect of females by Satmar and other Hasidic courts—communities in which religion is so central to their lives—is also reflected in the stringent restrictions women face in Orthodox syn-agogues. There women sit in a high walled-off section separated from men because, it is thought, their presence can arouse male worshippers and dis-tract them from their religious obligations. Writes one observer of this prac-tice: "Women sit behind screens in synagogue services, or behind curtains or half-screens, or upstairs, or sometimes separately in another room. They never take an active part in the services. They are never called to read from the scrolls of the law, the essential reason for the service. And they remain invisible throughout the proceedings" (Kaye 1987:17).

This religious exclusion may be the reason some women grow disaffected with Satmar life. When they are very young—usually under the age of six—Satmar girls often accompany their fathers to synagogue on the Sabbath but once they turn seven they have to stay home with their mothers to help prepare the Sabbath meal. At about this age it also becomes clear to some girls how much more their parents value their brothers' education than their own. There is yet another singular sign of their limited presence in religious life. When married women want to make a request to the Satmar Rebbe or ask for his blessing, they can only do so through their husbands.

Even the prayers of women are not as highly valued as those of men. Women are not required to pray because their prayers do not have the sort of holiness that comes from prayers that are fulfilling a religious commandment. Only men's prayers can attain such holiness. This is why Hasidic women have long been told that "when they supported their husbands as spiritual leaders, their own needs would be met" (Fader 2009:207).

Said one former Hasidic woman about her own experience with these religious limitations: By the age of seven or eight, "it became clearer and more obvious that I had no place within the Orthodox religious world; I was unable to publicly express my religion. I understood that all public religious rituals and honors were exclusively the province of men and there would never be any participatory religion for me" (quoted in Davidman 2015:61). Of relevance here is the fact that every morning a Hasidic man says a prayer thanking God that he has not made him a woman.

Satmar women are told that they are "spiritually stronger" than men and so have less need for the constant renewal of formal rituals. "Instead of taking part in daily services and donning prayer shawls or ascending to the Torah," writes one Satmar woman, "we were supposed to be ennobled by hiding our bodies and public silence, elevated by having babies without end and creating a Jewish home" (Lax 2015:345).

How can such a large number of offspring, boys and girls alike, be educated, especially since all Satmar children attend private Jewish schools and most households have only one wage earner? One answer is low teacher salaries. At Bais Rochel, the Satmar girls school, teachers, most of them young women, earn less than $10,000 a year. Economizing is a way of life at the school. Sparse classrooms are filled with row upon row of desks, and former storage closets are turned into resource rooms where students can get extra help. Furniture and textbooks are all secondhand. This is how tuition at Satmar schools is kept extremely low, often just $2,000 a year. "Our tuition is the lowest in the United States. It's about $200 per month, besides those who get in free," said Bais Rochel's male principal. Still, tuition cannot cover utility bills or holiday food packages or other costs. Contributions are made by better-off members of the Satmar community. "There are some people who do well who make nice contributions and help. The school depends on it," the principal added (Cohen 2012).

As we have seen, with all of these mouths to feed and bodies to clothe, many Satmar families are not only dependent on the charity of their wealthier co-religionists for school tuition, but also on government subsidies that sup-

Satmar women and their children
Source: Alamy.com

port their costly lifestyle. Recall that with large Satmar families but very limited job opportunities, poverty is widespread. Kiryas Joel is now the poorest community in the United States, with two-thirds of its residents living below the poverty line and a near majority receiving food stamps. They have been described as engaging in the "poverty of choice"—that is, because they shun a quality secular education, which limits their job opportunities, and are committed to religious study over employment they are, in effect, choosing to be poor (Biale at al. 2018:758).

Satmar Williamsburg is not far behind Kiryas Joel in terms of its level of poverty and need for outside support. As with the FLDS, the cost of rampant procreation is necessarily borne, in part, through state and federal assistance programs (King 2009).

NIDDAH SEPARATION

When menstruation is treated as normal, it becomes more than a nuisance, a
punch line or a weapon wielded to keep women in their place.
                    —Chris Bobel, "When Pads Can't Fix Prejudice," 2018

You shall not approach a woman to uncover her nakedness while she is in her
menstrual uncleanness.
                                        —Leviticus 18:19

One practice related to reproduction among the Satmar and other Hasidic
sects has no counterpart among the FLDS and the Pashtun. These are the
laws of *niddah* separation of husband and wife. The term *niddah* refers to a
menstruating woman and the term also means "removed" or "separated."
Ultra-Orthodox men and women remain apart physically when a woman is
menstruating and continue to avoid one another for an additional "clean
week." This means that during roughly twelve to fourteen days a month a
very rigorous separation of the sexes is maintained.

When wives are menstruating, they must shun all physical contact with
their husbands. Says one former Satmar woman: "He can't hand you a glass,
even if your fingers don't touch. He has to put it down on the table and then
you pick it up. Secondary contact can't happen. If you're sitting on a sofa,
you have a divider between you. It makes you feel so gross. You feel like this
animal in the room" (Stewart 2012).

A menstruating woman's contamination extends to her household and its
contents. Her husband is not supposed to eat with her at the same table lest
something she touched touches him. He cannot drink from her cup nor can
she pour him a glass of wine. They must sleep in their own beds and the beds
must be separated. This is the reason all Hasidic couples sleep in twin beds
rather than double beds. When traveling in a car, taxi, bus, train, or plane
they must sit in such a way that they do not come into direct contact with one
another. Moreover, during this time of sustained abstinence a husband is not
even supposed to glance at his wife's body. She is simply forbidden to him
(Kaye 1987).

Some Hasidic women change their sheets to indicate their degree of purity. They use colored or printed sheets when they are not in *niddah*, changing
them to white sheets when they are menstruating. White sheets are said to
show bloodstains more clearly, thus alerting a woman's husband that she is
unavailable for sexual relations (Winston 2005).

After a Hasidic woman ceases menstruating, she is supposed to wear white underwear for seven days, checking constantly to see if there is any discharge. Here is the way one writer described the practice of *niddah* by a female acquaintance: "[She] counted five days of blood and seven clean days. During the seven clean days, she wore white underwear and slept on white sheets. Morning and evening, she inserted a white cloth, deep; she turned, retrieved, examined as prescribed. Were she to find a reddish spot, she would have to label the cloth or underwear with the time and day" (Markovits 2013:157).

It is well established among the Satmar and other Hasidic courts that it is their respective Rebbes who rule on private matters, even when the domain is the female body. This is why, according to one Satmar woman, "if there's a question about your period, you take the underwear and put it in a zip-lock bag, and give it to your husband. He takes it to the synagogue and pushes it into this special window and the rabbi looks at it and pronounces it kosher or non-kosher" (Stewart 2012).

Rather than sending the cloth to a rabbi, there is now an application (app) that can be used instead. It is called *Tahor* (Pure) and allows a woman to send digital photos of her menstrual cloth to her Rebbe—although its user guide warns that "very complicated stains cannot always be answered" (Simms 2019).

Some scholars of Jewish culture reject the notion that women are considered impure or contaminated during menstruation, insisting it is the concept of *tameh*—a word that indicates a spiritual change as the result of the loss of potential life—that is responsible for the separation of husbands and wives during the wife's menses. They point out that when men ejaculate, they also become *tameh* and require immersion in a ritual bath. In neither case is there any assumption of being unclean or lacking purity, according to this interpretation of the practice (Jacobs 2012). But others disagree. "Where I come from," says one ex-Satmar woman, "rabbis believed that menstruation rendered women into unclean beings, who therefore had to be regulated in order to protect the male community from contamination" (Feldman 2014:176).

One member of the faculty at a Jewish theological seminary did not mince words in this regard: "Menstrual discharge is repulsive. Among the men who will oppose the presence of women on the *bimah* (the altar at the front of the synagogue) will be many who fear that a menstruating woman will contaminate them and the sacred objects, especially the Torah" (quoted in Kaye 1987:147). Because of this belief and the uncertainty of the timing of menstruation, in ancient days women were completely prohibited from entering the temple.

Once a woman has stopped spotting and is deemed clean by a rabbinical authority, she goes to a *mikvah*, the ritual bath that is ubiquitous in every Hasidic community. By immersing herself in a *mikvah* a woman moves from a state of impurity (*tumah* in Hebrew) to a state of purity (*taharah*). *Tumah* and *taharah*, however, are not correlates of "dirty" and "clean." *Tumah* refers to the fact that the woman menstruated because she did not become pregnant in the past month; it is a recognition of the absence of a new life in her body. The *mikvah* restores her to a state of *taharah*, in that she now has the potential to bring new life into the world (Markoe 2014).

Immersion in a *mikvah* does not mean just a quick dip in a small indoor pool of water. As with so many other mandates of Jewish law that affect women, the *mikvah* requirements are legion. The water in a *mikvah* must be pure rainwater untouched by human hands. Rainwater is collected into a filter system that renders the water highly transparent. This clarity is crucial because a basic principle of the *mikvah* is that there be absolutely no barrier between the woman and the surrounding water. This means not only must a woman enter the water completely unclothed, but she cannot have anything touching her skin, including jewelry—not even her wedding ring. She also must remove all nail polish, makeup, and any beauty products on her hair and skin. In *mikvahs* run by Hasidic Jews, a "*mikvah* lady" (attendant) will carefully check to make sure these requirements are closely followed. Then once the *mikvah* is concluded, a woman is free to have sex with her husband. Perhaps not coincidentally, it is believed that at this point in a woman's menstrual cycle she is at her most fertile (Markoe 2014).

A woman's preparations for the *mikvah,* like so much else in the life of Hasidic females, is greatly elaborated by rabbinical authorities. Here is an exhaustive checklist demanded by one Rebbe prior to a woman entering a *mikvah*:

Brush and floss teeth [and] rinse mouth well

Remove nail polish from fingernails and toenails

Cut and clean nails, fingers and toes

When washing, start from your head and go downwards in order not to forget anything

Remove all jewelry and makeup (eyeliner, eye shadow, mascara, lipstick, etc.)

Soak body (you can work on your face and finger nails and underarm hair
at the same time as you soak)

Wash hair with a mild shampoo that could remove any residue

Eyes—clean inner corners

Ears—pay extra attention to external part that can be seen

Nose—blow and clean

Clean other bodily hair well (getting rid of deodorant and/or other residue)

Clean navel with Q-tip

Scrub the entire body, paying attention to folds between the thighs, armpits, areas between fingers and toes and removing glue from band-aids, lotions, etc.

Remove artificial teeth etc.

Clean vagina internally with warm water

Rinse your entire body thoroughly from soap and shampoo before immersion

Comb head hair and separate by hand all other bodily hair

Check yourself (pay extra attention to your face) and feel areas you cannot see

Total time needed to prepare: 1 hour and 10 minutes (Yerushalmi n.d.)

Similar checklists are taped to the walls in nearly all Hasidic *mikvahs* and may include additional instructions such as the following: "Rabbinic advice should be sought for temporary fillings, root-canal work, or capping in progress, nits in the hair, casts . . . unremovable scabs, unusual skin eruptions" (Harris 1985).

As it turns out the invasive *mikvahs* conducted by Satmar "*mikvah* ladies" are a lot more stringent than those in other branches of Orthodox Judaism. In no other *mikvah* are women required to expose themselves completely to the attendant while she clips their toenails. In other *mikvahs* women put on a robe before calling for the attendant to inspect their nails. Then they are escorted to the *mikvah*, while the attendant holds up the robes to shield the view until they are fully immersed in the water (Goldberger 2014f).

Once a woman emerges from a *mikvah* she is ready to have "kosher sex" with her husband. It appears to be considered unseemly to take too much notice of a woman leaving a *mikvah*, the implication being that she is going home to have sexual relations with her husband. And if one does comment about seeing her there, it is the same thing as saying—to put it less politely— "I know who's going to get some tonight!"

Yet the concept of *niddah* is not limited to menstruation. When a woman gives birth, she enters a state of *niddah*. This begins from the first sign of blood or from the time she feels the first labor contractions. The *niddah* state then lasts for seven days after the birth of a boy and fourteen days after the birth of a girl. As with menstruation, what is important here is that from the moment a woman becomes *niddah*, her husband cannot touch her while she is in labor, not even hold her hand. Moreover, since he may not see any part of her body that is normally covered, it is considered highly improper for him to be present at the actual birth of his children (Lobell 2014).

WOMEN AS BROODMARES AMONG THE PASHTUN

> The child comes out of the mother's womb, but in no document relating to the
> child—from infancy to old age—does the mother's name get registered.
> —Mujib Mashal, "Their Identities Denied, Afghan Women Ask,
> 'Where Is My Name?'" 2017

In the last chapter we learned that many Pashtun women endure an existence of almost unremitted pain and suffering. This is largely due to their lack of control over their lives as wives and mothers in a society that appears to place relatively little value on the female sex. One central element of this suffering is their inability to determine when and how often they give birth.

Like the Satmar and the Fundamentalist Church of Jesus Christ of Latter-Day Saints, the Pashtun adhere to a belief in unrestrained reproduction although in their case, especially in the rural areas of southern Afghanistan, the actual means of preventing a pregnancy are limited or nonexistent.

Also, unlike the Satmar and FLDS, relatively healthy communities embedded in an advanced industrial country, the maternal mortality rate of 1,400 maternal deaths for every 100,000 live births in Afghanistan is the highest in the world and over twice the average found among other low-income countries.[3] This makes Afghanistan one of the unhealthiest places on earth to be a woman. Given this, it comes as no surprise that life expectancy for Afghan women is only forty-four years (Pessala 2012).

How many offspring a Pashtun woman bears is influenced by the number of male children to which she gives birth. In Pashtun society gaining prestige and influence within the extended family rests on how many heirs a woman

---

3. This figure is for the country as a whole. I was unable to find a figure specifically for the Pashtun.

produces for the family, namely, sons. Writes one observer of the Pashtun, "A woman who cannot birth a son in a patrilineal culture is—in the eyes of society and often herself—fundamentally flawed" (Nordberg 2014:13).

Hence, the ultimate size of a family often depends on the number of sons a woman bears. While some couples know how to limit pregnancy, they will only do so—despite any health issues a woman might face—if a sufficient number of sons already have been born. If a woman has two or three sons, she will not be pressured to have additional children, but if she only has daughters she will be urged to try again and again. "A total of four or five children is perfectly acceptable to most parents in Afghanistan—but only if that number includes mostly boys," writes an observer of Pashtun culture (Nordberg 2014:42). In essence, having at least one son is said to "straighten" the family, lending it prestige and, given patrilineal descent, ensuring the continuance of the male line. For this reason, families are considered incomplete if they have no male children.

"A baby boy is triumph, success. A baby girl is humiliation, failure," notes this same observer of Pashtun life (Nordberg 2014:39). When a boy is born the news spreads like wildfire in the neighborhood and the happy tidings are carried far and wide. Such a birth is greeted with cries of joy, celebrations, congratulatory gifts, and visits to the mother. When a woman gives birth to a son she is fêted and abundant food and drink are brought to her along with gifts to acknowledge her signal achievement.

The birth of a daughter, in contrast, is greeted with shame. Here the new mother is often kept hidden rather than being proudly presented to guests. Some women cry when a daughter is born, and when they leave the household they may bow their heads in shame. Such a woman might not be given food for several days after the birth and might even be beaten. And if she already has a number of daughters her husband will also be subject to ridicule (Grima 1992).

Writes Sayd Bahodine Majrouh, one of Afghanistan's most revered poets, about such attitudes: Pashtun women, he asserts, "feel repressed, scorned and thought of as second-rate human beings. From the cradle on, they are received with sadness and shame. The father who learns of such an unwelcome arrival seems to go into mourning, whereas he gives a party and fires off a salvo of gunshots at the birth of a boy" (quoted in Rubin 2005).

The birth of a female child is greeted in this manner because the existence of an individual in a tribal system depends, in part, upon the number and strength of the males in the family. Moreover, as we know, the Pashtun are a patriarchal society where power rests with men and descent and inheritance are passed exclusively through the male line. This is why the birth of a son has far greater consequences for the extended family than the birth of a daughter (Afridi 2010). Again, as the observer cited above remarks, "one kind of child arrives with the promise of ownership and a world waiting outside. The other is born with a single asset, which must be strictly curtailed and controlled, the ability to one day give birth to sons of her own" (Nordberg 2014:40).

Because of the intense cultural preference for boys, women who bear many daughters but no sons will sometimes raise a daughter—until she reaches puberty—as though she were a son. Instead of donning a headscarf and a dress, a little girl will get her hair cut short and will wear pants. The *bacha posh*—literally "dressed up as a boy," as such children are called— learn from an early age to behave like boys and play boy's games. Their parents treat them as boys and while close relatives and friends are often aware of the "gender switch," little is made of it and those outside the familial unit have no idea they are dealing with a "boy" who is actually a biological girl (Nordberg 2014).

A whole new world opens up for a Pashtun girl posing as a boy. It allows her freedom of movement and may mean a chance to attend school. In almost every case it allows these *bacha posh* to experience a way of life that is closed to girls and young women. One mother of a *bacha posh* said she wanted her young daughter to know "what life was like on the other side"— to be able to run and jump and play freely, fly a kite, sit in the front seat of a vehicle, speak up, look people in the eye, all impossible for a Pashtun girl (Nordberg 2014:15). Then, too, in poor families *bacha posh* can work to help support the family, something a girl can never do.

Patterns of child-rearing among the Pashtun help reinforce these double standards. As in many male-dominated cultures, a daughter always comes second to her brothers—in the food she is given, in the education she is provided, and in the medical care she receives. In Pashtun homes boys re-main under the care of their mothers until about age seven, after which their fathers become the primary parent. As a consequence, later on boys often have difficulty relating to females and come to accept the negative stereo-types of girls and women that are so pervasive in Pashtun society. Ironically, once a boy reaches seven and the parental role is taken over by his father, his mother—out of habit and tradition—is still identified by the child. As a consequence, a woman whose name is entirely absent in law and is never spoken in public becomes "the mother of Ahmad" or "the mother of Mahmoud," a practice that anthropologists refer to as "teknonymy" (Mashal 2017).

SEEKING SEX OUTSIDE: THE PASHTUN AND THE SATMAR

Women are for children, boys are for pleasure.

—Pashtun saying

Homosexual pederasty accompanies extreme gender apartheid.

—Phyllis Chesler, *Islamic Gender Apartheid*, 2017

"In an environment where sex is never discussed, where men and women are strictly separated, sex is, ironically on everybody's mind all the time," writes one observer of Pashtun culture (Nordberg 2014:101). And the same might well be said of the Satmar, among whom relationships between males and females are equally strained. Consequently, the question becomes: When women are simply off-limits, does this constraint lead men to seek sex from other individuals, such as from boys and young men or from prostitutes? In some cases, it apparently does. Among the Pashtun, for example, the sexual molestation of boys by wealthy and powerful men is so widespread that it has its own designation, *bacha bazi,* literally meaning "boy play," which refers to the sexual relationship between older men and adolescent boys. Among the Satmar in the last several years a number of scandals have erupted involving claims that boys were being molested by adult men, including by some of their own yeshiva teachers (Otterman and Rivera 2012).

In the tradition of *bacha bazi* boys are groomed for sexual relationships with adult men and are bought—or sometimes kidnapped—from their families. Among high-status Pashtun men, beautiful prepubescent boys, typically nine- and ten-year-olds, are greatly desired as sexual partners. The better looking and the more talented the boy, the more prestige accrues to his patron. The practice of *bacha bazi* is often ritualized at festivities during which young boys are made to dance using alluring feminine motions while wearing face makeup and girls' clothes before being sexually assaulted by older men. Such a boy is expected to engage in sexual acts with his suitor, often remaining the sexual plaything of a man or a small group of men for a number of months or sometimes longer (Goldstein 2015; Mondloch 2013a).

Asne Seierstad (2003), in her book about living with an Afghan family in Kabul, notes that many military commanders take young male lovers—boys adorned with flowers in their hair and thick lines of kohl around their eyes. At times jealous dramas arise between such commanders if one of their young male lovers appears to divide his affections, a circumstance that can lead to a blood feud.

Bacha bazi is essentially a system of gender role reversal. As we have seen, Pashtun society is intensely misogynistic and male-dominated, the result of deeply ingrained Islamic mores combined with strong Pashtun tribal norms. As a product of these entrenched and often negative attitudes towards women, *bacha bazi* can be read as the substitution of young males for females as objects of desire. Likewise, strong feelings of companionship and affection have often been reported among Pashtun men, men who lack similar intimate experiences with women in their families and their communities.

This appropriation of female roles by males must be understood within the wider normative context of Pashtun society. There can be little doubt that *bacha bazi* is related to the severe segregation of females, the absolute prohibition of heterosexual sexual activity outside of marriage, and the high cost of marriage itself, which requires a man to provide extensive gifts to the bride and her family. A report commissioned by a U.S. agency operating in Afghanistan makes this link evident in its conclusion that the social conditions that have made women unavailable—extreme veiling and their segregation and exclusion from public life—are usually attributed to Islam, but also are cultural artifacts handed down and embellished through Pashtun local tradition. Consequently, when women can neither be sources of companionship nor objects of sexual desire, they become alien beings with whom men have difficulty having warm human relationships. The report goes on to suggest that where "women are foreign and categorized by religious teachers as, at best, unclean or undesirable," a practice like *bacha bazi* becomes intelligible (Human Terrain Team n.d.).

Pashtun social norms assert that *bacha bazi* does *not* contradict Islamic teachings condemning homosexuality because if a man is *not in love with* the boy with whom he is having sexual relations, the act in and of itself is not sinful. According to this logic, such an act is far more principled than dishonoring a woman. Here homosexuality is narrowly defined as one man being the love object of another man. Consequently, its Pashtun practitioners insist that *bacha bazi* does not involve homosexual acts, which indeed are strictly prohibited in Islam. Cultural interpretations of Islam among the Pashtun tacitly excuse *bacha bazi*, seeing it as far less fraught than certain heterosexual relationships. While sex between two males is widely considered problematic, it is not nearly as scandalous as having sex with an ineligible woman, an act that within the context of the Pashtun code of honor might well result in revenge and an honor killing.

Historically somewhat isolated in their mountainous redoubts and unable to speak or read Arabic—the language of all Islamic texts—many Pashtun allow social customs to trump religious principles, including those in the Koran that eschew homosexuality. Moreover, some warlords in the country, having exploited Islam for both political and personal gains, have also promulgated tolerance towards *bacha bazi* (Mondloch 2013b).

Because *bacha bazi* is a longstanding practice among the Pashtun, it is said that many Pashtun men have lost their natural attraction towards members of the opposite sex. Although social and religious customs demand that all men marry and father children, such marriages are often devoid of love and affection and are viewed with a jaundiced eye as practical arrangements required by society. It is also likely that the ongoing normalization of *bacha bazi* will perpetuate the traditional view of women as second-class beings, as domestic drudges meant for child-rearing and menial labor, and unworthy of male attraction and affection (Mondloch 2013a).

What are the psychological consequences, if any, of *bacha bazi* for its practitioners? Because the practice appears to be so widespread, a significant percentage of Pashtun males potentially bear psychological scars stemming from childhood sexual abuse, abuse that thrusts them into a place where they are at least temporarily shorn of their masculine identity. Some estimates suggest that as many as half of all men in the rural Pashtun tribal areas of Afghanistan take on boy lovers or have themselves been *bacha bazi*, making it likely that pedophilia is pervasive and affects entire rural communities (Mondloch 2013a).

Additionally, *bacha bazi* seems to play a role in the perpetual state of conflict in Afghanistan, especially in the southern Pashtun-dominated countryside. Indeed, the practice has actually grown more widespread since 2001, after the initial defeat of the Taliban. Still, because pedophilia and sodomy remain strong points of contention between the Islamist Taliban and traditional Pashtun warlords, the widespread nature of *bacha bazi* probably fuels the Taliban's desire to reassert Sharia law throughout Afghanistan. Finally, the reported American policy of treating child sexual abuse as a "cultural issue" about which little or nothing can be done certainly has the potential of alienating those Pashtun whose young sons are being preyed upon (Goldstein 2015; Nordland 2018a).

Although research is limited, scholars believe that the rate of child and adolescent sexual abuse within ultra-Orthodox circles is virtually the same as in the general U.S. population and has been so for many years. Yet Hasidim have a strong tendency to silence all discourse related to sexuality, in general, and to sexual abuse, in particular, especially when it implicates men since such abuse involves the strong religious condemnation of homosexual activity (Zalcberg 2017).

Indeed, in recent years there has been a spate of reports on the sexual abuse of young boys by adult men belonging to various Hasidic sects, including the Satmar. In one especially egregious case an ultra-Orthodox rabbi was accused of sexually molesting as many as twenty boys over the course of several years. Nevertheless, the head rabbi of the yeshiva where the perpetrator taught took forceful measures to derail a rabbinical court's action against him. The rabbi informed the parents of a number of the alleged victims that if they dared to come forward and report him to the authorities, they would be shunned by their fellow Hasidim and their other children would be expelled from his yeshiva and kept from enrolling in any other Jewish school (Aviv 2014; Kolker 2006).

In another case a young Satmar rabbi was accused of molesting four teenage boys whom he then blamed for trying to seduce him! In one widely reported incident the FBI investigated a school principal in Kiryas Joel for molesting a young male student, an incident that was caught on videotape (Heilman 2016). Of these proclivities said one Orthodox Jew with close ties to the Satmar—whose leaders he refers to as the "Talibanowitz"—"There is no community more homoerotic than the Hasidim" (quoted in Idov 2010).

It is not only boys in some Hasidic courts who are the victims of sexual abuse. In the case described in chapter 3 it was a young Satmar girl who was repeatedly molested by a "counselor" in that community, a man whom her parents were forced to hire as a therapist by the principal of the girl's school after the girl committed a number of minor infractions involving improper dress and reading material. The counselor, who had no training in counseling, psychology, or any related field, was eventually convicted on fifty-nine counts of sexual abuse. Then there was the truly horrifying case of a Satmar rabbi who raped his daughter over a period of years starting when she was barely ten years old and then fled the country to escape prosecution by U.S. authorities (Lesher 2015).

In *Unchosen: The Hidden Lives of Hasidic Rebels*, sociologist Hella Winston (2005) scrutinizes Hasidic enclaves in Brooklyn through the eyes of some rebellious members who have come to struggle with the dictates of their insular sects. In an interview about her research Winston turns to the issue of sexual abuse in these communities. "I heard more from men than from women. What was really shocking was how many boys—*so many boys*—have had this experience. People I've interviewed have told me every Hasidic kid has heard about this happening to someone" (quoted in Kolker 2006). Likewise, in a 2017 documentary film, *One of Us*, about several young people who have left the confines of their Hasidic communities, one nineteen-year-old reported that as a young boy he had been repeatedly raped by a counselor at a Satmar summer camp in the Catskill Mountains.

Then there is the psychiatrist who treats Hasidim and notes a good deal of what he refers to as "casual incest"—sexual activity between siblings—among his patients. He attributes this to the fact that boys reaching puberty are denied what would be considered healthy contact with girls apart from close female relatives and, with masturbation considered a dreadful transgression, end up acting out sexually with whoever is close at hand (Winston 2006–2007). According to several observers, it is the extreme sexual repression so common among the ultra-Orthodox that creates fertile ground for these types of deviance.

One concept in traditional Jewish law has impacted the way in which the Satmar and other ultra-Orthodox communities have dealt with the issue of child sexual abuse. The prohibition against *lashon ha-ra* (literally "evil tongue" in Hebrew)—meaning slander, gossip, and rumors—has frequently been used to silence the victims of child sexual abuse along with their supporters. "You cannot spread derogatory gossip," they are told. "There's no proof of what you claim. There are no witnesses." The thinking behind this stance is that virtually any public complaint about another person, especially a fellow Hasid, amounts to slander. As a consequence, victims and their allies are silenced and their abusers go unpunished and often go on to molest again (Dratch 2009).

Another tenet of Jewish law, *mesirah*—the suspicion of secular authorities—also has contributed to the vast underreporting of child sexual abuse. Jews have often lived in places where governments oppressed them and at times even murdered them. The concept of *mesirah* dates back to the days of the *shtetl* in eastern Europe when Jews rightfully feared reporting wrongdoing to state authorities. Thus, protecting one's co-religionists from government scrutiny was often a matter of life and death. As such, the concept of *mesirah* was a source of protection within the Jewish community. Among many Hasidim it is still seen as unconditional and reporting transgressions to outside authorities is an excommunicable offense (Katzenstein and Fontes 2017).

Going to the police is generally frowned on in the Hasidic world; all legal matters between Jews should be brought before rabbinical courts, *not* secular ones, or so tradition dictates. According to this logic, religious Jews should only utilize the Jewish legal system overseen by rabbis. "Satmar never calls the police. No matter what happens. Never," says one former Satmar. Therefore, turning a Jew over to secular authorities—no matter what the crime—is considered a grave offense. Today the notion of *mesirah* equates going to outsiders with treason (Dratch 2009; Golan 2018).

Still other Jewish religious norms also weigh against reporting child sexual abuse. *Shondah*, or shame, is one. This is the intense concern with being shamed. In this context a child or parent who makes a claim of sexual abuse may be thought of as bringing shame on the entire family. Here there is also the realistic fear that reporting sexual abuse will adversely affect a family's standing in the community as well as the marital prospects of family members (Katzenstein and Fontes 2017).

There is also the rule of *shalom bayit* (literally "peace of the home") or the mandate to maintain peaceful domestic relations. Here women and children are made to feel that it is their responsibility to maintain harmony by not turning in their abusers. Then there is the notion of *chillul Hashem*—desecrating God's name—which is a commandment not to air the community's dirty laundry in public or allow the judgment of Jews in non-Jewish courts (Kolker 2006).

These ultra-Orthodox tenets have meant that child molestation, including that perpetrated by rabbis and yeshiva teachers, is a seemingly widespread but unreported problem and one that has long been covered up. Then, too, underreporting sexual abuse is more prevalent among male victims than female victims because of its implied homosexual conduct. While some ultra-Orthodox rabbis today argue that a child molester should be reported to the police, others strictly adhere to the ancient prohibition against *mesirah*, and consider publicly airing allegations against fellow Jews to be *chillul Hashem*, a defilement of God's name (Kolker 2006; Zalcberg 2017).

In addition, those who do come forward to report such abuse to secular authorities often encounter intense intimidation from their relatives and friends and from rabbinical authorities as well—all of whom pressure would-be informers to drop their accusations. Abuse victims and their families have been expelled from religious schools and synagogues, shunned by fellow ultra-Orthodox Jews, and boycotted and harassed with the goal of destroying their businesses. Some victims' families have even been offered money—ostensibly to help pay for a victim's therapy—but actually meant to put an end to the pursuit of criminal charges (Otterman and Rivera 2012). Former Brooklyn district attorney Charles Hynes described "Mafia-like intimidation" of child sexual abuse victims and their families who spoke out against the abuse (Katzenstein and Fontes 2017).

As recently as 2011, Agudath Israel of America, a large and powerful ultra-Orthodox organization, decreed that observant Jews should not report such allegations to the police. The organization issued guidelines that prohibit parents, teachers, and social workers from directly contacting civil authorities about child sexual abuse. They must first seek out the advice of a rabbi *before* even contemplating such a move (Fishman 2012).

Likewise, in 2012 Satmar authorities in Williamsburg took what advocates said was an unprecedented step. They posted a sign in Yiddish in their synagogues warning children and adults to avoid a member of the Satmar community who was said to be molesting young men. But the sign did not urge victims to go to the police: "With great pain we must, according to the request of the brilliant rabbis (may they live long and good lives), inform you that the young man," who was then named, "is, unfortunately, an injurious person and he is a great danger to our community" (quoted in Otterman and Rivera 2012).

"They are more afraid of the outside world than the deviants within their own community," notes Professor Samuel Heilman, a scholar of Hasidic life. "The deviants threaten individuals here or there, but the outside world threatens everyone and the entire structure of their world." He goes on to suggest that sexual repression, the resistance to modernity, and the barriers to outsiders foster an atmosphere conducive to both abuse and to maintaining silence about it (quoted in Otterman and Rivera 2012).

However, there is a glimmer of hope concerning the near-absolute silence about child abuse in these communities. Access to the Internet has given voice to some individuals who once were silent victims (Finkel 2013).

But children and adolescents are not the only outlets for whatever pent-up sexual frustration is present among Hasidic men. Some also frequent prostitutes. A close friend who lived in Williamsburg, Brooklyn, in the mid-1990s told me how night after night black vans would pull up on the block in front of his building. The vans were filled with Hasidic men—men who were very likely Satmar since Williamsburg is primarily a Satmar neighborhood. The men in the vans were serviced one after another by what appeared to be crack-addicted, street-level sex workers who performed oral sex on each of them in turn (personal communication, Gregory Henderson, July 2016).

My friend's observation was confirmed by others. A Brooklyn-based prostitute told an interviewer that over the years she has serviced several Hasidic clients from Williamsburg. A former New York City police detective who once worked in the neighborhood remarked, "A lot of times one of the officers will see a car pulled over, and sees a Hasidic guy with a prostitute. That's common. Years ago, it was even more common, when there were more prostitutes out. But the need is still there, that desire" (quoted in Gabel 2012).

So here we have it: the turn towards other sources for sexual satisfaction when women are out-of-bounds. The highly repressive character of Pashtun and Satmar culture in terms of sex has led some men to seek sexual stimulation elsewhere, be it from children and adolescents or from sex workers. This is just one of the unfortunate outcomes of societies that treat women as little more than domestic drudges and that impose strict limits on when and with whom they may associate.

THAT'S JUST WHAT WOMEN ARE LIKE

Dehumanizing women is a key component of fundamentalist cults, from hardcore Muslims to certain Republicans.

—Jesse Kornbluth, "Unorthodox:
The Satmars v. Feldman and Kornbluth," 2012

The question now is: How do the components of womanhood in these three fundamentalist religious communities—the demands made on women for extreme modesty, the trials of marriage at a young age to men they barely know, and the consequences of motherhood on demand—coalesce around what is thought to be "women's nature"? In other words, what are women like? What are their natural propensities? In each of these cases we see evidence of the persistent belief that men's and women's natures can be handily split into two categories or "natural kinds" that are distinct, timeless, and deeply grounded in biology. Here my goal is explicit: to illustrate how representations of girls and women—along with the ideologies surrounding these portrayals—provide a rationale for the ways in which they are treated.

All three hold fast to the view that by their very nature, women, when it comes to religion, are limited in their ability not only to participate in religious rituals but also to fully appreciate complex religious concepts. "Why were the scriptures so hard for me to understand?" one female FLDS devotee queried plaintively. "Maybe it's because I was a woman and didn't have the benefit of a man's sharp brain. Maybe that's why the men insisted that women leave the heavy scripture studying to them" (Schmidt 2006:351). In a similar vein, Pashtun women are thought to be less able than men to reason, to act rationally, and, therefore, to achieve a deep understanding of sacred Islamic texts.

And, as with so much else we have been covering here, the rabbinical wise men of Satmar and other Hasidic courts go to considerable lengths to elaborate on women's nature and why it is incompatible not only with their participation in hallowed rituals but also with profound religious understanding. "The ancient Jewish sages," according to one student of Hasidism, were "puzzled by these 'others'—the women—who, among numerous other issues, bled monthly, entering a state of ritual impurity that, if not carefully managed, could transfer [it] to their husbands or other men" (Davidman 2015:169). Women are not considered to have the "proper mind" for the serious study of religious texts. There is an explicit rule, in fact, that prohibits women from reading the Hebrew text of the Talmud, the body of Jewish civil and ritual law. Then there is this: "He who teaches his daughter Torah, it is as though he teaches her lewdness," declares the Mishna—the written form of Jewish oral tradition (cited in Landau 1993:243). Then, too, Jewish women, according to rabbinical thinking, are ill-equipped to carry out the many religious duties required of Jewish men. Among the Satmar the traditional ban on religious education for females is still strictly enforced.

To the FLDS, women—the daughters of Eve—are almost always the root cause of sin and the source of sickness. This is one reason why only FLDS males age twelve and above can be administered the priestly sacrament and why the priesthood is closed to women. While the fall of Adam and Eve in the Garden of Eden cursed both transgressors, it was far more catastrophic for women (Quinn 1993). "The curse placed on women was that when they had children, they would suffer nearly to death," according to a text in the FLDS school, which goes on to insist that "the blessing on the woman . . .

and the only way she could ever be happy was—that she would let her husband, a faithful man, rule over her." After the fall, "that was the only way back to Heavenly Father for the woman." The text concludes with the admonition that "the woman is to obey her husband as he obeys the prophet" (*FLDS 101* 2009c).

In the 1970s these teachings were reinforced when FLDS women discovered the book *Fascinating Womanhood: A Guide to a Happy Marriage* (Andelin 1963), a work that taught that subservience and helplessness are the real secrets behind a woman's attractiveness to men. First published in the 1960s, that book—which has since gone through six editions—still appears to be read by FLDS women today and a course based on the book, known as the "Ladies Class," was long taught in FLDS schools (*FLDS 101* 2009c).

The book teaches that "a man is by nature and temperament a born leader, who tends to be decisive and have the courage of his convictions. A woman, on the other hand, tends to vacillate." For this reason it is much better "to surrender your point of view to a man than win an argument." To do so is simply more feminine. Remember, notes the book's author, "that by nature you are *not* capable." If you do, in fact, have any "masculine capabilities" you must have acquired them "unnaturally" because "God did not create woman for the strenuous masculine responsibilities." Finally, the book's closing pages sternly warn women that "you can't change your husband, only yourself" (Andelin 1963).

The FLDS course based on the book taught girls to "be skilled in the feminine arts of the household, caring for children, handling money wisely and doing more than is required." The leadership role is not for you, FLDS females were warned. "Stop giving him suggestions. If you obey your husband, even if you disagree, things will turn out all right" (*FLDS 101* 2009c). You must adjust to whatever circumstances your husband provides for you, and avoid any set notions you may have about what you want or any fixed plans you have for your children.

These passages clearly delineate women's "natural role" in the FLDS community. They are to be led, not lead. They are to obey without complaint. They are to adjust to whatever situation they find themselves in, whether decreed by their husbands, fathers, or other male relatives. And, perhaps most pointedly, they are to subsume all their personal desires and behave in a manner that is pleasing to Heavenly Father.

The Pashtun view of women is perhaps best summarized by the statement of a high-level official of Afghanistan's constitutional convention, the *loya jir-ga*. After women delegates complained about being underrepresented at this critical convocation, the official warned them not to "try to put yourself on a level with men. Even God has not given you equal rights." Under God's direction, he averred, "two women are counted as equal to one man" (quoted in Waldman 2003). Here he was referring to a provision in Islamic law that decrees that, in some cases, the testimony of two women is equivalent to that of one man. The reason for this pronouncement is that women are said to be less able than men to reason and to act rationally—hence one requires the testimony of two women to equal that of one man.

Women are also said to have less self-control than men, which is why modesty in dress and behavior is so essential to female life. Moreover, it is claimed that women are often beset by emotions like grief, another sign of feminine weakness and a trait that is considered taboo among men. "By fostering a strong expectation of women's laments . . . men and women reinforce a notion of women as weak and uncontrolled, thereby needing the control of men," writes one observer of Pashtun culture (Grima 1992:11).

Despite their inherent frailty, women are also considered dangerous be-cause they always pose a potential threat to the reputations of the men in their lives. Women carry men's honor in their every action, which is the reason their behavior is so closely monitored. Women are essentially impotent ex-cept in their power to humiliate their husbands and other male relatives (Lindholm 1982).

Still, there is an odd twist to this analysis. The gossip of neighbors about a woman is even *more* feared than the woman's actual behavior. Gossip can effectively erode a man's honor and is very difficult or impossible to rein in. This is one reason why women are best kept indoors and under wraps where no one can see them, there to remain invisible behind the high concealing walls of the family compound (Glatzer 1998).

The earlier statement by the Pashtun official concerning women's participa-tion in the *loya jirga* is reminiscent of that of the Satmar and other Hasidic courts and provides us with insight about their take on women. Perhaps nothing better reveals how the ultra-Orthodox view women's nature than the pronouncement that the testimony of a mentally ill man is more credible before a rabbinical court than that of a sane woman, a clear denigration of women's ability to reason. In their very essence women are different from men, according to the Hasidic sages, in that they have *bina*, a wisdom that stems from intuition and entails deep instinctive knowledge, which is unlike the inherent cerebral intelligence of men. It comes as no surprise that these same sages assert that this type of intuitive wisdom is particularly well-suited to caregiving (Winston 2005; Mann 2007).

Hasidic ideology suggests that at the core of Satmar women's lives—their very reason for being—is the ability to oversee a Jewish home. Because the role of women in Hasidic communities is to look after the family and ensure that their husbands are able to devote themselves to the study of the Talmud and other religious texts, from childhood on Satmar women are taught that their intellect is not equal to that of men nor is their capacity to reason.

Accordingly, the division of labor by sex, in which men study sacred texts and hold all important public positions in the Satmar community while women tend to hearth and home, is seen as predestined, as both natural and inevitable. This reinforces the widely held view among Hasidim that women are intrinsically suited to certain roles and not others, a conviction that helps sustain the gendered status quo.

We can conclude, then, that the FLDS, Pashtun, and Satmar belief systems are singularly important in helping to preserve their existing gender arrangements, ones in which male and female roles are sharply differentiated. In all three instances women are subject to strenuous rules of modesty, they have little say as to when and whom they marry, and they are expected to spend nearly all of their adult lives procreating.

The roles of women in these communities, along with the ideological underpinnings of these roles, are not indeterminate in nature. Ideas about what women are like—about their dispositions and temperament—are not arbitrary; they are highly correlated with and help undergird the actual roles women play. The societal institutions in which women are ensconced, along with beliefs about women's nature, reinforce their subordinate positions in these fundamentalist populations.

In the last few decades, what have always been extreme regimes when it comes to the treatment of girls and women in these groups have become even more so in the sense that more rigorous standards of dress and behavior have come to be demanded of women in them. The next chapter describes these trends.

Chapter Six

Even More Extreme

In the preceding chapters we have seen the severe strictures in multiple domains placed on the lives of girls and women among adherents of the Fundamentalist Church of Jesus Christ of Latter-Day Saints and the Hasidic Satmar as well as members of the Pashtun ethnic community. In each case such impositions have become even more extreme in recent years.

Take the Satmar, for example. In the decades following World War II their Grand Rebbes—first Joel Teitelbaum, followed by his nephew Moses and Moses's sons Zalman and Aaron—have all become increasingly strict in their reading of Jewish religious law. The generation of Satmar now reaching college age as well as the court's young adults are generally more stringent in their religious observance than their parents. Today it is not uncommon for the children of Hasidic college graduates to renounce higher education for themselves and for their own children (Davidman 2015).

Or ponder the FLDS where, early in the new millennium, Prophet Warren Jeffs was no longer content just to demand women's complete submission and obedience to their husbands. He subsequently decreed that women should not work outside the home and should not even leave the house without their husbands' explicit permission (Jessop 2007). Then there are the Pashtun. In the last three decades, the extremes to which certain segments in the Pashtun community have gone in terms of gender roles can be summarized in two words: the Taliban.

A NEW EXTREME: THE FLDS UNDER WARREN JEFFS

Under Warren Jeffs clothing requirements of the FLDS became even more extreme.

—Caroline Jessop, *Escape*, 2007

Some of the new strictures decreed by Prophet Jeffs were fairly minor. As we know, women's clothing was limited to pastel colors and the wearing of red was strictly forbidden. More recently, Jeffs added additional limits on the clothing choices of his female adherents, banning all prints and plaids. Then, by the Prophet's orders, toddlers who were not yet potty-trained were made to wear long underwear over their diapers even in the sweltering heat of Southwestern summers (Jessop 2007).

Next came the directive that all FLDS children cease attending public schools. Being educated by gentile teachers, declared the Prophet, could contaminate the sect's children with evil notions and sinful desires. Instead they were only permitted to attend church-run academies called "private priesthood schools." As we have seen, the result was that the public schools in the twin towns ceased operation for more than a decade (Jessop 2007).

In addition, the list of items that the Prophet forbade to his flock continued to grow. Flying the American flag was prohibited, as were children's toys and bicycles, all sports, dancing, and holiday celebrations including Christmas and the Fourth of July. Smiling was okay, but laughing was banned. He even forbade his followers from saying they were having "fun." "Fun," he said, was too unrestrained and should be replaced with a more placid word: "enjoyable" (Bennion 2011a).

During the final years that Jeffs directly ruled his theocratic fiefdom almost every property in the twin towns was set up with feeds for security cameras. The feeds all went back to a room full of TV screens in Jeffs's house where he could monitor the intimate lives of his followers to make certain they were not disobeying the rules of his unimaginably restrictive religious cult. Much like the Satmar's Vaad, Jeffs also organized a security force, the "God Squad," to enforce his wishes in Hildale and Colorado City and to track outsiders who happened to show up in one of the towns (Anderson 2018).

In December 2011, about four months after he started serving a life sentence in prison, Jeffs had a revelation. He told his followers that God ordered him to create a "United Order" that was to consist of the FLDS members most worthy of heaven, essentially an elite group within the faith. This new order was made up of selected church leaders and their chosen followers. The Prophet himself was to decide who would be included and Warren Jeffs's brother and right-hand man, Lyle Jeffs, immediately began questioning FLDS members about their lives and their faith to determine who was, indeed, worthy of inclusion. The chosen were then instructed to hand over all their worldly goods and told that in the future the church would provide for all their earthly needs (Hyde 2016).

"There was so much class distinction and shunning of people," said a former cook for the Lyle Jeffs family. She told the FBI that while she prepared feasts of lobster and shrimp for the family, her own children "lived off toast" (quoted in O'Neill 2016). The United Order created a highly stratified society that included a male elite at its pinnacle, then ordinary male FLDS members, followed by people "on restoral" who were trying to earn their way back into the good graces of the Prophet, and, finally, apostates. Elite individuals were rewarded while the rank and file faced extreme hardship.

So Warren Jeffs's presence still loomed large despite his having been in prison for several years. In one very odd demonstration of their continued allegiance to Jeffs, some of the faithful began performing a ritual in recognition of his plight. This involved building a small room made of wood from trees they had felled themselves. Then his acolytes would remain within this confined space for hours on end. The exercise was meant to enhance their understanding of and sympathy for their Prophet's suffering in his jail cell (Anderson 2018). To understand this bizarre behavior, it is well to recall that Jeffs has long told his followers that the bars of his cell will melt away and that he will be returned to them, a belief that is still firmly held by FLDS loyalists.

Still, it was in the realm of sexual relations that Jeffs's newest proclamations took their most extreme form. We already know that sex was only to take place for the purpose of procreation and was not permitted when a woman was pregnant. Given that FLDS women were expected to bear an unlimited number of children and remained pregnant for most of their adult lives, this certainly stymied whatever sexual desires they may have had.

Even more recently Jeffs decreed from his prison cell—through an order transmitted by Lyle—that husbands and wives were no longer permitted to have sexual relations with each other at any time. The no-contact rule was so strict that a married couple were not even allowed to hold hands! Any form of contact—from a simple hug to sexual intercourse—could be construed as adultery under Jeffs's new dictum. The FLDS faithful assumed that the ban on marital sex was meant to help free Warren Jeffs from prison. "The perceived reason was everyone was supposed to conserve their energies for the deliverance of the Prophet," according to one FLDS member (Carlisle 2015a).

What is more, the prohibition seems to have been taken seriously. Between 2009 and 2013, after Jeffs gave his directive, the number of babies born in the twin towns declined sharply. In 2009 there were 467 live births, but by 2013 only 42 live births were recorded. In fact, the decline in births was so precipitous that the local birthing center nearly closed (Carlisle 2015a).

But Warren Jeffs did not stop there. Charlene Jeffs, an estranged wife of Lyle, described a group of FLDS followers who were chosen to be "seed bearers." "A seed bearer," she testified in court, "is an elect man of a worthy bloodline chosen by the Priesthood to impregnate the FLDS woman." Not to mince words, men deemed to have "worthy" bloodlines were those who expressed unquestioned fealty to the Prophet as well as to FLDS principles. As a consequence, only fifteen FLDS men were deemed sufficiently worthy to be impregnators of FLDS women (Patterson 2015).

Under this new directive, "FLDS men are no longer permitted to have children with their multiple wives. That privilege belongs to the seed bearer alone," according to the testimony of Charlene Jeffs. She went on, "It is the husband's responsibility to hold the hands of their wives while the seed bearer 'spreads his seed.'" In more explicit terms, the husband is required to be present while the chosen seed bearer(s) rapes his wife or wives (Wagner 2015).

Clearly, these new directives promulgated from prison by Warren Jeffs impacted not only female adherents of the sect, but males as well—the vast majority of whom were now expected to remain celibate under the Prophet's orders. This is why—as we will see in the final chapter—so many men in the FLDS viewed this as the final straw and began leaving the cult, along with their wives and children, in droves.

PASHTUN EXTREMES

There probably is no more egregious and systematic trampling of fundamental rights of women today than what is happening in Afghanistan under the iron rule of the Taliban.

—Hillary Rodham Clinton, 1998 (quoted in Skaine 2002)

A denier of the veil is an infidel and an unveiled woman is lewd.
—Taliban proclamation

The extremes of Pashtun society's treatment of girls and women are reflected in the rise of the Taliban, a Sunni fundamentalist movement whose members were trained in an austere form of Islam in *madrassas* (religious schools) in Pakistan in the late 1980s and early 1990s. The term "Taliban" means "students" in Pashto. From 1996 to 2001 the Taliban held power over approximately three-quarters of Afghanistan and enforced their own strict interpretation of Sharia (Islamic law) throughout the region. The movement eventually gained control over most of the country until it was overthrown after the American-led invasion of Afghanistan in December 2001 following the September 11 attacks in New York City and Washington, D.C.

The Taliban are essentially an all-male brotherhood that had very minimal contact with girls and women. One result is that, under their purview, women were almost completely erased from public life. Of critical importance for an understanding of the Taliban's stance towards females is the fact that the vast majority of them are ethnic Pashtun. As such, this movement not only had its roots in an extreme form of Islam—based on militant jihadism—but also in the tribal conventions of Pashtunwali. In other words, the Taliban's fundamentalist religious ideology is overlain with a robust version of the Pashtun tribal code. And this relationship is especially important when analyzing the Taliban's beliefs about and treatment of girls and women. If we recall the ways in which Pashtun society devalued women and treated them as the lesser sex constrained by all manner of tribally based restrictions, we can understand the evolution of the Taliban and their attitudes toward women.

Because of this grounding in fundamentalist religious and tribal codes, it comes as no surprise that the constraints on females in many parts of Afghanistan under Taliban rule were—and still are—extraordinarily severe and all-encompassing. These multiple restrictions can be best summarized by dividing them into three categories: dress, behavior, and treatment.

Dress

The requirement that outside the home women wear an all-enveloping cloak, a *burqa*, covering them from head to toe with only a latticed cloth across the eyes allowing for limited vision.

A ban on women wearing brightly colored clothes. To the Taliban, these are "sexually attracting colors."

Women's clothes should not be adorned in any way.

A ban on flared or wide pant legs, even when worn under a *burqa*.

Women's clothes must not be narrow and tight "to prevent the seditious limbs from being noticed."

A ban on wearing high-heeled shoes which produce a clicking sound when women are walking. A man must not hear a woman's footsteps.

Women's foot ornaments must not produce any sound and women must not wear sound-producing garments of any kind.

All cosmetics are banned, including nail polish. Some Afghan women with painted nails had their offending fingers cut off.

Women must not use perfume. If a perfumed woman passes by a crowd of men, she is considered to be an adulteress.

Women's clothes must not resemble men's clothes.

Muslim women's clothes must not resemble non-Muslim women's clothes.

Male tailors are banned from taking women's measurements or sewing women's clothes.

Behavior

A complete ban on women working outside the home, which applies to female teachers and most professionals. A handful of female doctors and nurses were allowed to serve in a few hospitals in Kabul.

A ban on women studying at schools, universities, or any other educational institution.

Young girls can only receive schooling up to the age of eight and even then their education should be limited to the Koran.

A ban on women's activity outside the home unless accompanied by a *mahram*—a close male relative such as a father, brother, or husband.

Women must not leave their houses without their husband's permission.

They must not walk in the middle of the street.

They must not talk to strange men and if it is necessary to talk, they must talk in a low voice.

A ban on women laughing loudly and singing. No stranger should hear a woman's voice.

A ban on women talking or shaking hands with non-*mahram* males or looking at or mixing with strangers.

Women may not deal with male shopkeepers.

Women may not be treated by male doctors.

A ban on women riding in a taxi without a *mahram*.

A ban on males and females traveling on the same bus. Public buses have been designated "males only" and "females only."

A ban on women riding bicycles or motorcycles, even with their *mahrams*.

A ban on women washing clothes next to rivers or in a public place.

A ban on female public baths.

A ban on women appearing on the balconies of their apartments or houses.

The compulsory painting of all windows in houses so women cannot be seen from the street outside their homes.

A ban on women playing sports or entering a sports center or club.

A ban on women gathering for festive occasions such as the Eid holiday, or for any recreational purpose.

A ban on women's presence on radio and television or at public gatherings of any kind.

A ban on photographing or filming women.

A ban on women's pictures printed in newspapers and books or hung on the walls of houses and shops.

The modification of all place names that include the word "woman." For example, "woman's garden" must be renamed "spring garden."

Treatment

The whipping, beating, and verbal abuse of women not clothed in accordance with Taliban rules, or of women unaccompanied by a *mahram*.

The whipping of women in public for having uncovered ankles.

The public stoning of women accused of having sex outside marriage.

Men were also under the Taliban's thumb and were punished for any infractions of the rules outlined above committed by their female relatives. Men are responsible for controlling women's behavior. Given the austerity of the Taliban lifestyle and apart from the multiple restrictions on women's dress and activities, there were some dress requirements for boys and men as well:

An order requiring only approved haircuts for Afghan youth.

An order that all male students must wear turbans. "No turban, no education" was a Taliban motto.

An order that men wear Islamic clothes and an Islamic cap.

An order that men not shave or trim their beards, which should grow long enough to protrude from a fist clasped at the point of the chin.

The general population was also subjected to severe restrictions:

A ban on listening to music and musical instruments.

A total ban on watching movies, television, and videos.

A ban on the use of the Internet by both Afghans and foreigners.

A ban on celebrating the traditional New Year, Nowruz, on March 21. The Taliban proclaimed the holiday un-Islamic.

A disavowal of Labor Day on May 1, deemed a "communist holiday."

An order that all people with non-Islamic names change them to Islamic ones.

An order that all males attend prayers in mosques five times a day.

A ban on keeping pigeons and playing with birds, describing such pastimes as un-Islamic. The violators will be imprisoned and the birds shall be killed.

A ban on certain games, including flying kites; such games are un-Islamic.

An order that all onlookers, when encouraging sportsmen, refrain from clapping and instead chant "*Allah-o-Akbar*" (God is great).

An order that anyone who is found to possess objectionable literature will be executed.

An order that anyone who converts from Islam to any other religion will be executed.

An order that non-Muslim minorities must wear a distinct badge or stitch a yellow cloth onto their clothes to be differentiated from the majority Muslim population. [1]

This long list does not provide a complete picture of the trials the Afghan population, most especially women, had to endure during the Taliban era. In the regime's attempt to install a purely Islamic state many women were detained and beaten for such "egregious acts" against Islam as not having

---

1. All of these rules and orders were compiled by the Revolutionary Association of the Women of Afghanistan (n.d.).

their ankles properly covered in public, for wearing white socks, or for other alleged infractions of the Taliban's harsh dress code. Moreover, the rules governing women's lives were not just restrictive; sometimes they were life-threatening as well. For example, women were not permitted to seek medical treatment from male physicians even if they were the only health practitioners available. Because women were terrified of leaving their homes and being arrested and beaten for minor infractions, many were reluctant to go out in public at all, even to receive needed medical treatment. Because some women were simply too poor to afford to buy a *burqa*, they were confined to their homes at all times (Skaine 2002).

Wearing a *burqa* also caused multiple problems for women. Aside from the danger of falling or bumping into objects because of the very limited vision afforded by the mesh cloth covering the eyes, other problems involved difficulty hearing, skin irritations including heat rashes, headaches, and problems breathing under the thick folds of this enveloping garment, a particular issue for women with asthma (Skaine 2002).

In 1998, at the height of the Taliban's power in Afghanistan, the executive director of the organization Physicians for Human Rights asserted that under Taliban rule he was unaware of "any place in the world in recent history where women have so systematically been deprived of every opportunity to survive in the society—from working to getting an education to walking on the street to getting health care." "People were drained of hope." They were "living zombies," one woman recalled (Jakes 2019). Or as one contemporary observer described women under the Taliban: "They have become selfless physical nonbeings that have to live. They have become nonbeings yet they exist. They exist. They breathe, but it's a life full of torture" (cited in Skaine 2002:22, 64).

And so it goes. While the Taliban no longer control the whole of Afghanistan, many of the constraints on the general population and especially on women are still enforced to a large extent in those areas of the country that the Taliban do control. In other words, the Taliban's austere restrictions not only had a major impact on the general Afghan population, but they also largely succeeded in their attempt to completely erase females from public life.

SATMAR EXTREMES

Over the past 10 or 20 years the Hasidic community has gone from being
extreme to being ultra-extreme.
—Sara Stewart, "I Was a Hasidic Jew—but I Broke Free," 2012

In recent years several Hasidic women have remarked on the growing strictures on girls and women in their own communities. "They've passed more
laws from out of nowhere, limiting women," averred a Satmar female who
had abandoned the sect and then wrote a book about growing up Satmar
(Feldman 2011). "There's a rule that women can't be on the street after a
certain hour. That was new when I was growing up." She went on to note the
greater stringency in the female dress code. "When I was 11, they changed
the clothing rules. You used to be able to wear a long-sleeve, high-neck T-
shirt. Now you can only wear high-neck blouses, with woven fabrics, because their theory is that woven fabrics don't cling. T-shirts show boobs"
(Feldman quoted in Stewart 2012).

There is no question that compared to earlier generations the two most
recent generations of Satmar in Williamsburg and Kiryas Joel have been
subject to stricter requirements regarding the complete separation of the sexes and the call for extreme female modesty. Today in Kiryas Joel the stipula-
tion that women and men keep to their own side of the street to prevent them
from walking or talking together in public is vigorously enforced.

In terms of modesty, by the late 1980s little girls as young as three were
made to wear long stockings, while in earlier times such "modest dress" was
only required for girls of eight or even older. Then, too, the Vaad Hatznius—
the squad of modesty enforcers—has been very active in the last few decades
in seeing that the new standards are followed to the letter, especially by
women. The group now is known to resort to extreme measures. They slash
car tires, for example, when warnings and threats do not work to restore the
decree of modesty they demand (Mintz 1992; Goldberger 2013a).

It is not only the dress code that has become more stringent in recent
years. There also has been a decline in the level of education that the Satmar's Rebbes have deemed appropriate for their court's female members.
Recall the relatively recent ban on Satmar girls attending teacher education
classes after they complete high school.

"The lives of Satmar women were not always so cloistered," according to
a woman who was raised as a Satmar. "My mother was among the first
generation of Satmar-educated girls in America. She grew up in Brooklyn's

Williamsburg, the daughter of Holocaust survivors, in those early years when the Satmar community was finding its footing. Her academic and cultural experiences were radically different from mine: New York City public school teachers staffed the English department of Bais Rochel, the Satmar girls school. My mother spoke English with her siblings and peers [not Yiddish], read secular literature, visited the library regularly, attended movies occasionally, listened to the radio and dressed fashionably." All freedoms that are unimaginable among contemporary Satmar (Goldberger 2014a).

The community was less constrained for both men and women in her parents' day, opined another Satmar woman. Here she was referring to what is now considered unacceptable reading material. As we know, secular books, magazines, and newspapers are strictly off-limits. In contrast, when she was a young child living with her father on the Lower East Side he regularly read the *New York Times* and *U.S. News and World Report*, publications that are prohibited to Satmar today (Winston 2005).

Additional strictures have also evolved in the religious realm. In keeping with the traditional ban on substantive Torah lessons for girls, Biblical studies in Hebrew are now completely forbidden for females, and their knowledge of Hebrew texts is restricted to that used in prayers. The dictum of the Jewish sages that "He who teaches his daughter Torah teaches her foolishness" is a bedrock of contemporary Satmar religious thought. Then, too, the censorship of textbooks is ongoing with permanent markers and crayons blocking out material perceived as a threat to the sheltered female brain (cited in Deen 2015:43; Goldberger 2014a).

It is in the realm of technology that the religious gatekeepers of Satmar have become the most active and the most vociferous in their condemnation. Using technology is a *bitul z'man*—a waste of time—according to this thinking, time that would be better spent on religious study. Most notably, the gatekeepers' denunciations have been squarely aimed at the Internet, which they consider a particularly insidious innovation. One ultra-Orthodox rabbi dubbed it a "huge Trojan horse" because surfing the Web can be done privately and secretly, which makes it especially perilous for a person living in a hermetically sealed Hasidic space. The Internet provides anonymity and isolation while allowing access to the world at large (Berger 2005).

In recent years Aaron Teitelbaum, the Rebbe of Kiryas Joel, has imposed a blanket ban on access to the Internet within the homes of his fellow Satmar. If it is absolutely necessary to go online, the Rebbe decreed, then Satmar must only use meticulously filtered connections to the World Wide Web on a computer *outside* the home. This refers to the religious ruling that obliges any Satmar with Internet access to pay a monthly fee for a filter that reports the individual's browsing history to the court's religious authorities (Nathan-Kazis 2012).

Meshimer—the Satmar-approved Web filter—is "an Internet Filtering Solutions Company" that wards off the Internet's power to "cause spiritual and practical destruction in your home and business," according to its advertisements. This filtering software has features like "skin color blocking," which scans Web pages for immodest quantities of female flesh, and "accountability solutions," which send a user's browsing history to a third party. Given the Rebbe's resolve to erect a robust wall between his followers and the threat of the Internet, the Satmar leadership spends around $50,000 a month to set up and maintain this filtering service. The Rebbe "requires everyone, that if you want to send your kids to our schools you need this filter." A subsequent Satmar warning threatened that "those caught using the Internet for nonbusiness purposes, or without content filters, would have their children expelled from the Satmar yeshivah." As one observer has pointed out, it is a lot more difficult to enforce the approved use of the Internet than it was to enforce the late Satmar Rebbe Joel Teitelbaum's ban on television in 1955 (Bronstein 2015; cited in Biale et al. 2018:784).

A Satmar-owned computer store in Williamsburg plays a central role in this directive. While it looks very much like any other store selling laptops and iPads, this store also has several computer kiosks in the back that charge for Internet access, access that blocks forbidden sites through the use of what has been dubbed a "kosher filter." It comes as no surprise that Playboy.com and similar sites are blocked, but Yahoo! News is also off-limits because the site mixes entertainment news with hard news, and news about popular personalities, current movies, and television programs is anathema to the insular Satmar. In essence, such a filter creates a virtual ultra-Orthodox enclave by reducing the expansive World Wide Web down to a tiny number of *frum*-friendly sites (Nathan-Kazis 2012; Finkel 2013).

This store is at the forefront of the Satmar Rebbe's efforts to keep Web access out of his adherents' homes. If he gets his way, kiosks like these will be almost the *only* means that his thousands of followers will have to access the Internet. However, as an alternative to going online using these kiosks, the Rebbe is demanding that those who do own computers and must have them to conduct business keep them *outside* the home and safely away from their children.

Satmar parents, in particular, have been constantly harangued about the dangers that the Internet poses to their children, especially when a computer is present in the home. Aside from filters to "kosherize" the Web, there is also a technological device called Web Shadow that reports children's activity online. Web Shadow tracks the sites they visit and records the time spent on them. As soon as a child visits a questionable site or searches for inappropriate content, a parent can receive an instant email and SMS alert. Weekly reports keep parents informed about their children's online activity so they can intervene immediately if they learn that they are looking at inappropriate Web sites. The company's Web site advertises: "You Wouldn't Let Your Kids Roam The Streets Alone. Why Let Them Do It Online?"

Escalating his commands regarding the Internet, Rebbe Aaron announced in Kiryas Joel in 2012 that following a six-month grace period, children whose families have an Internet connection in the home will be barred from the Jewish schools affiliated with Satmar—a serious form of shunning that is widely feared in the community. According to a Williamsburg community leader, the schools have set up committees to authorize exceptions on a case-by-case basis, usually for families that rely on income provided by family members doing computer work at home. The logistics of implementing the ban have been difficult, such that the six-month grace period was extended for an additional six months and now is in effect (Nathan-Kazis 2012; Llorente 2018).

How is this directive enforced? "It's the Vaad. They don't let you have smart phones, computers, laptops, or DVD players," said a Kiryas Joel resident. "I wasn't even saying anything bad on social media. I was asking a question. But you are not to question anything" concerning Hasidism. "It's like we're in North Korea or China," he said (Llorente 2018).

Wearing masks, the Vaad Hatznius broke into the bedroom of a fifteen-year-old girl one night to confiscate her cell phone. The Vaad are, of course, the Satmar's "moral police" who carefully monitor any dress or behavior considered immodest. Members of the Vaad disable Web browsers and install filters on cell phones to block access to Google, YouTube, many Wikipedia pages, and porn Web sites, among other content (Yarrow 2012).

On one occasion in 2015 religious authorities in Kiryas Joel sent parents a contract to sign, declaring that their cell phones "are in accordance to the rules of the community and yeshiva," and adding, "We also confirm that we do not possess in our home another cell phone." Anyone who does not comply with this order, the Rebbe warned, will no longer be permitted "to continue in their position with any Satmar institution" (quoted in Llorente 2018). Some Satmar skirt this ban by having two phones, a "kosher" one that does not connect to the Internet or receive text messages, and a smartphone whose number is not given out to their children's school.

Women bear the brunt of these prohibitions. The Rebbe decreed that no woman may own a smartphone. They are allowed to have "basic" or flip phones, but not smartphones that connect to the Internet "under any circumstances and without exception, not even for work." And posters put up in public spaces in Williamsburg actually suggest that "mothers with smart phones" are to blame for teens who have "gone off the *derech*" (path), that is, who have strayed from Hasidic orthodoxy (Sokol 2015; Kahn 2012).

In 2017 the Satmar Committee of Technology issued a notice indicating it was completing its work eradicating smartphones "owned by the mothers of students of our holy schools." It went on to demand that if members of the community knew "such a person"—that is, a woman who owned a smartphone—they should get in touch with the committee without delay so that the phone could be immediately confiscated (Vizel 2017).

The fear and loathing of the Internet stretch far beyond the Satmar, the most traditional and anti-modern of Hasidic courts. All manner of interventions have been promoted by other ultra-Orthodox authorities to thwart access to the Internet and limit the damage that, they insist, it is doing. For example: "Today with the internet in every pocket, we risk losing the battle. This *kedusha* [holiness] crisis is unique to our generation and has wreaked havoc on untold families and individuals," proclaims an online advertisement for a counseling service. "Our organization is determined to find a solution and has already helped thousands." The organization referred to here "is battling the *kedusha* crisis on every front, by providing treatment for those already drowning and prevention to protect others from falling in." The service will help individuals "break free of lust-related behaviors."

This statement is from the Web site of a company called GuardYourEyes, which advertises a program that purports to cure ultra-Orthodox Jews of their Internet addiction. The program is available in English, Hebrew, Yiddish, French, and Spanish. According to a YouTube video that is linked to the Web site, Internet addiction is even more powerful than addiction to hard drugs and the only way to cure it is to join the twelve-step Porn Anonymous Program, "which will rid your life of *shmutz* [filth]."

Again, abhorrence of the Internet is not limited to Satmar. In fact, the most well-known attempt to rein in Internet usage and warn against the dangers of the World Wide Web took place in 2012 at a massive all-male rally at Citi Field Stadium in New York City, a rally attended by tens of thousands of Hasidic Jews belonging to a number of Hasidic courts. While roughly fifty thousand ultra-Orthodox men went to the rally, women—in keeping with the rules of gender segregation—held at-home viewing parties in Orthodox neighborhoods in Brooklyn and New Jersey to watch the event (ironically) live-streamed over the Internet. This was the first of two outdoor anti-Internet *asifas* ("gatherings" in Yiddish) organized by leaders of the Satmar community in Williamsburg (Eller 2012).

During the gathering, which raised $1.5 million for the cause, speakers emphasized the "evil" of the Internet. Rabbis led attendees in evening prayers and then gave fiery exhortations to abjure the "filth" that is found on the World Wide Web. A pamphlet handed out at the rally declared that "providing your children with an internet-accessible cell phone is giving

Satmar anti-Internet demonstration, New York, 2012
Source: **Rabbi Jason Miller**

them directly into the hands of Satan." Said one attendee: "Desires are out there. . . . We have to learn how to control ourselves!" A spokesman for the event informed reporters that "the siren song of the Internet entices us! It brings out the worst of us!" (quoted in Grynbaum 2012).

Satmar Rebbe Aaron of Kiryas Joel did not attend the rally. He boycotted the event because he had been told that the rally would not call for a *total* ban on the Internet. He also took issue with the fact that the *asifa* would be conducted in English, saying, "Our forefathers fought against having speeches in the languages of other nations and I do not want to send my followers to a place where they will be speaking a foreign language." (English!) It is also important to point out that the Satmar Rebbe has taken a much more extreme stance against the Web than the scores of other ultra-Orthodox leaders who supported the Citi Field event. After all, he is demanding an absolute prohibition on access to the Internet except in a very limited number of cases related to business (Biale et al. 2018:783; Eller 2012).

As we will see in the next and final chapter, the fight against modernity engaged in by each of these fundamentalist religious communities has had only limited success. In recent years external forces, particularly among the FLDS and the Satmar, have posed serious threats to their traditional, encapsulated ways of life.

Chapter Seven

And the Future?

There is no getting around the fact that the relationship between gender equality and fertility is very strong: There are no high-fertility countries that are gender equal.

—Philip Cohen (quoted in Miller 2018)

In this final chapter we turn to prognostications for future developments in these three fundamentalist communities, paying particular attention to what might be in store for the female portions of their populations. I will also describe some important shifts in these communities, particularly among the Satmar and the FLDS, as they confront external forces with which they have had to contend in recent years.

THE PASHTUN FUTURE

No doubt the war on terror toppled the misogynist and barbaric regime of Taliban. But it did not remove Islamic fundamentalism . . . it just replaced one fundamentalist regime with another.

—Member of the Revolutionary Association of the
Women of Afghanistan (quoted in Skaine 2008)

The future does not look bright for Afghanistan—the country, its people, and most especially its girls and women. By 2008 Taliban insurgents had regained control over much of the southern region of the nation, especially Kandahar and Helmand Provinces—home to a majority of Pashtun—and by 2018 the Taliban dominated almost 44 percent of the country, the most territory it had controlled since 2001. But even earlier, after the Taliban had been temporarily vanquished, nothing had changed for the better for women in Kabul, according to Asne Seierstad (2003), who lived there two years after the Taliban retreat. And the violent conflict for control of the nation is ongoing (Chughtai 2019; Nordland 2018c).

Knowing what we do about Taliban beliefs and practices, it comes as no surprise that the Taliban resurgence has greatly impacted women's political, social, and economic prospects in those areas of Afghanistan under Taliban control. This is especially true of women who are politically active and who attempt to resist traditional gender roles. These women are often intimidated and threatened by the Taliban as well as by other social conservatives. A number of female leaders in the country have, in fact, been assassinated by militants (de Leede 2014; Rubin and Zahori 2012).

What do we know about the fate of Afghan women since the rout of the Taliban in late 2001? There were some advances for women in terms of education and participation in economic and political life—at least for a while. By 2007, for example, over a quarter of the members of the Afghan parliament were women. Then, too, millions of girls returned to school, some 400,000 for the first time. Yet at about the same time Human Rights Watch reported that various indicators still ranked Afghan women as among the most unfortunate on earth. While infant mortality had decreased, maternal mortality was still among the highest in the world with 1,600 deaths per 100,000 births, a figure that translates into about one in seven women dying during pregnancy and childbirth (Skaine 2008; USAID 2017).

The Afghan constitution guarantees rights and a specified number of seats for women in the country's parliament, but such "paper rights" can be misleading because women, especially in rural areas, have little or no contact with the state and with civil society in general. So while women were guaranteed the right to vote, 87 percent of those surveyed said that women can only vote if a male relative permits them to do so and 35 percent believe that women would be denied the right to vote by their male relatives (Skaine 2008).

In 2009 several prominent Afghan women's rights activists, members of civil society groups, and lawmakers came together to draft a bill to better protect girls and women through legal channels by defining crimes of violence against them. The bill, known as the Elimination of Violence Against Women Act (EVAW), would have led to new penalties for underage and forced marriage, rape, mandatory prostitution, and similar abuses. It was temporarily passed that same year, but the EVAW later hit a roadblock when a number of conservative members of the Afghan parliament opposed it, arguing that the act was against "Islamic teaching." This was followed by Afghan president Ashraf Ghani ordering the Ministry of Justice to remove the EVAW chapter from the nation's new penal code. Ever since his controversial reversal, the status of the act has been in limbo (Human Rights Watch 2018; Koofi 2015).

In addition, a long-promised plan by the Afghan government to implement a UN Security Council Resolution that calls for women's equal participation in issues surrounding peace and security was largely ignored. The several rounds of peace talks involving the country included only *two* women among forty-seven government and international representatives.

Other statistics provide a grim picture of women's rights in that nation. In 2016 the Afghanistan Independent Human Rights Commission (AIHRC) investigated close to 5,600 cases of violence against women. Then, in the first six months of 2017, the AIHRC reported thousands of cases of violence against women and girls across the country, including beatings, killings, and acid attacks, with few resulting in prosecutions. A similar report was filed by Afghanistan's Ministry of Women's Affairs on an increase in cases of gender-based violence against women, especially in areas under Taliban control. Yet another report suggested an intensification of the public punishment of women by armed groups applying Sharia law. Against the backdrop of the general failure to investigate these abuses, cases of violence against women remained grossly underreported, a result of traditional practices as well as fear of the consequences of reporting by the victims themselves (Amnesty International 2018).

Other potential reforms fell by the wayside. A long-term effort to modernize family law, including the provisions for granting divorce, remained stalled. Promised reforms to end the use of unscientific and abusive "virginity examinations" for women taken into custody, along with their imprisonment for so-called "morality crimes"—like running away from home—also never materialized (Human Rights Watch 2018).

Then, in 2017, threats forced the closure of girls schools in several villages in Farah Province, temporarily denying education to more than 3,500 girls. When the schools reopened, the vast majority of parents were initially afraid to allow their daughters to return to class. Lack of security due to violent attacks by the Taliban on government forces and retaliatory responses by the latter also have led to the closing of thousands of schools formerly attended by both boys and girls. Two years later an education official in the same province was warned by local Taliban leaders that he should fire all male teachers at girls schools since men should not teach girls. He did as he was told, saying, "We didn't want to give them an excuse" to shut down the schools by force. Still, the schools were not spared. Armed men set fire to two girls schools just outside Farah city, the provincial capital. Both schools were badly damaged and their teaching materials were destroyed. This ended classes indefinitely for almost 1,700 girls. Today an estimated 3.5 million school-age children are not in school across Afghanistan, 75 percent of them girls (Amnesty International 2018; Rahm and Zucchino 2019).

Perhaps even more shocking is the fact that some 87 percent of Afghan women are *still* illiterate. Despite efforts to educate girls by the Afghan government and international donors, an estimated two-thirds of Afghan girls still do not attend school. This dismaying figure is due not only to wide-spread violence and the absence of security but also to a lack of female teachers and conservative social restrictions that have kept girls from attending school (Amnesty International 2018; Bohn 2018).

There have been a few bright spots for the female population in Afghanistan although they may prove to be illusory. Since the temporary demise of the Taliban, about forty women's shelters housing several thousand women have been established by NGOs with the financial aid of foreign donors, especially the United States. It is noteworthy, however, that while women's shelters have been set up in eleven provinces across Afghanistan none are in southern Afghanistan, the Pashtun heartland.

Moreover, the establishment of such shelters has been met with a great deal of controversy. In 2011 the Afghan parliament nearly passed harsh limitations on the shelters and lawmakers only backed down after pressure from the United States and other donor nations. Attempts also have been made by the Afghan government to wrest control of the shelters by obliging donors to pay into a fund at the Ministry of Women's Affairs, which, in turn, would disburse money to shelter operators. This would essentially put the sites under government control, a move that has been vehemently opposed by women who run the shelters (Kramer 2018).

Conservative figures in the government, including Islamic mullahs serving in the Afghan parliament, have bridled over the existence of the shelters, viewing them as examples of foreign meddling and an "imperialist imposition" on Afghan society. "People are calling them centers of prostitution," noted the manager of a large consortium of shelters with evident disgust.

Officials in the Ministry of Women's Affairs have struggled to adjudicate disagreements between the shelters' foreign donors and conservative members of the Afghan government. The latter are intensely critical of the shelters, where women live unsupervised by men. They have also spoken darkly of them as "brothels." Taliban insurgents and conservative members of the Afghan government have sometimes made common cause in their loathing of and adamant stance against any progress made in terms of women's rights in the country, most of which have come about through foreign pressure tied to international funding (quoted in Kramer 2018; Nordland 2014b).

This resistance to women's progress, along with many of the problems Afghan women face today, is rooted not in Afghan or Islamic law, but in the nation's ethnic and local traditions such as those I have described for the Pashtun. One example is forced marriage, an ongoing practice. The UN Development Fund for Women reports that between 70 and 80 percent of marriages in the country are arranged regardless of the desires of the girls and women involved and, for females, just under 60 percent occur before the legal age of sixteen (Skaine 2008).

One aspect of Afghan society meant to improve women's status has had a modicum of success, at least in terms of the attention it has received. This is the campaign widely aired on social media to change the Pashtun custom of never mentioning the names of women in public. The campaign, initiated by a group of young women, comes with a hashtag in Pashto and Dari that addresses the core issue and translates as #WhereIsMyName. The aim of the activists is to challenge women to reclaim their basic identity by shattering the deep-rooted taboo that prevents men from mentioning the names of their female relatives in public. A well-known male singer wrote about his personal experience after choosing to defy the taboo: "On many occasions in front of a crowd that doesn't have family relations to me [sic], I have noticed how the foreheads of men sour by what they see as my cowardice in mentioning the name of my mother or my wife. They stare at me in such a way as if I am the leader of all of the world's cowards and I know nothing of 'Afghan honor and traditions'" (quoted in Mashal 2017).

In the last few years, as the withdrawal of the United States and other Western nations from Afghanistan has accelerated, advocates for women's rights are seeing a downturn in funding for women's programs. "We already see the signs of losing the support of the international community," said one advocate in an interview before she resigned her position with an NGO. "No one's funding new civil society programs anymore. None of the foreigners show up anymore; they're all in hiding. And I think what gains we have achieved the last thirteen years, we're slowly losing all of them," she noted dejectedly (quoted in Nordland 2014b).

The events in 2019 at a traditional Afghan assembly, a *loya jirga*, intended to debate Afghanistan's road to peace, certainly do not inspire confidence that things are improving for women in that country. A number of female delegates said they were patronized or ignored at the proceedings and were told that only men should preside over the fifty-one committees at the gathering, while women should serve as secretaries. Then there was the outburst of a bearded delegate who told a woman who tried to speak about peace to "shut up." "Peace has nothing to do with you," he said. "Sit down! You should be in the kitchen cooking!" (quoted in Faizi and Zucchino 2019).

At the same time, peace talks between the Taliban and representatives of American forces in Afghanistan appeared to be on the road to success, an eventuality that would mean the withdrawal of all American forces from the country. Among many Afghan women, however, the hopes raised by a possible end to the fighting are mixed with an undeniable sense of dread. "We don't want a peace that will make the situation worse for women's rights compared to now," said the head of the legal department of the Afghan Women's Network. A female member of the Afghan parliament agreed: "Afghan women want peace too. But not at any cost." Nevertheless, as an Afghan prosecutor noted sorrowfully: "A Talib is a Talib. They have proven what type of people they are, what their ideology is. And if they return with the same ideology, everything will be the same again" (quoted in Nordland, Faizi, and Abed 2019; quoted in Engelbrecht 2019).

A *New York Times* headline says it all about the peace negotiations: "Women Here Are Very, Very Worried." The reason is clear. Afghan women's issues are not on the American agenda in its peace talks with the Taliban, which are limited to discussions concerning terrorism and security following the departure of American military forces. And the signs from the Taliban are not encouraging. While they agree that women can go to school and hold some political offices, they are adamant that women cannot become judges or serve as president. Moreover, they view the Afghan Constitution and its promise of women's equality as an illegitimate document that was imposed by the United States. Still, there is a slight ray of hope. According to a woman currently involved in Afghan peace negotiations, "Women in Afghanistan are more empowered now. They have access to social media and have built a very strong network around the world. They will not let anyone take them backward" (Chira 2019; quoted in Kumar 2019).

Most of this overview of the position of women in Afghanistan over the last two decades has referred to women in general, both Pashtun and those of other ethnicities as well. However, it is still worth recalling that Pashtun women have long led extremely constrained lives and it appears that not much has changed in this regard. A male-dominated tribal culture in which women often have been treated as little more than chattel, combined with a conservative practice of Islam and a nationwide lack of education, has meant that long before the Taliban arrived in the mid-1990s, women had few opportunities beyond the home.

As of this writing very little has changed in women's lives in the Pashtun areas of Afghanistan. Women are simply not considered or treated as full human beings in Pashtun society. This is one reason why over the last decade Afghanistan has been called "the most dangerous country for women on earth" by a poll of international experts on gender issues. High levels of violence, poor health care, low levels of education, and poverty make Afghanistan the most benighted place on earth to be a woman (BBC News 2011).

WHAT'S IN STORE FOR THE FLDS?

One day they're going to wake up and realize that what they believed isn't true.

—Former FLDS member (quoted in Hannaford 2018)

As we know from earlier discussions, membership in the Fundamentalist Church of Jesus Christ of Latter-Day Saints has been on the decline since Warren Jeffs became Prophet in the early years of the new millennium. This decline has been particularly steep since 2011, when Jeffs began issuing a series of proclamations from his prison cell, directives that severely limited the lifestyles of his followers, most especially in the realm of sex. Nevertheless, as recently as 2018 he was still maintaining his iron grip on the FLDS from prison.

In 2015 a private investigator in Utah estimated that between 500 and 1,000 FLDS adherents had left in the previous two years, concluding that about 10,000 believers remained. Another estimate of the twin towns' populations that same year put the total number at around 7,750. And the exodus has continued ever since. Several events account for these departures (Johnson 2018).

The sect had to deal with a new challenge in 2016 as the law finally caught up with Lyle Jeffs, Warren's brother and the de facto leader of the FLDS for over a decade. After Lyle's arrest the faithful came to believe that the walls of the courtroom where he was to be tried in a major fraud case would collapse when he appeared before the judge. At the same hour an earthquake would befall Texas and demolish the prison holding Warren Jeffs, allowing him to walk out a free man. "I am hearing from people inside the FLDS that . . . there is going to be a kind of apocalypse," said one observer of the sect (quoted in Walters 2016b).

But the only signs of an apocalypse have been the series of criminal and civil cases that have suddenly befallen the FLDS leadership. Lyle Jeffs was one of nearly a dozen senior FLDS figures arrested in early 2016. He and his cronies were charged in a welfare fraud scheme and accused of money laundering and swindling the U.S. government out of millions of dollars in federal food stamps. Jeffs was subsequently sentenced to almost five years in prison for the key role he played in carrying out this elaborate food stamp theft. His sentence came at the end of a major government case that took several years to investigate and found that some $11 million in food stamp benefits had been diverted to an FLDS communal storehouse as well as to several of its front companies. In other litigation the FLDS has been accused of using child labor in construction projects (Walters 2016b; Associated Press 2017).

The jailing of Lyle Jeffs was an enormous blow to the FLDS faithful because, as we have seen, it was Lyle who conveyed to the community the orders issued from behind bars by his brother Warren, and it was Warren, his followers were convinced, who directly channeled the word of God. "The community is absolutely paralyzed with Lyle in jail," noted one former FLDS member (quoted in Walters 2016b).

Yet another, even more cataclysmic event engulfed the sect in recent years. Since 2005 the FLDS land trust, the United Effort Plan (UEP), has been involved in disputes with federal authorities. The UEP was once controlled by Warren Jeffs and subsequently managed by the FLDS leadership. At the time, the land trust owned most of the properties in Hildale and Colorado City, which were said to be worth well over $100 million (Bennion 2012).

Because of the charge that the UEP was financing criminal activities, especially welfare and food stamp fraud, a court in Utah transferred control of the trust in 2005 from the FLDS to a state-appointed board of trustees. Since then the board has taken control of homes, businesses, and other properties wherever FLDS members refused to sign occupancy agreements or have allowed their property taxes to go unpaid (Carlisle 2017).[1]

Members of the new board resolved that rather than continue to hold many homes, businesses, and acres of land in trust, most would be sold. Some homes could be retained by the individuals who had actually built them if they were willing to pay surveying and closing costs. They could remain in their homes if they agreed to the following requirements: sign an occupancy agreement, pay a $100 monthly fee, and pay up all property taxes that were in arrears. Refusing to do so placed the homes at risk of seizure and their inhabitants threatened with eviction (Woods 2018).

FLDS members were not excluded from property ownership under this plan; the terms of the reformed UEP specified that it was "religiously neutral." Nevertheless, many FLDS adherents refused to go along with these requirements. The transfer of the trust to non-FLDS administrators, they charged, was simply a tool for the outside world to take over the twin towns. The church, they were convinced, had paid all the requisite taxes and the land and all the structures on it had long ago been consecrated to God. As a consequence, no individual or family or land trust had a "right" to any of this property. Moreover, their faith prohibited them from even speaking to nonbelievers about such a plan and any agreement with the UEP trustees risked their very salvation (Carlisle 2017).

These events have led some to allege that the UEP was purposely driving FLDS members from their homes and their community. The mayor of Colorado City, who remains an FLDS stalwart, said his fellow believers are being given an impossible choice: "Either they enter into agreements with apostates to their faith, or they lose their homes." Another FLDS member believes the UEP has created policies to drive believers out so that people unaffiliated with the church can vote themselves into office in future municipal elections. "Every believer is in the same situation," according to yet another FLDS adherent. "It feels like they pretty much want us out of here" (quoted in Carlisle 2017; quoted in Woods 2018).

---

1. In June 2019, the court-monitored oversight of the UEP Trust ended. After fourteen years it finally came time for the community to run itself again (Danovich 2019).

Many FLDS members did, in fact, lose their homes once eviction notices were served. After multiple families were evicted, they gathered together and began taking refuge in unoccupied dwellings, often cramming two, three, even four families along with their many children into a single household. This is what the church referred to as being "stacked up" in crowded, cramped lodgings. One such residence housed 185 people until they, too, were evicted (Woods 2018).

Estimates suggest that evictions may have impacted almost 90 percent of Hildale's FLDS residents, with a single family often made up of dozens of wives and children. Nevertheless, most families stayed in town. They bounced from one house to another, squatting for a few weeks until a new eviction notice arrived. Soon the FLDS Church could only offer trailers and shipping containers to house its homeless followers. FLDS supporters who remained were forced into the same impossible choice between heaven and hell: Would they violate their faith to stay in a home, or lose everything for their beliefs? And what was to become of God's sacred land? (Hannaford 2018)

Some FLDS believers left town in search of a new place to live and work. This exodus was also related to the litigation and court-ordered reforms in Hildale and Colorado City. In essence, the FLDS moved from a single core site to several smaller settlements in various locales. They spread across neighboring venues with some of the faithful creating enclaves in southern Utah, on the Oklahoma plains, in Minnesota, in North and South Dakota, and across the Canadian border, all starting over in an alien world of which they had no understanding (Winslow 2019).

One such FLDS enclave is a 140-acre compound in the remote Black Hills near Pringle, South Dakota. Founded by one of Warren Jeffs's myriad brothers, the compound is surrounded by barbed wire, and a manned lookout tower looms large over the complex. South Dakota officials have charged that the compound's residents have never complied with a state law requiring them to report all births and deaths, so it is unclear how many people actually live there. By establishing a penalty for failing to report this information, state lawmakers hope to clarify what remains hidden behind the compound's walls (McDonell-Parry 2019).

It was not just the legal trials and tribulations of the twin towns that caused FLDS members to flee. Like the Satmar, some FLDS adherents were first exposed to the world outside their religious milieu by the Internet, which became the catalyst for their departure. Said one twenty-two-year-old: "I finally heard about this thing called Facebook. I had no idea what it was. I sneaked a look on a computer, even though that was forbidden, and I found some old friends who'd got out. I was, like, 'Wow, they've been living here in town all this time.' That's when I knew I could leave." Web sites like Facebook and Snapchat have been called "the new highway" for FLDS members leaving the sect because they allow them to reconnect with others who left earlier. Because of these connections, one former sect member noted how much easier it is to leave the FLDS now than it was a decade ago. Or as another former member put it with tongue in cheek: "Thank goodness for the Internet! I learned how to put on mascara from watching YouTube" (quoted in Walters 2015a, 2015b).

As outsiders began moving into town the ambiance slowly started to change. Walls and gates erected by the FLDS to shield outsiders' views were torn down. Religious structures slipped from the church's grasp. Soon more women were appearing on the street wearing conventional attire rather than the distinctive prairie dress of the FLDS faithful. As FLDS families were evicted from their homes, they began filling up with outsiders, all of whom were deemed apostates. Today it is estimated that FLDS members make up only about 20 percent of Hildale residents, although Colorado City remains a bastion of the FLDS faithful. These changes have meant that Hildale has now taken on a new, decidedly more secular and middle-American character (Hannaford 2018).

The remaining FLDS followers in Hildale tried to recede from view by erecting tall fences around their houses and hanging wooden "Zion" signs above their doors, indicating that these are homes of the faithful. The sign is a signal for outsiders to stay away. The goal is to protect themselves from the apostates moving into town, some of whom live right next door (Sanders 2018).

As more people moved into town, some started local businesses in Hildale. An outsized house once owned by Warren Jeffs was auctioned off and repurposed as "America's Most Wanted Bed & Breakfast," offering guests the opportunity to stay in the once off-limits mansion for just $99 a night. Soon thereafter Airbnb listings began to dot the town, as well as a few motels. A karate studio opened along with a Subway franchise, the Merry Wives Cafe & Coffee, a Dollar General store, a bakery, a vape shop, five restaurants, and a bar—Edge of the World Brewery—that received the town's first liquor license. But the changes were not limited to retail establishments. In mid-2019, a company that manufactures X-ray protection equipment confirmed plans to open a plant in Hildale, a move that will provide ninety new jobs for the community. In short, with each passing day the outside world slipped deeper into the twin towns, most especially Hildale, bringing FLDS members into contact with people who had virtually no understanding of the FLDS and its way of life (Woods 2018; Danovich 2019).

FLDS adherents viewed these events as an alarming invasion. For the first time the two remote towns were no longer the exclusive domain of the church and its followers. Former FLDS members, once dismissed as apostates, began trickling back into their old homes, settling down among neighbors who would not speak to them. Local FLDS adherents who remained faithful to the sect would have nothing to do with the newcomers who were not fellow believers, even those who had once been members of the FLDS in good standing.

Yet another incident signaled an important shift in this FLDS redoubt. In 2014, for the first time in thirteen years, a public school was reestablished in the town of Hildale. "That school renewed hope," said one local. "It changed Hildale." A kindergarten teacher described how parents slowly came to allow their children to attend the newly opened public school. "The courage that it took even for them to take their children and enroll them into public school. . . . It was huge," she said. Recall that Warren Jeffs had pronounced public schools as strictly off-limits, dens of iniquity that would sully the minds of believers (quoted in Havens 2017; quoted in Woods 2018).

After classes started the school tested every child who enrolled, evaluating the scars left from a childhood with little or no education. Some students who had attended the FLDS-run school scored up to four grades behind their age level. Many children were entering school for the first time and had never learned to read or write their own name or even to hold a pencil. A generation of FLDS children—now teenagers—was lost. When they finally returned to school, the challenges the students faced were immense. High school students even had to be taught how to sit in class and how to raise their hands to answer questions (Woods 2018).

Other changes were taking place as well. For as long as a municipal government existed in the twin towns, it was closed to all but elite members of the FLDS. Put simply, the church controlled the local government. FLDS leaders appointed mayors and town councils, instructing adherents to vote for their preferred candidates. Given this history, a striking event took place in 2017. In that year, for the first time ever, a woman—an ex–church member who was considered an apostate by the FLDS faithful—ran as a candidate for mayor of the town of Hildale and won. This was an absolutely unimaginable turn of events! While the new mayor thought she could bring the people of Hildale together, her government faced many obstacles. The town treasurer, a devout FLDS believer, quit before she took office. He refused to work for an apostate—no less for a woman. Then the two town clerks quit along with the billing director; the utility and gas managers and the park director decided to take early retirement. Said one city official at the time: "It has come to a point where I have to choose between my religion and participation in city government, and I choose my religion. My religion teaches me that I should not follow a woman for a leader in a public or family capacity." Nevertheless, the mayor persisted and she still serves in office in Hildale (Hannaford 2018; quoted in Anderson 2018).

A year earlier, a new police chief—an outsider with no ties to the community—was sworn in after a jury ruled that the previous police force, made up entirely of church members, was guilty of religious discrimination. A federal jury determined that residents who were not members of the FLDS were routinely singled out. They were not issued permits or water hookups, and when FLDS squatters took possession of houses and would not allow their legal owners to move in, the local police refused to evict the squatters and turned allegations against the accusers, charging them with filing false police reports. In short, the legal proceedings found that the local police were an enforcement arm of the church and, by extension, of its former leader, Warren Jeffs (Kiefer 2016; Walters 2016a).

Perhaps no group has been more affected by all of these developments than the twin towns' female population. A number of groups formed to help women adapt to the changes going on all around them. In 2009 an organization devoted to helping those escaping polygamy, called Holding Out Hands, began operating to assist FLDS women. It smuggled cell phones into the community when it received word, usually from friends or relatives on the outside, that someone wanted to escape the sect. The group then aided individuals, or occasionally whole families, to relocate to safehouses where FLDS officials would not be able to track them down and pressure them to return to the suffocating fold of fellow believers. It also helped find schooling or job training for those who chose to remain in the area. "They're pretty much refugees," said one member of the support group, "except they speak English" (quoted in Carlisle 2018).

In 2017 one of Jeffs's former wives turned the forty-four-room mansion where she had once lived with dozens of sister-wives and their children into a refuge for other women fleeing the FLDS.[2] The mansion, now named the Dream Center, received financial support from a California-based Christian charity. During one month in 2018 four women and their children lived full-time at the center—one woman accompanied by her eleven children—and at times as many as 150 former church members attended the center's potluck supper. Every week trauma counselors drove up from Phoenix to provide therapy sessions to residents who expressed a need for emotional support (Hannaford 2018).

But change did not come overnight. The lack of socialization to the wider world plagued many FLDS women, even those who had left the sect years earlier. "I've heard a lot of the young girls, they say that they can't even go to work without taking a shot of whiskey or vodka to even speak up or get a job," remarked one local. The culture shock felt by those who fled the FLDS was profound because they knew so little about the world outside their insular cult. The fact that some 70 percent of adults in the two towns had not gone past eighth grade helps explain this dearth of experience. Lacking social skills, confidence, and education, FLDS women were flummoxed when trying to adjust to secular society. The communal edifice under which decisions were made for them was gone. Decisions about where to work, whom to marry, how many children to have, and where to live were all directives that they were once required to obey. The structure of their lives no longer existed. "When a person loses that sense of belonging," said one member of the Holding Out Hands support group, "there's a sense of hopelessness" (quoted in Havens 2017; quoted in Carlisle 2018).

One sixty-two-year-old woman who had left the FLDS three years earlier still considered herself "a teenager." Women who have departed the cult often think of themselves in these terms. They laugh that their emotional development was arrested at an early age. Consequently, when they leave the FLDS they go through the same stages that every child goes through, from teenage rebellion, to exploration in their twenties, to feeling more confident by the time they reach their thirties (Petersen 2018).

Former FLDS members were at sea. "When you leave, you are like a big baby with no idea how the outside world works," said one lapsed follower. "I feel like I'm starting from zero," she said. Abandoning the FLDS way of life

---

2. By the time he was jailed Jeffs had eighty wives, each of whom had an average of ten children (Anderson 2018).

felt like being "deprogrammed" and even after time had passed she still feels "a bit alien" living in the world outside the sect. Even knowing what to wear can be a problem for some women. As one who still feels uncomfortable in non-prairie dress remarked, "Gentiles growing up get to try something on, and try something else on, and see someone wearing a different style and say, 'Oh, I like that!' But we never developed taste. There's all this other trauma when we leave the FLDS—and then we have to figure out how to dress, too" (quoted in Walters 2015b; quoted in Petersen 2018).

Given their doctrinaire upbringing, it is not surprising that some women who had left the FLDS returned to their husbands who remained in the sect. Sometimes these were the very abusers from whom they had fled. The teachings of the FLDS do much to explain this behavior. They dictate that all hard decisions *must* be left to men. Women are simply incapable of making them for themselves. This belief is drummed into the heads of little girls from early childhood on. And it meshes neatly with another FLDS dictum that tells women, "I'm nothing without a man. . . . I'm never getting into heaven without a man" (Schmidt 2006; Jessop 2009:244).

Some of those who have tried to help FLDS women questioned whether they were really doing any good. One therapist who counseled local women worried about how they could possibly become self-sufficient in twenty-first-century America. "When you've grown up sewing and you don't know how to do a checkbook," she said, "and all of a sudden to have to go out and support yourself, I would say, yes, there's a crisis." And the sect's children will not necessarily fare any better in adapting to the outside world. On a trip to a local Wal-Mart with FLDS children who had grown up in a money-free environment, one child asked after taking an item down from a shelf, "Mother, can I take this?" (quoted in Dark 2017).

Others worried about the risks girls and women face when they leave the sect and interact with men they meet in the outside world. Some struggle to figure out how to reject unwanted advances. The option of saying no was never available to them. This sometimes resulted in date rape and sexual harassment by men whom they met since leaving the FLDS. It is even worse for adolescents who were raised under the dictum to "keep sweet," which taught them that as "priesthood people" they were not to fight, disagree, or resist. When men they encounter learn that ex-FLDS women do not know how to say no, the women become easy prey. "We're getting so much worldly attention that all these young girls are getting taken advantage of. They've never dated, they don't know it's OK to not be submissive," said the woman who established the Creekers Foundation,[3] another local group designed to assist FLDS women. "They're scared that if they leave, they're going to live on the streets or in prison because they can't make it alone," she said (Petersen 2018; quoted in Havens 2017).

Within this environment it is not surprising that suicide has become more common among former members of the FLDS, both men and women. Drug abuse is another scourge. Many people who have spent a lifetime never being permitted to make personal decisions for themselves have fallen into one addiction or another since leaving the cult and entering a world full of perilous choices. The self-destructive behavior displayed by many former FLDS members is rooted in the many years of lives lived without personal autonomy (Anderson 2018).

The Creekers Foundation, a nonprofit organization, was started in 2016 as a way for women in the twin towns to gain social skills, receive support from women who had had similar experiences, and otherwise fill a void while recovering from what it termed "religious brainwashing." Said the founder of Creekers: "I think we are at least one or two generations behind the rest of the world in women's empowerment here" (quoted in Havens 2017).

The Creekers seeks to help both ex-FLDS and current FLDS women. The group has a philosophy of viewing its members and others whom it tries to help as "survivors" rather than as "victims." Each week women come together for a group meeting under the rubric "Overcoming Obstacles." They share their own stories with the aim of creating an atmosphere to encourage personal growth as well as to provide a safe space for other women seeking a way to break free from the sect. A "Brave Women Camp" is another group that meets periodically and is for female members who have survived sexual abuse. Perhaps the most important reason for the success of this organization is that its sway comes from within, that is, from other women who have themselves escaped the FLDS (Scott 2017; Anderson 2018).

"It's bizarre to watch adults in the community process out of the religion," said a member of the Creeker Foundation. "On one hand, they'll make the leap, but then they'll hang on to certain pieces." Referring to the state and federal lawsuits brought against the FLDS leadership, another said, "The feds are not going to shut down the FLDS, but it's a mindset and more and more people are leaving the religion and those that are still inside the faith are

---

3. The name of the Creeker Foundation is taken from Short Creek, the original name of the twin towns whose residents are sometimes referred to as "Creekers."

bewildered and don't know what to do or what is going to happen next"
(quoted in Walters 2016b).

These groups are helping to bring about a very slow transfer of control
from the sect to the individual. The gradual withering of the FLDS as a
religious institution has created an opening space in the community and
growing economic opportunity has become fertile ground for the major
changes that have started to take place there. Yet, given the absolute control
that the FLDS has had over the minds and bodies of its believers over several
decades, most especially its girls and women, it is difficult to be terribly
optimistic about the future, at least in the near term.

THREATS TO THE SATMAR ENCLAVE

> I think the rabbis are right. Foreign influences are highly toxic to the Orthodox
> mindset. Even the smallest crack in the perfectly cultivated shell can cause
> corrosion throughout the system.
>> —Ari Mandel, "A Piece of Unsolicited Advice for the
>> Hasidic Community," 2015

> I had to rebuild my world literally from zero, and to this day there are still
> people who won't speak to me.
>> —Chaim Potok, "Ultra-Orthodox Jewish Groups," n.d.

Somewhat akin to the Creekers Foundation is Footsteps, a group established
to help Hasidic and other ultra-Orthodox women and men adjust to life on
the outside after leaving their respective religious communities. The organization was founded in 2003 by a woman who left the Lubavitch Hasidic sect
in Brooklyn in order to attend college, which, as we know, is a level of
education prohibited by many Hasidic Rebbes. Footsteps now has around
1,400 members, a number that has been growing by some 35 percent a year.

Footsteps helps its clients by providing a range of services including
social and emotional support, educational and vocational guidance, work-
shops, social activities, and access to a variety of resources. At times it also
provides legal representation and advice in custody cases. Footsteps even
puts on the occasional fashion night during which members learn about modern styles of dress as distinct from the somber, all-concealing clothes for
women and the black suits and hats and white tie-less shirts for men—the
only couture with which they are familiar as lifelong Hasidim.

Footsteps is located in a skyscraper in downtown Manhattan and its address is kept secret in order to protect its clients' safety. To become a member of Footsteps, there is a one-time fee of $25 in addition to a signed agreement stating that the member will not share information about any other member or "out" them for being associated with the organization. The reason for these precautions is that Footsteps is infamous among many thousands of ultra-Orthodox Jews in the United States who look upon it as a perilous influence and an insidious evil. When an individual leaves his or her insular Hasidic community, the person is sometimes said to have "joined Footsteps." The organization has been accused of aggressively wrenching people away from their comfortable lives as religious Jews. But the fact is that Footsteps does not advertise or proselytize in these communities, nor does it require members to renounce their religion in order to use its services or participate in its get-togethers. "We don't care if they go back to Hasidism afterward. We don't have an agenda," said a Footsteps spokesperson. "And contrary to the rumors, we don't force men to cut off their *payos* [sidelocks], nor do we feed anyone bacon as part of an initiation rite," she said. "We just want people to have choices" (quoted in Simms 2019).

Of particular interest here is that by 2012 over one-quarter of Footsteps members had previously belonged to the Satmar court. Even though the Satmar community is, in fact, the largest contemporary Hasidic sect in the United States, this number nevertheless is a telling indication of growing disenchantment within the sect since, as we have seen, Satmar practices have become even more extreme in recent years (Goldberger 2013b).

When Satmar and other Hasidim leave their respective religious folds they confront American society not unlike immigrants who have just arrived in the United States. Their strict separation and isolation from the surrounding culture make it difficult to navigate a new way of life. This is why Footsteps's assistance is so essential. Most of its clients have little secular education, no marketable skills, and no experience with contemporary gender roles, including informal male-female friendships (nor are they accustomed to shaking hands with the opposite sex). Then, too, in some cases they have a poor command of English, and what they do know is spoken with a heavy Yiddish accent. They have little or no experience with people unlike themselves, be they of other races, religions, or ethnicities. Moreover, many are taught from an early age to shun gentiles. They "want to kill us," they are told, and the lessons of the Holocaust are cited.

Because they lack access to secular media in their cloistered ultra-Orthodox enclaves, they typically know little or nothing about contemporary culture; popular films, music, and books; well-known personalities in the arts and politics; or current events. There are many ubiquitous cultural signposts with which those growing up Satmar are completely unfamiliar: the Beatles, Martin Luther King Jr., *The Wizard of Oz*, *Sesame Street*, Michael Jackson, *Star Wars*, *The Sopranos*, Lady Gaga, Disneyland, Madonna, and the Yankees—to name just a few. There are also a number of unknown or forbidden words both in Satmar schools and in polite conversation—dinosaur, universe, pregnancy, globalism, evolution, vagina, gymnasium, lesbian, among others. Several subjects are simply off-limits. Sex and sexuality do not exist. There is little or no study of history beyond Jewish history. In short, they have limited familiarity with American life beyond their insular communities.

Leaving the Satmar and other similar religious redoubts to explore the world beyond almost always elicits extremely negative reactions from family and friends. And the leave-takers are generally shunned and ostracized by their larger Hasidic communities as well. In fact, people who depart such groups are said to be committing "social suicide." One man who left said that "leaving makes you a pariah. You might as well be boarding a one-way rocket to another planet" (quoted in Simms 2019). Or as another man put it in the aforementioned documentary film *One of Us*, about three young people who abandoned their Hasidic sects, "Nobody leaves the Hasidic community, unless they're willing to pay the price."

Moreover, those who leave must also struggle with the dire predictions hurled at them from all sides: that they are bound to be "failures," that they will be "utterly miserable" in the outside world, and that they will eventually "die alone." Said one ex-Hasid: "Coming away from the ultra-Orthodox world, you have all the voices in your head that say you will go out and you will fail and you will probably kill yourself . . . these are the recordings we have in our heads and they're very difficult to get rid of" (quoted in Lavin 2015).

Such once ultra-Orthodox Jews are said to have gone "off the *derech*." *Derech* means "path" in Hebrew, and "off the *derech*," or OTD for short, and "going off the *derech*" are how their ultra-Orthodox families and friends refer to them when they depart their tight-knit religious communities. The Hebrew word *derech* carries an even more specific religious connotation. In the synagogue and the yeshiva, it means the correct way, the observant way, the devout way, the *only* way. A more loaded term for those who have fallen away from their religious redoubts is *apikorsim*, or apostates.

The term OTD was once used derisively to describe young Hasidim who were illicitly experimenting with drugs and sex. But the term has been reclaimed by some of the ex-Orthodox themselves to mean "Yes, I have left your path—and now I must find my own way." In addition to OTD the term "closeted" is used to refer to people still living in ultra-Orthodox communities who have doubts about their religious beliefs and practices and who are thinking of abandoning their religious sects (Friedman 2014; Lavin 2015).

OTDs often gather together on their own blogs and in Facebook groups in which their favored hashtag is #itgetsbesser—*besser* meaning "better" in Yiddish. In 2010 Footsteps began a video project using the same rubric, "It Gets Besser," which was meant to echo the "It Gets Better" campaign, which seeks to support at-risk LGBT youth. "It Gets Besser" videos portray a variety of successful journeys out of Orthodoxy (Brodesser-Akner 2017).

There are over forty Off the *Derech* groups on Facebook ranging from OTD Sisterhood to OTD Foodies, OTD Singles, LGBT and OTD, OTD Parenting, OTD Divorcees, OTD Book Club, and OTD Political Discussions. Once online, Hasidim often use bogus names to establish accounts on Facebook, where they quickly encounter other budding OTDs like themselves who are curious about the larger world beyond their religious enclaves and who have begun to be disillusioned with the life they have been living. Many exchange stories about why they left or are thinking of leaving (Copeland 2012).

Aside from the numerous OTD Facebook groups, there is also a Secret OTD Support Group on Reddit and an OTD Meetup that sponsors happy hours and outings to sporting events and barbecues for the OTD community. The Internet has spawned a host of fringe Orthodox blogs and e-mail lists with names like "Jewish Atheists," "Hasidic Rebel," and "Frum Skeptics." There are also nomadic get-togethers like Chulent, named after a classic Jewish bean-based stew, which until 2010 met at the Millinery Center Synagogue in Manhattan's garment district and after losing its synagogue location began gathering periodically at members' homes and commercial spaces around New York City. Chulent advertises itself on the Web as a group that is "an extraordinary gathering of X-O's—ex-orthodox—exploring the narrow margins where secular and haredi,[4] atheist and Chasidic, deepest depths

---

4. *Haredi*, from the Biblical Hebrew "one who quakes," is a term commonly used in Israel that encompasses Hasidim as well as ultra-Orthodox Jews who are not followers of a Rebbe.

and most foolish foolery, overlap." Chulent is a drop-in lounge for individuals who have strayed from the Hasidic fold, whether in spirit, mind, or body. Yet, some show up at such gatherings still wearing the black hats and long skirts that are the traditional garb of Hasidim (Bleyer 2007; Weichselbaum 2010).

Footsteps administrators note that some reject ultra-Orthodoxy because they desire a more egalitarian life course than the stringent gender-defined roles of their upbringing. Abandoning rigid readings of gender is one of the most difficult problems an ultra-Orthodox woman faces when seeking to transition to a new life. As we have seen among the Satmar and other Hasidic communities, girls are raised with the sole purpose of becoming mothers and wives, while boys are raised to study Torah and other Jewish texts with the goal, for some, of eventually becoming religious scholars. Given such constrained childhoods in which alternative roles are never even mentioned, it becomes clear why these transitions are so difficult. The executive director of Footsteps explains this succinctly: "The community is held together by conformity. The biggest emotional piece is working through the idea that having a voice of one's own is okay, that it's good to express opinions or ideas" (quoted in Bader 2012).

The sentiment regarding gender roles was confirmed in one major study of religious Jews who had left their ultra-Orthodox communities. It queried over three hundred respondents who had once belonged to several Hasidic courts. The study found that men and women had different motivations for leaving; the biggest difference was the status and role of women. The position of women, with all of its limitations, was the primary reason women gave for their exit. But it was cited by only 3 percent of men. Other key motives for leaving their Hasidic enclaves included abuse and domestic violence, communal "hypocrisy" and double standards, and the scope and stringent nature of the religion as practiced in their own communities (Trencher 2016).

Somewhat surprisingly, only 2 percent of respondents mentioned the Internet as the catalyst for their departure despite the fact that it has become such a cause célèbre among Hasidic gatekeepers. Many more mentioned learning about science or books they had read that influenced their exit or people outside their own community who led them to question and ultimately leave their sects. It is entirely possible that contact with the larger society outside the ultra-Orthodox world has a greater impact than the Internet *per se*, although, of course, a great deal of information about the larger world is found on the Internet (Trencher 2016).

Here is how one Hasidic woman in an anonymous blog posted on the Internet expressed her own growing disenchantment with the religious status quo: "I was tired of the Torah lessons trying to demonize feminism yet convince us that women really do have a special role to play that is highly valued and in line with our natural abilities and desires—baby making and homemaking. I was tired of sitting in the back of the *shul* [synagogue] behind a barrier. I was tired of my vagina dictating when I could pass the car keys to my husband. I was tired. At first I was mad, but then I was just tired. So I stopped" (Anonymous 2017).

Complaints about the lifestyle and myriad rules surrounding Hasidic life are not limited to women. Said one Satmar male with evident disgust: "What our eyeglasses were made of was very important. Metal is bad; plastic is good. What counts is the color of your socks, which shoe you tie first in the morning. Wearing a watch is discouraged before bar mitzvah; after that it is completely banned" (quoted in Golan 2018).

The issue of children can also be an excruciating one for those choosing to abandon the sect of their birth and upbringing. The risk of losing one's children may well explain why the majority of those leaving ultra-Orthodoxy are men, not women. Most Satmar women are married by age eighteen or nineteen and some are mothers by then. But men usually marry slightly later—around twenty or twenty-one—which provides them with a bit more time to begin questioning their beliefs and to start forming a sense of self unburdened by the obligations of having a spouse and children.

Those with children who seek to escape Orthodoxy are not looked on kindly by their religious communities, whose members often band together to provide legal and financial support to the parent who remains true to the faith. In any case, the community considers each child a "Jewish soul" that must not be lost. For this reason, the parent who departs can rarely compete with the resources and influence of the communities they are leaving behind. Many Hasidic groups raise substantial amounts of money for legal battles in support of the Orthodox parent and frequently organize their co-religionists to intimidate the leave-taking parent, who may be labeled a "heretic" or a "whore" in an effort to wrest custody of the children from the parent who has strayed from the religious fold.

Sometimes custody cases brought before secular courts rule against the parent leaving the Hasidic sect. Courts frequently view *gets* (religious divorce decrees) as legally enforceable contracts. If a parent has agreed in the *get* to raise the children in a strictly Orthodox fashion and then fails to do so, he or she may be at risk of losing custody.

Some examples: A woman in a Hasidic couple with three children began questioning her faith and she and her husband eventually divorced. Although he had not seen the children for many months, he sued for full custody once he learned from members of the woman's family that she was allowing her daughters to wear pants and was calling them by their English, rather than their Hebrew, names. As a consequence, she very nearly lost custody of her children. Something similar happened to another Hasidic woman who also came close to being denied custody of her seven children after her husband accused her of allowing their daughters to wear socks embroidered with snowmen, which, he insisted, were symbols of Christmas. And at least one religious court issued an order refusing a formerly ultra-Orthodox father visitation rights because he showed up for a parental visit wearing blue jeans, an item of clothing that is prohibited by most Hasidic Rebbes (Raphelson 2018; Otterman 2018).

Writes one ex-Satmar woman about these extreme stances that may lead to an offending parent being denied custody of her own children: "This behavior is a byproduct of the indoctrination they have been indirectly fed their entire lives: that keeping children in the ways of the Torah is more important than love for one's own child. Tribe before offspring" (Goldberger 2017).

For parents and others escaping Orthodoxy, the pathway out sometimes begins with the Internet. As we have seen, the biggest problem for the powers that be among the insular Satmar may be access to the Internet; it is perhaps more indirectly responsible than anything else for the burgeoning number of OTDs in the community. As one observer referring to the Satmar put it, "The reality is that while the ultra-Orthodox primarily use their electronic devices for work-related matters, once the Internet is in their pockets, the world becomes vastly more accessible. And alluring" (quoted in Bronstein 2015).

The director of Footsteps agrees. She traces the explosive growth of membership in her organization to the influence of the Internet. This, she says, is often the first place where people learn that it is possible to leave their ultra-Orthodox enclaves, that others have already done so and that, for the most part, they have survived. Then, too, there is evidence that a number of Satmar women have reached out to a counseling service via the Internet to bemoan what their lives are like. Time and again they tell their own stories about the monotony and suffocation of their roles as housewives and mothers of many children. Via the Internet they discover others with experiences similar to their own and, like other nascent OTDs, some begin considering a life change. "So they got a computer and it had Internet installed, and that's it—then it's over," notes one observer of this trend (Copeland 2012; quoted in Bronstein 2015).

For some of the first Satmar led astray by the Internet, it took a decade or more to resolve conflicts within their own marriages as well as to settle any child custody disputes that may have arisen. As a consequence, it is only in more recent years that such early adopters have begun to share their exile stories on the Internet with other would-be OTDs. While the first wave of Internet-influenced OTDs had to rely on the surreptitious use of workplace or library computers or perhaps a borrowed laptop, today young Satmars have it much easier. They only need a smartphone in their pocket or purse. Because of today's ease of access to the Internet, the drumbeat of the disaffected is very likely to continue (Copeland 2012).

According to one Satmar father who regularly uses the Internet to conduct business, Hasidim who surf the Web become open to the ideas of foreign people, cultures, even moral codes. "The problem is, a lot of the leaders in the community . . . just say, 'Run away from the Internet—just close your eyes and run away.' It's not going to help you," he said. "It's going to run *after* you, and it's going to run faster than you can. It's going to catch up with you" (quoted in Bronstein 2015).

Still, the organized effort to counter this encroachment is ongoing and the Satmar battle against the Internet is as fierce as ever. Lately, for example, a group of ultra-Orthodox rabbis issued a ruling against using the mobile application WhatsApp, which they characterized as "a great spiritual danger" because it allows two people to chat without anyone else knowing about the conversation. The Satmar-linked Web filtering company also has sought to block filtered phones from sharing video, audio, and photos through WhatsApp. "It's not something they can control," said one Satmar. "Anything they can't be in control of makes them nervous." So it comes as no surprise that Rebbe Zalman declared in a speech in 2014 that belonging to social groups on WhatsApp destroys one's "Jewish spirit" (quoted in Nathan-Kazis 2014).

Then there is the notice posted on a street in Williamsburg—the original was in Hebrew—warning that "there is an instrument that is liable to bring terrible destruction to the entire family and it is father-in-chief of impurity of our time. It is called the '*internet*.' It is sin crouching at the door and [most] who enter its door never return." The poster goes on to suggest that the Internet is "at present the great cause for the majority of divorces" within the Satmar community (cited in Fishman 2012:162).

Says one Satmar man about such attempts to stop his co-religionists' use of the Internet: "Even if the Satmar Rebbe talks to his community—let's say he is going to be successful—40 percent [of the community] is going to listen to him." But even that segment of the population, "in five, ten years down the road, they're going to do it anyway, since the Internet is coming more and more into our life" (quoted in Bronstein 2015).

Similar concerns have been expressed in the Satmar redoubt of Kiryas Joel, where access to the Internet is rightly seen as a dire threat to the community's insularity. The Internet provides access into a world of "corrosive influences," including but not limited to pornography, warn the Satmar gatekeepers who "know full well that it allows one to go virtually anywhere, far beyond the limitations of Haredi culture, without ever leaving the physical confines of the enclave and with no one besides the Web surfer knowing—a dangerous possibility for a society that seeks solidarity and insularity," writes Professor Samuel Heilman (2006), a scholar of Jewish Orthodoxy. In short, the speed of technological change and innovation and the ability to access it in the privacy of one's home will almost always prevail over whatever barriers to entry exist in this closed society.

I will conclude with a thought experiment. What if Satmar and other Hasidim were still entirely reliant on furtive visits to the public library to secretly read books and magazines as a way of learning about the world beyond their own communities—as had been the case for decades? If it were not for the speed and ease of the Internet so readily at hand on cell phones, would as many Satmar or other Hasidim become OTDs? It is a question without an answer, but one worth pondering.

Postscript

Why extremists always focus on women remains a mystery to me. But they all seem to. It doesn't matter what country they're in or what religion they claim. They want to control women. They want to control how we dress. They want to control how we act. They even want to control the decisions we make about our own health and bodies.

—Hillary Rodham Clinton (quoted in Dowd 2012)

To bring this book to a close and to give its ending a contemporary twist, I want to mention the recent call for unrestrained reproduction among today's white nationalists in the United States, the same phenomenon that we have found and analyzed among the Satmar, the FLDS, and the Pashtun. These U.S.-based far-right groups view the declining birth rate among white women with deep alarm, an alarm that was central to the marchers' chants, "You will not replace us," at the white nationalist rally in Charlottesville, Virginia, in 2017. Underlying this fear is a racist premise termed "the replacement theory." The theory is based on the idea that white women are not having a sufficient number of children and that their falling birth rate inevitably will lead to white people being replaced by people of color (Bowles 2019).

For male devotees of this theory everything is framed around the issues of gender and reproduction. As a consequence, and like so many fundamentalist ideologies, including those described in this book, the foundation of this one demands the subjugation of women. Why are women taking jobs instead of staying home and raising lots of children, the theory's advocates want to know. Feminism is the culprit, they argue. Antifeminist blogs that tout unrestrained reproduction question the very notion of gender equality and relitigate debates that were settled long ago, such as whether women should be "allowed" to work and be involved in politics or whether their lives should be entirely circumscribed by home and family. Today, such misogynistic rhetoric and practice is not just found in extreme fundamentalist religious traditions, such as those analyzed in this book, but lurks in the conspiratorial thinking of certain segments of the male population. In other words: *plus ça change, plus c'est la même chose.*

References

Abraham, Pearl. 1996. *The Romance Reader*. New York: Riverhead Books.

Adlerstein, Yitzchok. 2016. "Satmar: Do They Take Us for Fools?" *Cross-Currents*, August 26. https://cross-currents.com/2016/08/26/satmar-do-they-take-us-for-fools/.

Afridi, Azim. 2010. "Pashtun Customs Regarding Birth, Marriage and Death." *Pashtun Culture and History* (blog), August. http://pashtuncultureandhistory.blogspot.com/2010/08/pashtun-customs-regarding-birth.html.

Ahmed, Azam, and Habib Zahori. 2013. "Despite West's Efforts, Afghan Youths Cling to Traditional Ways." *New York Times*, August 1, p. 1.

Ali, Yasmeen Aftab. 2013. "Understanding Pashtunwali." *The Nation*, August 6. https://nation.com.pk/06-Aug-2013/understanding-pashtunwali.

All Peoples Initiative. 2009. "Satmar Jews in the New York Metro Area." September. http://unreachednewyork.com/wp-content/uploads/2012/11/Satmar-Profile-Final.pdf.

Almond, Gabriel A., Emmanuel Sivan, and R. Scott Appleby. 1995a. "Examining the Cases." In *Fundamentalisms Comprehended*, edited by Martin E. Marty and R. Scott Appleby, 445–82. Chicago, IL: University of Chicago Press.

Almond, Gabriel A., Emmanuel Sivan, and R. Scott Appleby. 1995b. "Explaining Fundamentalisms." In *Fundamentalisms Comprehended*, edited by Martin E. Marty and R. Scott Appleby, 425–44. Chicago, IL: University of Chicago Press.

American Academy of Arts and Sciences. 2000. *The Fundamentalism Project*. Chicago, IL: University of Chicago Press.

Ammerman, Nancy T. 1994. "The Dynamics of Christian Fundamentalism: An Introduction." In *Accounting for Fundamentalisms: The Dynamic Character of Movements*, edited by Martin E. Marty and R. Scott Appleby, 13–17. Chicago, IL: University of Chicago Press.

Amnesty International. 2018. "Afghanistan 2017/2018." https://www.amnesty.org/en/countries/asia-and-the-pacific/afghanistan/report-afghanistan/.

Andelin, Helen B. 1963. *Fascinating Womanhood: A Guide to a Happy Marriage*. New York: Random House.

Anderson, Sulome. 2018. "Paedophile Cult Leader Warren Jeffs Tore This Town Apart. Now His Victims Are Putting It Back Together." *New Statesman America*, September 17. https://www.newstatesman.com/world/north-america/2018/09/paedophile-cult-leader-warren-jeffs-tore-town-apart-now-his-victims-are.

Angel, Marc D. 2012. "A Modesty Proposal: Rethinking Tseniut." *Conversations* 12 (Winter): 38–49, reposted at IDEAS: Institute for Jewish Ideas and Ideals. https://www.jewishideas. org/article/modesty-proposal-rethinking-tseniut.

Angel, Marc D. 2016. "Thoughts on the Scandal on an El Al Airplane: Blog by Rabbi Marc D. Angel." IDEAS: Institute for Jewish Ideas and Ideals, April 1. https://www.jewishideas.org/ blog/thoughts-scandal-el-al-airplane-blog-rabbi-marc-d-angel#.VtXmUCcRw18.facebook.

Anonymous. 2017. "Off the Derech on the Down Low." Neshamas. http://neshamas.com/off-derech-low/.

Associated Press. 2015a. "Divisions Open Up in Towns Once Led by Polygamist Leader Warren Jeffs." *The Guardian*, January 23. https://www.theguardian.com/world/2015/jan/23/ warren-jeffs-mormon-utah-arizona.

Associated Press. 2015b. "New Utah School Open to FLDS Community Continues to Grow." *Salt Lake Tribune*, August 17. http://www.sltrib.com/home/2844580-155/new-school-in-utah-polygamous-community.

Associated Press. 2016. "Leaders of Utah Polygamous Sect Arrested and Accused of Fraud." *The Guardian*, February 23. https://www.theguardian.com/us-news/2016/feb/23/warren-jeffs-leaders-arrested-utah-polygamous-sect-fraud.

Associated Press. 2017. "Ex-polygamous Sect Leader Lyle Jeffs Gets Nearly 5 Years in Fraud Case." *USA Today*, December 13. https://www.usatoday.com/story/news/local/arizona/ 2017/12/13/ex-polygamous-sect-leader-gets-nearly-5-years-fraud-case/949760001/.

Atwood, Margaret. (1985) 1998. *The Handmaid's Tale*. New York: Anchor Books.

Aviv, Rachel. 2014. "The Outcast." *New Yorker*, November 10.

Azami, Muhammad Dawood. 2006. "Reporter's Story." BBC World Service. http://www.bbc. co.uk/worldservice/people/features/ihavearightto/four_b/report-azami.shtml.

Bader, Eleanor J. 2012. "Footsteps into a New Life." *The Brooklyn Rail*, June 4.

Bahrampour, Tara. 2004. "'Plague of Artists' a Battle Cry for Brooklyn Hasidim." *New York Times*, February 17.

Banting, Erinn. 2003. *Afghanistan: The People*. New York: Crabtree Publishing Company.

Barth, Frederick. 1998. *Ethnic Groups and Boundaries: The Social Organization of Cultural Difference*. Prospect Heights, IL: Waveland Press.

BBC News. 2011. "Poll Says Afghanistan 'Most Dangerous' for Women." June 15. http:// www.bbc.com/news/world-south-asia-13773274.

BBC News. 2013. "Ethnic Groups." June 7. http://news.bbc.co.uk/hi/english/static/in_depth/ world/2001/war_on_terror/key_maps/ethnic_pashtun.stm.

Beagley, David. 2008. *One Lost Boy, His Escape from Polygamy: A Memoir*. Springfield, UT: CFI.

Beinart, Peter. 2014. "'At Home in Exile' and 'The Pious Ones.'" *New York Times Book Review*, November 6. https://www.nytimes.com/2014/11/09/books/review/at-home-in-exile-and-the-pious-ones.html.

Belcove-Shalin, Janet S. 1995. "Introduction: New World Hasidim." In *New World Hasidim: Ethnographic Studies of Hasidic Jews in America*, edited by Janet S. Belcove-Shalin, 1–30. Albany: SUNY Press.

Bellafante, Ginia. 2016. "Educational Orthodoxy." *New York Times*, Metro section, September 4, pp. 1, 5.

Bennion, Janet. 2011a. "History, Culture, and Variability of Mormon Schismatic Groups." In *Modern Polygamy in the United States: Historical, Cultural, and Legal Issues*, edited by Cardell K. Jacobson and Lara Burton, 101–24. New York: Oxford University Press.

Bennion, Janet 2011b. "The Many Faces of Polygamy: An Analysis of the Variability in Modern Mormon Fundamentalism in the Intermountain West." In *Modern Polygamy in the*

United States: Historical, Cultural, and Legal Issues, edited by Cardell K. Jacobson and Lara Burton, 163–84. New York: Oxford University Press.

Bennion, Janet. 2012. *Polygamy in Primetime: Media, Gender, and Politics in Mormon Fundamentalism*. Waltham, MA: Brandeis University Press.

Benor, Sarah Bunin. 2012. *Becoming Frum: How Newcomers Learn the Language and Culture of Orthodox Judaism*. New Brunswick, NJ: Rutgers University Press.

Berger, Joseph. 2005. "Staying Connected, with the Internet at Bay; Orthodox Jews Grapple with the Web." *New York Times*, November 23, p. B1.

Berger, Joseph. 2010. "God Said Multiply, and Did She Ever." *New York Times*, February 19, p. M7.

Berger, Joseph. 2012. "Divisions in Satmar Sect Complicate Politics of Brooklyn Hasidim." *New York Times*, July 6, p. 19.

Berger, Joseph. 2013. "Modesty in Hasidic Brooklyn Is Enforced by Secret Squads." *New York Times*, January 30, pp. 1, 25.

Berger, Joseph. 2014a. "No Fines for Stores Displaying a Dress Code." *New York Times*, January 21.

Berger, Joseph. 2014b. *The Pious Ones: The World of Hasidim and Their Battles with America*. New York: Harper Perennial.

Bergner, Daniel. 2015. "Flesh of My Flesh." *New York Times Magazine*, January 25, pp. 24–27.

Berkowitz, Bill. 2015. "Attack on Charlie Hebdo Was God's Divine Retribution for Mocking Christianity, Says Religious Right Broadcaster." BuzzFlash.com, January 14. http://www.truth-out.org/buzzflash/commentary/attack-on-charlie-hebdo-was-god-s-divine-retribution-for-mocking-christianity-says-religious-right-broadcaster.

Bezhan, Frud. 2013. "Loya Jirga—An Afghan Tradition Explained." Radio Free Europe, November 20. http://www.rferl.org/a/afghanistan-loya-jirga-explainer/25174483.html.

Biale, David, David Assaf, Benjamin Brown, Uriel Gellman, Samuel Heilman, Moshe Rosman, Gadi Sagiy, and Marcin Wodzinski. 2018. *Hasidim: A New History*. Princeton, NJ: Princeton University Press.

Billaud, Julie. 2015. *Kabul Carnival: Gender Politics in Postwar Afghanistan*. Philadelphia: University of Pennsylvania Press.

Blank, Jonah. 2013. "How to Negotiate Like a Pashtun." *Rand Blog*, June 4. http://www.rand.org/blog/2013/06/how-to-negotiate-like-a-pashtun.html.

Bleyer, Jennifer. 2007. "Chulent Times: City of Refuge." *New York Times*, March 18, p. C1.

Bobel, Chris. 2018. "When Pads Can't Fix Prejudice." *New York Times*, April 1, Sunday Review, p. 6.

Bohn, Lauren. 2018. "'We're All Handcuffed in This Country.' Why Afghanistan Is Still the Worst Place in the World to Be a Woman." *Time*, December 8. http://time.com/5472411/afghanistan-women-justice-war/.

Borger, Julian. 2005. "The Lost Boys, Thrown Out of U.S. Sect So That Older Men Can Marry More Wives." *The Guardian*, June 14. https://www.theguardian.com/world/2005/jun/14/usa.julianborger.

Bowles, Nellie. 2019. "'Replacement Theory,' a Racist, Sexist Doctrine Spreads in Far-Right Circles." *New York Times*, March 18, p. 8.

Bradley, Martha Sonntag. 1993. *Kidnapped from That Land: The Government Raids on the Short Creek Polygamists*. Salt Lake City: University of Utah Press.

Bramham, Daphne. 2009. *The Secret Lives of Saints: Child Brides and Lost Boys in Canada's Polygamous Mormon Sect*. Toronto, Canada: Vintage.

Briggs, Kenneth A. 1983. "2 Hasidic Groups in Brooklyn Involved in Complex Conflict." *New York Times*, June 21, p. 3.

Brodesser-Akner, Taffy. 2017. "The High Price of Leaving Ultra-Orthodox Life." *New York Times Magazine*, March 30, pp. 36–41.

Bronstein, Dani. 2015. "The Satmar Evolution." *Shoe Leather*, June. http://shoeleath ermagazine.com/2015/the-satmar-revolution/.

Brostoff, Marissa. 2007. "Apparent Decision in Satmar Succession Feud." *Forward*, November 21. http://forward.com/news/12074/apparent-decision-in-satmar-succession-feud-00828/.

Brower, Sam. 2012. *Prophet's Prey*. New York: Bloomsbury.

Brown, Judith K. 1970. "A Note on the Division of Labor by Sex." *American Anthropologist* 72, no. 5: 1073–78.

Brown, Judy. 2013. "Cracks in a Holy Vessel." *Forward*, March 11. http://forward.com/articles/172568/cracks-in-a-holy-vessel/.

Brown, Judy. 2015. *This Is Not a Love Story: A Memoir*. New York: Little, Brown and Company.

Cable News Network (CNN). 2007. "Sect Leader Indicted on Sexual Conduct with Minor, Incest Charges." July 12. http://www.cnn.com/2007/US/07/12/polygamy.charges/index.html.

Cable News Network (CNN). 2008. "219 Children, Women Taken from Sect's Ranch." April 6. http://www.bishop-accountability.org/news2008/03_04/2008_04_06_CNN_219Children.htm.

Callimachi, Rukmini. 2016. "For Women under ISIS, a Tyranny of Dress Code and Punishment." *New York Times*, December 12.

Carlisle, Nate. 2014. "Demolition Starts on Old FLDS Polygamous School." *Salt Lake Tribune*, September 4. http://archive.sltrib.com/story.php?ref=/sltrib/news/58340109-78/jeffs-acade my-alta-flds.html.csp.

Carlisle, Nate. 2015a. "Births in Polygamous Towns on Utah-Arizona Line Slow to a Crawl." *Salt Lake Tribune*, October 12. http://www.sltrib.com/home/3038619-155/births-in-polygamous-towns-on-utah-arizona.

Carlisle, Nate. 2015b. "Here's the 'Application' an FLDS School Told Girls to Fill Out." *Salt Lake Tribune*, October 26. http://www.sltrib.com/home/3098244-155/heres-the-application-an-flds-school.

Carlisle, Nate. 2017. "For a Polygamous Sect, Homes Have Gone and 'Apostates' Have Come." *Salt Lake Tribune*, April 10. http://archive.sltrib.com/article.php?id=4843521& itype=CMSID.

Carlisle, Nate. 2018. "There's More Support Than Ever for Those 'Escaping Polygamy.'" *Salt Lake Tribune*, June 24. https://www.sltrib.com/news/polygamy/2018/06/24/theres-more-support-than-ever-for-those-escaping-polygamy/.

Chesler, Phyllis. 2014. *An American Bride in Kabul*. New York: St. Martin's Griffin.

Chesler, Phyllis. 2017. *Islamic Gender Apartheid: Exposing a Veiled War against Women*. Nashville, TN: New English Review Press.

Chira, Susan. 2019. "'Women Here Are Very, Very Worried.'" *New York Times*, March 24, Sunday Review, p. 7.

Chizhik-Goldschmidt, Avital. 2015. "The 'Shidduch Crisis' Has Led to an Orthodox Obsession with Female Beauty." *Forward*, September 3. https://forward.com/sisterhood/320209/the-shidduch-crisis-has-led-to-an-orthodox-obsession-with-female-beauty/.

Chughtai, Alia. 2019. "Afghanistan: Who Controls What." *Al Jazeera*, June 23. https://www.aljazeera.com/indepth/interactive/2016/08/afghanistan-controls-160823083528213.html.

Clevstrom, Jenny. 2005. "Family Feud: Will the Real Satmar Please Stand Up?" *Brooklyn Rail*, December 10. http://www.brooklynrail.org/2005/12/local/family-feud-will-the-real-satmar-please-.

Cohen, Debra Nussbaum. 2012. "New York Ultra-Orthodox Discover the Downside of Being Fruitful and Multiplying." *Haaretz*, September 24. http://www.haaretz.com/israel-news/new-york-ultra-orthodox-discover-the-downside-of-being-fruitful-and-multiplying-1. 466458.

Copeland, Libby. 2012. "Google vs. God." *Slate*, August 21. http://www.slate.com/articles/double_x/doublex/2012/08/hasidic_jews_and_the_internet_a_bad_combination_.single.html.

Crain's New York Business. 2012. "Blood Feud Dampens Satmar Power." November 12. https://www.crainsnewyork.com/article/20121113/BLOGS04/311139993/blood-feud-dampens-satmar-power.

Danovich, Tove K. "The Forest Hidden behind the Canyons." *The Ringer*, June 24. https://www.theringer.com/2019/6/24/18692816/flds-short-creek-polygamy-feature.

Dark, Stephen. 2017. "As a Polygamist Community Crumbles, 'Sister Wives' Are Forced from Homes." *The Guardian*, November 17. https://www.theguardian.com/society/2017/nov/17/fundamentalist-mormons-sister-wives-homelessness.

Davidman, Lynn. 2015. *Becoming Un-Orthodox: Stories of Ex-Hasidic Jews*. New York: Oxford University Press.

Daynes, Kathryn M. 2011. "Differing Polygamous Patterns: Nineteenth-Century LDS and Twenty-First-Century FLDS Marriage Systems." In *Modern Polygamy in the United States: Historical, Cultural, and Legal Issues*, edited by Cardell K. Jacobson and Lara Burton, 125–48. New York: Oxford University Press.

Deen, Shulem. 2015. *All Who Go Do Not Return*. Minneapolis, MI: Graywolf Press.

Deen, Shulem. 2018. "Why Is New York Condoning Illiteracy?" *New York Times*, April 4.

Deitsch, Chaya. 2015. *Here and There: Leaving Hasidim, Keeping My Family*. New York: Schocken Books.

de Leede, Seran. 2014. *Afghan Women and the Taliban: An Exploratory Assessment*. Policy brief, International Centre for Counter-Terrorism, The Hague. https://www.icct.nl/download/file/ICCT-Leede-Afghan-Women-and-the-Taliban-April-2014.pdf.

Dias, Elizabeth. 2019. "'Mormon' No More: Faithful Reflect on Church's Move to Scrap a Moniker." *New York Times*, June 29. https://www.nytimes.com/2019/06/29/us/mormon-church-name-change.html.

Dominguez, Virginia. 1993. "Questioning Jews." *American Ethnologist* 20, no. 3: 618–24.

Dowd, Maureen. 2012. "Don't Tread on Us." *New York Times*, March 14, p. 27.

Dratch, Mark. 2009. "A Community of Co-enablers." In *Tempest in the Temple: Jewish Communities & Child Sex Scandals*, edited by Amy Neustein, 101–25. Lebanon, NH: Brandeis University Press.

Driggs, Ken. 2011. "Twenty Years of Observations about the Fundamentalist Polygamists." In *Modern Polygamy in the United States: Historical, Cultural, and Legal Issues*, edited by Cardell K. Jacobson and Lara Burton, 77–100. New York: Oxford University Press.

Edsall, Thomas B. 2019. "Why the Fight Over Abortion Is Unrelenting." *New York Times*, May 29, p. 25.

Eller, Sandy. 2012. "Kiryas Joel, NY—Satmar Rebbe: Internet Asifa or Siyum Hashas Event Not for 'Satmar' Chasidim." *Vos Iz Neias*? (What Is News?), May 17. https://www.vosizneias.com/106533/2012/05/17/kiryas-joel-ny-satmar-rebbe-internet-asifa-or-siyum-hashas-event-not-for-reb-yoels-ztl-chasidim/.

Engelbrecht, Cora. 2019. "Women Fear Return of Taliban, and Old Ways." *New York Times*, July 14, p. 6.

Fader, Ayala. 2009. *Mitzvah Girls: Bringing Up the Next Generation of Hasidic Jews in Brooklyn*. Princeton, NJ: Princeton University Press.

Failed Messiah (blog). 2014a. "Kiryas Joel Satmar Bans 3-Year-Old Girls from Wearing Short Socks." January 29. https://failedmessiah.typepad.com/failed_messiahcom/2014/06/kiryas-joel-satmar-bans-3-year-old-girls-from-wearing-short-socks-123.html.

Failed Messiah (blog). 2014b. "Hasidic Modesty Squad Warns Hasidim to Stay Inside During the 'Dirty' Marathon." November 3. https://failedmessiah.typepad.com/failed_messiahcom/2014/11/hasidic-modesty-squad-warns-hasidim-to-stay-inside-during-the-dirty-marathon-234.html.

Failed Messiah (blog). 2015. "Women Shouldn't Talk Loudly or Laugh in Public, Satmar Rebbe Says." January 29. https://failedmessiah.typepad.com/failed_messiahcom/2015/01/women-shouldnt-talk-loudly-or-laugh-in-public-satmar-rebbe-says-567.html.

Faizi, Fatima, and David Zucchino. 2019. "Afghan Assembly on Peace Sees Women as Irrelevant." *New York Times*, May 4, p. 6.

Feldman, Ari. 2017. "Hasidic Village's Massive Condo Development Will Be Denser Than Manhattan." Forward, December 14. https://forward.com/fast-forward/390018/hasidic-villages-massive-condo-development-will-be-denser-than-manhattan/.

Feldman, Deborah. 2011. *Unorthodox: The Scandalous Rejection of My Hasidic Roots*. New York: Simon and Schuster.

Feldman, Deborah. 2014. *Exodus: A Memoir*. New York: Penguin.

Ferris-Rotman, Amie, and Jodie Evans. 2015. "After Over a Decade of Occupation and $1.5 Billion in US Aid, the Reality Facing Women in Afghanistan Has Barely Changed." *AlterNet*, October 5. https://www.alternet.org/activism/after-over-decade-occupation-and-15-billion-us-aid-reality-facing-women-afghanistan-has/.

Finkel, Rebecca. 2013. "The Messiah Will Be Tweeted." *Slate*, June 19. https://slate.com/human-interest/2013/06/the-internet-isnt-the-problem-for-the-hasidic-community-its-its-best-chance-for-survival.html.

Fishman, Phillip. 2012. *A Sukkah Is Burning: Remembering Williamsburg's Hasidic Transformation*. Minneapolis, MN: Mill City Press.

FLDS 101 (blog). 2009a. "FLDS Beliefs 101—Arranged Marriages." May 7. http://flds101.blogspot.com/2008/05/flds-beliefs-101-arranged-marriages.html.

FLDS 101 (blog). 2009b. "FLDS Beliefs 101—The Family." May 8. http://flds101.blogspot.com/2008/05/flds-beliefs-101-family.html.

FLDS 101 (blog). 2009c. "FLDS Beliefs 101—Role of Women." May 11. http://flds101.blogspot.com/2008/05/flds-beliefs-101-role-of-women.html.

FLDS 101 (blog). 2009d. "FLDS Life 101—Alta Academy." May 17. http://flds101.blogspot.com/2008/05/flds-life-101-alta-academy.html.

Foderaro, Lisa W. 2017. "Call It Splitsville, NY: Hasidic Enclave to Get Its Own Town." *New York Times*, November 19, p. 17.

Friedman, Samuel G. 2014. "Stepping Off the Path and Redefining Faith." *New York Times*, October 18, p. 17.

Fuller, Graham E. 2003. *The Future of Political Islam*. London: Palgrave MacMillan.

Gabel, Pearl. 2012. "Heretic Hasidim." Narratively, December 13. http://narrative.ly/heretic-hasidim/.

Gersh, Harry. 1959. "Satmar in Williamsburg: A Zealot Community." *Commentary*, November 1.

Giustozzi, Antonio. 2009. *Decoding the New Taliban: Insights from the Afghan Field.* New York: Columbia University Press.

Glatzer, Bernt. 1998. "Being Pashtun–Being Muslim: Concepts of Person and War in Afghanistan." In *Essays in South Asian Society: Culture and Politics II*, edited by Bernt Glatzer, 83–94. Berlin: Das Arabische Buch. http://www.khyber.org/publications/021-025/glat zer1998.pdf.

Glatzer, Bernt, and Michael J. Casimir. 1983. "Herds and Households among Pashtun Pastoral Nomads: Limits of Growth." *Ethnology* 22, no. 4: 307–25.

Golan, Ori. 2018. "Former Satmar Hasidic Jew Now Tours World to Expose Sect's Dark Underbelly." *Times of Israel*, July 17. https://www.timesofisrael.com/former-satmar-hasidic-jew-now-tours-world-to-expose-sects-dark-underbelly/.

Goldberger, Frimet. 2013a. "Ex-Hasidic Woman Marks Five Years Since She Shaved Her Head." *Forward*, November 7. http://forward.com/articles/187128/ex-hasidic-woman-marks-five-years-since-she-shaved.

Goldberger, Frimet. 2013b. "A Community of Exes—Hasids, That Is." *Forward*, December 12. http://blogs.forward.com/forward-thinking/189210/a-community-of-exes-hasids-that-is/.

Goldberger, Frimet. 2014a. "One Hasidic Housewife's Inspiring—and Unusual—Journey to College and Beyond." *Forward*, January 9. http://forward.com/articles/190267/one-hasidic-housewifes-inspiring-and-unusual-j/.

Goldberger, Frimet. 2014b. "Satmar Rebbe Blames Cancer on Makeup." *Forward*, February 13. http://blogs.forward.com/sisterhood-blog/192744/satmar-rebbe-blames-cancer-on-make up/.

Goldberger, Frimet. 2014c. "The Perils of Working Out While Hasidic." *Forward*, May 20. http://forward.com/sisterhood/198513/the-perils-of-working-out-while-hasidic/.

Goldberger, Frimet. 2014d. "Taxonomy of the Sheitel." *Forward*, August 8. http://forward. com/articles/203226/taxonomy-of-the-sheitel/.

Goldberger, Frimet. 2014e. "A Satmar Girl Remembers Rosh Hashanah With Honey and Fear." *Forward*, September 26. http://forward.com/articles/206002/a-satmar-girl-remembers-rosh-hashanah-with-honey-a/?p=all#ixzz3PxsB9s8C.

Goldberger, Frimet. 2014f. "When the Mikveh Is an Ordeal of Faith." *Forward*, October 30. https://forward.com/sisterhood/208148/when-the-mikveh-is-an-ordeal-of-faith/.

Goldberger, Frimet. 2015. "I'm a Woman in America, and I Wasn't Allowed to Drive." PRI's *The World*, January 22. http://www.pri.org/stories/2015-01-22/im-woman-america-and-i-wasnt-allowed-drive.

Goldberger, Frimet. 2017. "What Makes the Hasidic Community Choose Tribe over Off-spring?" *Forward*, October 27. https://forward.com/life/faith/386288/what-makes-the-hasidic-community-choose-tribe-over-offspring/.

Goldberger, Frimet, and Shimon Steinmetz. 2014. "The Complete History of the Sheitel." *Forward*, August 13. http://forward.com/sisterhood/203981/the-complete-history-of-the-sheitel/.

Goldman, Ari L. 1990. "Brooklyn Project Shakes Hispanic-Hasidic Peace." *New York Times*, October 1, p. 1.

Goldstein, Joseph. 2015. "U.S. Soldiers Told to Ignore Afghan Allies' Abuse of Boys." *New York Times*, September 20, p. 1.

Gorvett, Zaria. 2017. "The Polygamous Town Facing Genetic Disaster." BBC.com, July 26. http://www.bbc.com/future/story/20170726-the-polygamous-town-facing-genetic-disaster.

Green, Arthur. 2009. "Hasidism: Satmar Hasidism." In *Encyclopedia of Religion*, 3793–94. New York: Macmillan Reference.

Grima, Benedicte. 1992. *The Performance of Emotion among Paxtun Women.* Austin: University of Texas Press.

Grima, Benedicte. 2004. *Secrets from the Field: An Ethnographer's Notes from North Western Pakistan.* Bloomington, IN: AuthorHouse.

Gross, Terry. 2009. "From Polygamist Royalty to FLDS Lost Boy." *Fresh Air*, National Public Radio, May 21. http://www.npr.org/templates/story/story.php?storyId=104359348.

Grumet, Louis, and John Caher. 2016. *The Curious Case of Kiryas Joel.* Chicago: Chicago Review Press.

Grynbaum, Michael. 2012. "Ultra-Orthodox Jews Rally to Discuss Risks of Internet." *New York Times*, May 20, p. 17.

Guidère, Mathieu. 2012. *Historical Dictionary of Islamic Fundamentalism.* Lanham, MD: Scarecrow Press.

Haider, Murtaza. 2014. "The Continued Abuse of the Pashtun Woman." *Dawn*, February 21. http://www.dawn.com/news/1088086.

Hamilton, Marci A. 2014. *God vs. the Gavel: The Perils of Extreme Religious Liberty.* New York: Cambridge University Press.

Hannaford, Alex. 2018. "The Woman Who Escaped a Polygamous Cult—and Turned Its HQ into a Refuge." *The Guardian*, October 13. https://www.theguardian.com/world/2018/oct/13/woman-escaped-cult-hq-flds-refuge.

Hardacre, Helen. 1993. "The Impact of Fundamentalisms on Women, the Family, and Interpersonal Relations." In *Fundamentalisms and Society: Reclaiming the Sciences, the Family, and Education*, edited by Martin E. Marty and R. Scott Appleby, 129–50. Chicago: University of Chicago Press.

Harris, Lis. 1985. *Holy Days: The World of a Hasidic Family.* New York: Summit Books.

Havens, Emily. 2017. "FLDS Women Forgotten: Healing from the Inside Out." *The Spectrum*, April 21. https://www.thespectrum.com/story/news/2017/04/21/flds-women-forgotten-healing-inside-out/100700534/.

Heaton, Tim B., and Cardell K. Jacobson. 2011. "Demographic, Social, and Economic Characteristics of a Polygamous Community." In *Modern Polygamy in the United States: Historical, Cultural, and Legal Issues*, edited by Cardell K. Jacobson and Lara Burton, 151–61. New York: Oxford University Press.

Heilman, Samuel C. 1994. "Quiescent and Active Fundamentalisms: The Jewish Cases." In *Accounting for Fundamentalisms: The Dynamic Character of Movements*, edited by Martin E. Marty and R. Scott Appleby, 173–96. Chicago: University of Chicago Press.

Heilman, Samuel C. 2006. *Sliding to the Right: The Contest for the Future of American Jewish Orthodoxy.* Berkeley: University of California Press.

Heilman, Samuel C. 2017. *Who Will Lead Us? The Story of Five Hasidic Dynasties in America.* Oakland: University of California Press.

Heilman, Uriel. 2016. "Undercover Video of Hasidic Principal Handling Boy Prompts Sex Abuse Probe." *Jewish Telegraphic Agency*, May 3. https://www.jta.org/2016/05/03/united-states/undercover-video-of-hasidic-principal-handling-boy-prompts-sex-abuse-probe.

Human Rights Watch. 2018. "Afghanistan: Events of 2017." World Report 2018. https://www.hrw.org/world-report/2018/country-chapters/afghanistan.

Human Terrain Team AF-6. n.d. "Pashtun Sexuality." Research Update and Findings. https://info.publicintelligence.net/HTT-PashtunSexuality.pdf.

Hyde, Jesse. 2016. "A Polygamist Cult's Last Stand: The Rise and Fall of Warren Jeffs." *Rolling Stone*, February 9. http://www.rollingstone.com/culture/features/a-polygamist-cults-last-stand-the-rise-and-fall-of-warren-jeffs-20160209.

Idov, Michael. 2010. "Clash of the Bearded Ones." *New York Magazine*, April 11. http://nymag.com/realestate/neighborhoods/2010/65356/.

Jacobs, Adam. 2012. "The Secret Life of Hasidic Sexuality." *HuffPost*, April 22. https://www.huffpost.com/entry/the-secret-life-of-hasidic-sexuality_b_1284916.

Jacobson, Mark. 2008. "Escape from the Holy Shtetl." *New York Magazine*, July 13. http://nymag.com/news/features/48532/.

Jakes, Lara. 2019. "Peace Road Map for Afghanistan Will Let Taliban Negotiate Women's Rights." *New York Times*, August 17, p. 1.

Jamal, Aamir. 2014. "Men's Perception of Women's Role and Girl's Education Among Pashtun Tribes of Pakistan: A Qualitative Delphi Study." *Cultural and Pedagogical Inquiry* 6, no. 2: 17–34.

Jeffs, Rachel. 2017. *Breaking Free: How I Escaped Polygamy, the FLDS Cult, and My Father, Warren Jeffs*. New York: Harper LUXE.

Jessop, Caroline. 2007. *Escape*. New York: Broadway Books.

Jessop, Flora. 2009. *Church of Lies*. San Francisco: Jossey-Bass.

Johnson, G. David, and Lewellyn Hendrix. 1982. "A Cross-Cultural Test of Collins' Theory of Sexual Stratification." *Journal of Marriage and the Family* 44 (August): 675–84.

Johnson, Krista. 2018. "This Son of Prophet Warren Jeffs Has 54 Brothers and Sisters. Yet the Former FLDS Church Member Felt Alone." *USA Today*, April 18. https://www.usatoday.com/story/news/nation-now/2018/04/08/mormon-fundamentalist-yfz-ranch-raid/492767002/.

Jones, Abigail. 2013. "Divorce in the Orthodox Jewish Community Can Be Brutal, Degrading, and Endless." *Newsweek*, November 12. http://www.newsweek.com/divorce-orthodox-jewish-community-can-be-brutal-degrading-and-endless-3082.

Joyce, Kathryn. 2009. *Quiverfull: Inside the Christian Patriarchy Movement*. Boston: Beacon Press.

Kahn, Gabe. 2012. "Satmar Rebbe—It's Me or Your Smartphones." IsraelNationalNews.com, May 31. http://www.israelnationalnews.com/News/News.aspx/156402#.UBFAuXDR2I4.

Kahn, Hamid M. 2015. *Islamic Law, Customary Law and Afghan Informal Justice*. Special Report 363. United States Institute of Peace. March. http://www.usip.org/sites/default/files/SR363-Islamic-Law-CustomaryLaw-and-Afghan-Informal-Justice.pdf.

Kakar, Palwasha. 2005. "Tribal Law of Pashtunwali and Women's Legislative Authority." Islamic Legal Studies Program, Harvard Law School. https://beta.images.theglobeandmail.com/archive/00231/Tribal_Law_of_Pasht_231142a.pdf.

Kakar, Spogmay Waziri. 2014. "To Be Divorced—and Disgraced—in Afghanistan." Safe World for Women, January. https://www.asafeworldforwomen.org/safe-world-blogs/pvp/4441-to-be-divorced.html.

Katzenstein, David, and Lisa Aronson Fontes. 2017. "Twice Silenced: The Underreporting of Child Sexual Abuse in Orthodox Jewish Communities." *Journal of Child Sexual Abuse* 26, no. 6: 752–67.

Kaye, Evelyn. 1987. *A Hole in the Sheet: A Modern Woman Looks at Orthodox and Hasidic Judaism*. Secaucus, NJ: Lyle Stuart.

Keren-Kratz, Menachem. 2014a. "The Satmar Rebbe and the Destruction of Hungarian Jewry: Part 1." *Tablet*, July 16. http://www.tabletmag.com/jewish-arts-and-culture/books/178913/satmar-rebbe-1#LMveFs0VthDWGaSv.01.

Keren-Kratz, Menachem. 2014b. "The Satmar Rebbe and the Destruction of Hungarian Jewry: Part 2." *Tablet*, July 17. http://www.tabletmag.com/jewish-arts-and-culture/books/178925/satmar-rebbe-2.

Kershner, Isabel. 2017. "Israeli Court Rules for Woman in Airline Sexism Case." *New York Times*, June 22, p. A11.

Khattak, Raj Wali Shah, Mohammad Fida, and Richard Lee. 2009. "The Pashtun Code of Honour." *Central Asia* 65, no. 1 (Winter). http://www.asc-centralasia.edu.pk/Issue_65/01_ The%20Pashtun_Code_of_Honour.html.

Kiefer, Michael. 2016. "Feds Seek to Disband Polygamous Towns' Police Department." *The Republic*, October 27. https://www.azcentral.com/story/news/local/arizona/2016/10/24/doj-hildale-colorado-city-marshals-office-warren-jeffs-flds/92706630/.

King, Matt. 2009. "KJ Highest US Poverty Rate, Census Says." *Times Herald-Record*, January 30. http://www.recordonline.com/apps/pbcs.dll/article?AID=/20090130/NEWS/901300361.

Knafo, Nilaya. 2015. "Tribal Customs in Afghanistan Clash with the Modern World." *Morning Call*, May 28. http://www.mcall.com/opinion/ithink/mc-afghanistan-women-treatment-knafo-ithink-0529-20150528-story.html.

Kolker, Robert. 2006. "On the Rabbi's Knees." *New York Magazine*, May 12. http://nymag.com/news/features/17010/.

Koofi, Fawzia. 2015. "It's Time to Act for Afghan Women: Pass EVAW." ForeignPolicy.com, January 13. https://foreignpolicy.com/2015/01/13/its-time-to-act-for-afghan-women-pass-the-evaw/.

Kornbluth, Jesse. 2012. "Unorthodox: The Satmars v. Feldman and Kornbluth." Head Butler, March 6. http://headbutler.com/books/memoir/unorthodox-satmars-v-friedman-kornbluth.

Kottak, Conrad Phillip, and Kathryn A. Kozaitis. 2012. *On Being Different*. 4th edition. New York: McGraw-Hill.

Krakauer, Jon. 2004. *Under the Banner of Heaven*. New York: Doubleday.

Kramer, Andrew E. 2018. "Shelters Have Saved Countless Afghan Women. So Why Are They Afraid?" *New York Times*, March 17, p. 11.

Kristof, Nicholas. 2014. "What's So Scary About Smart Girls?" *New York Times*, May 10. https://www.nytimes.com/2014/05/11/opinion/sunday/kristof-whats-so-scary-about-smart-girls.html.

Kumar, Ruchi. 2019. "Women Have the Most to Lose in Afghan Peace Offer to the Taliban." The Lily, March 6. https://www.thelily.com/women-have-the-most-to-lose-in-the-afghan-peace-offer-to-the-taliban/.

Landau, David. 1993. *Piety & Power: The World of Jewish Fundamentalism*. New York: Hill and Wang.

Lavin, Talia. 2015. "Off the Path of Orthodoxy." *New Yorker*, July 31. https://www.newyorker.com/news/news-desk/off-the-path-of-orthodoxy.

Lax, Leah. 2015. *Uncovered*. Berkeley, CA: She Writes Press.

Lesher, Michael. 2015. *Sexual Abuse, Shonda, and Concealment in Orthodox Jewish Communities*. Jefferson, NC: McFarland & Company.

Levine, Stephanie Wellen. 2003. *Mystics, Mavericks, and Merrymakers: An Intimate Journey among Hasidic Girls*. New York: New York University Press.

Lewan, Todd. 2008. "How Hunting Ground Became a Polygamous Nightmare." FoxNews.com, April 19.

Lindholm, Charles. 1982. *Generosity and Jealousy: The Swat Pashtun of Northern Pakistan*. New York: Columbia University Press.

Lindholm, Charles, and Cherry Lindholm. 1979. "Marriage as Warfare." *Natural History* 88, no. 8: 11–21.

Llorente, Elizabeth. 2018. "Hasidic Leaders Sharply Limit Members' Web, Smartphone Use: 'It's Like We're in North Korea.'" FoxNews.com, June 12. http://www.foxnews.com/us/

2018/06/12/hasidic-leaders-sharply-limit-members-web-smartphone-use-its-like-were-in-north-korea.html.

Lobell, Kylie Ora. 2014. "Orthodox Women Turn to Other Orthodox Women During Pregnancy and Childbirth." *Tablet*, August 11. https://www.tabletmag.com/jewish-life-and-religion/180442/orthodox-women-doulas.

Lost Messiah. 2018. "Kiryas Joel Rabbi Declares War against NYS Education Department, Rich Hypocrisy." December 2. https://lostmessiahdotcom.wordpress.com/2018/12/02/kiryas-joel-rabbi-declares-war-against-nys-education-department-rich-hypocrisy/.

Lovett, Ian. 2015. "Deadly Flood Blurs Town's Religious Divisions, Even as Grief Highlights Them." *New York Times*, September 17, p. 19.

Mandel, Ari. 2015. "A Piece of Unsolicited Advice for the Hasidic Community." *Forward*, April 27. https://forward.com/culture/306399/unsolicited-advice-to-the-hasidic-community/.

Mann, Reva. 2007. *The Rabbi's Daughter*. New York: Dial Press.

Margolis, Maxine L. 1984. *Mothers and Such: Views of American Women and Why They Changed*. Berkeley and Los Angeles: University of California Press.

Margolis, Maxine L. 2000. *True to Her Nature: Changing Advice to American Women*. Prospect Heights, IL: Waveland Press.

Margolis, Maxine L. 2004. "The Relative Status of Men and Women." In *Encyclopedia of Sex and Gender: Men and Women in the World's Cultures*, edited by Carol Ember and Melvin Ember, 137–45. New York: Kluwer Academic/Plenum.

Markoe, Lauren. 2014. "What Is a Mikvah, and What Does It Have to Do with Sex?" *HuffPost*, November 1. https://www.huffingtonpost.com/2014/11/01/what-is-a-mikvah_n_6069556.html.

Markovits, Anouk. 2013. *I Am Forbidden*. New York: Hogarth.

Marty, Martin E., and R. Scott Appleby. 1993. "Introduction: A Sacred Cosmos, Scandalous Code, Defiant Society." In *Fundamentalisms and Society: Reclaiming the Sciences, the Family, and Education*, edited by Martin E. Marty and R. Scott Appleby, 1–19. Chicago: University of Chicago Press.

Mashal, Mujib. 2017. "Their Identities Denied, Afghan Women Ask, 'Where Is My Name?'" *New York Times*, July 31, p. 4.

McAfee, Eric. 2015. "Demography and Destiny: America's Youngest Community." NewGeography.com, March 21. http://www.newgeography.com/content/004873-demography-destiny-americas-youngest-county.

McDonell-Parry, Amelia. 2019. "Lawmakers Going After FLDS Polygamy Compound in South Dakota." *Rolling Stone*, February 1. https://www.rollingstone.com/culture/culture-news/warren-jeffs-flds-south-dakota-compound-788509/.

Milanich, Nara. 2019. *Paternity: The Elusive Quest for the Father*. Cambridge, MA: Harvard University Press.

Miles, Carrie A. 2011. "What's Love Got to Do with It? Earthly Experience of Celestial Marriage, Past and Present." In *Modern Polygamy in the United States: Historical, Cultural, and Legal Issues*, edited by Cardell K. Jacobson and Lara Burton, 185–207. New York: Oxford University Press.

Miller, Claire Cain. 2018. "A Baby Bust, Rooted in Economic Insecurity." *New York Times*, July 6. pp. B1, B5.

Miller, Jennifer. 2014. "Yiddish Isn't Enough." *New York Times*, November 22, p. 1.

Mintz, Jerome. 1992. *Hasidic People: A Place in the New World*. Cambridge, MA: Harvard University Press.

Molloy, Parker. 2019. "Tucker Carlson's Shock Jock Tapes Are R-rated Versions of What You'll Find on His Show." Media Matters for America, March 15. https://www.mediamatters.org/blog/2019/03/15/tucker-carlsons-shock-jock-tapes-are-r-rated-versions-what-youll-find-his-show/223143.

Mondloch, Chris. 2013a. "Bacha Bazi: An Afghan Tragedy." ForeignPolicy.com, October 28. http://foreignpolicy.com/2013/10/28/bacha-bazi-an-afghan-tragedy/.

Mondloch, Chris. 2013b. "An Afghan Tragedy: The Pashtun Practice of Having Sex with Young Boys." *Independent*, October 29. http://www.independent.co.uk/voices/comment/an-afghan-tragedy-the-pashtun-practice-of-having-sex-with-young-boys-8911529.html.

Moore-Emmett, Andrea. 2004. *God's Brothel*. San Francisco: Pince-Nez Press.

Morris, Bonnie. 1995. "Agents or Victims of Religious Ideology? Approaches to Locating Hasidic Women in Feminist Studies." In *New World Hasidim: Ethnographic Studies of Hasidic Jews in America*, edited by Janet S. Belcove-Shalin, 161–80. Albany: SUNY Press.

Musser, Rebecca, with M. Bridget Cook. 2013. *The Witness Wore Red*. New York: Grand Central Publishing.

Nachshoni, Kobi. 2015. "Ultra-Orthodox Jews Protest in NYC: 'Netanyahu Doesn't Represent Us.'" YnetNews.com, March 4. http://www.ynetnews.com/articles/0,7340,L-4633443,00.html.

Nader, Zahra, and Mujib Mashal. 2017. "Despite Ban, Invasive Virginity Tests Remain Prevalent in Afghanistan." *New York Times*, January 6, p. 6.

Nadler, Allan. 2011a. "The Riddle of the Satmar." *Jewish Ideas Daily*, February 17. http://www.jewishideasdaily.com/824/features/the-riddle-of-the-satmar/.

Nadler, Allan. 2011b. "The Riddle of Satmar and Palm Stockings." *Jewish Ideas Daily*, February 28. http://thinkingjewgirl.blogspot.com/2011/02/riddle-of-satmar-and-palm-stockings.html.

Nasimi, Shabnam. 2014. "The Devastating Truth of Women's Rights in Afghanistan." OpenDemocracy.com, July 11. https://www.opendemocracy.net/opensecurity/shabnam-nasimi/devastating-truth-of-women%e2%80%99s-rights-in-afghanistan.

Nathan-Kazis, Josh. 2012. "Internet Cafe on Front Line of Culture War." *Forward*, May 18. http://forward.com/news/156406/internet-cafe-on-front-line-of-culture-war/.

Nathan-Kazis, Josh. 2014. "WhatsApp Spreads Fast Among Ultra-Orthodox—and Rabbis Cry Foul." *Forward*, February 6. https://forward.com/news/192295/whatsapp-spreads-fast-among-ultra-orthodox-and-r/.

Nathan-Kazis, Josh. 2016a. "How the Hasids Won the Battle of Bloomingburg—and Everyone Else Lost." *Forward*, December 15. http://forward.com/news/357030/how-the-hasids-won-the-battle-of-bloomingburg-and-everyone-else-lost/.

Nathan-Kazis, Josh. 2016b. "What Does Developer's Arrest Mean for the Future of Hasidic Bloomingburg?" *Forward*, December 15. http://forward.com/news/357260/what-does-developers-arrest-mean-for-the-future-of-hasidic-bloomingburg/.

Nathan-Kazis, Josh. 2017. "Hasidic Bloomingburg Is Still Growing, Even After F.B.I. Arrests Its Builder." *Forward*, April 7. http://forward.com/news/368459/hasidic-yeshiva-opens-in-bloomingburg-months-after-fbi-arrests/.

National Geographic. 2011. "Ethnic Map of Afghanistan." July 15. https://web.archive.org/web/20110715231715/http://ngm.nationalgeographic.com/ngm/0311/feature2/images/mp_download.2.pdf.

Nir, Sarah Maslin. 2016. "Pool Rules: No Running, No Eating and, Three Times a Week, No Men." *New York Times*, June 29, p. 21.

Nordberg, Jenny. 2014. *The Underground Girls of Kabul: In Search of a Hidden Resistance in Afghanistan*. New York: Crown Publishers.

Nordland, Ron. 2014a. "In Spite of the Law, Afghan 'Honor Killings' of Women Continue." *New York Times*, May 3, p. 10.

Nordland, Ron. 2014b. "Struggling to Keep Afghan Girls Safe After a Mullah Is Accused of Rape." *New York Times*, July 19, p. 4.

Nordland, Ron. 2018a. "Afghan Pedophiles Get Free Pass from U.S. Military, Report Says." *New York Times*, January 23, p. 10.

Nordland, Ron. 2018b. "She Married 3 Brothers in Family Torn by War." *New York Times*, May 27, p. 6.

Nordland, Ron. 2018c. "Who's Winning the War in Afghanistan? Depends Which One." *New York Times*, August 19, p. 10.

Nordland, Ron, and Fatima Faizi. 2017. "Harassment All Around, Afghan Women Weigh Risks of Speaking Out." *New York Times*, December 10, p. 4.

Nordland, Rod, Fatima Faizi, and Fahim Abed. 2019. "Afghan Women Fear Peace with Taliban May Mean War on Them." *New York Times*, January 27, p. 1.

O'Neill, Ann. 2016. "Witnesses: Scallops for the Bishop, Toast for the Kids." CNN, April 6. http://www.cnn.com/2016/04/05/us/flds-secrets-warren-jeffs.

Orbala. 2013. "Introducing the Parruney: The Pashtun Woman's Body, Pashtun Men, and Harassment." Safe World for Women, June. http://www.asafeworldforwomen.org/safeworld-blogs/orbala/3679-introducing-the-parruney.html.

Oswaks, Molly. 2016. "The Journey Out: Women Who Escaped a Polygamist Mormon Cult Share Their Story." *Vice*, January 7. https://www.vice.com/en_us/article/ae5b7p/flds-celebrating-christmas-after-escaping-a-polygamist-mormon-cult.

Otterman, Sharon. 2012a. "Sex Abuse Trial of Brooklyn Man Begins." *New York Times*, November 27, p. 25.

Otterman, Sharon. 2012b. "Abuse Verdict Topples a Hasidic Wall of Secrecy." *New York Times*, December 11, pp. 1, 28.

Otterman, Sharon. 2018. "When Living Your Truth Can Mean Losing Your Children." *New York Times*, May 25, p. 1.

Otterman, Sharon. 2019. "Is a Town Fighting Growth, or a Hasidic Influx?" *New York Times*, August 14, p. 20.

Otterman, Sharon, and Ray Rivera. 2012. "Ultra-Orthodox Shun Their Own for Reporting Child Sexual Abuse." *New York Times*, May 9, p.1.

Pashtun Culture and History (blog). 2010. "Social Life of Pashtuns/Pukhtoons." August. http://pashtuncultureandhistory.blogspot.com/2010/08/social-life-of-pashtuns.html.

Patterson, Thom. 2015. "Polygamist Sect Limits Sex to 'Seed Bearers,' Court Document Says." CNN, October 1. https://www.cnn.com/2015/09/30/us/polygamist-flds-warren-jeffs-update/index.html.

Perkins, Nancy. 2007. "Warren Jeffs Resigns as Leader of the FLDS Church." *Deseret News*, December 5. https://www.deseretnews.com/article/695233512/Warren-Jeffs-resigns-as-leader-of-the-FLDS-Church.html.

Pessala, Anne. 2012. "Perspectives on Attitudes and Behaviors of Pashtun Women in Pakistan and Afghanistan." D3 Systems, Inc. http://www.d3systems.com/wp-content/uploads/2012/06/2012-AAPOR-Paper-Pessala-v4.pdf.

Petersen, Anne Helen. 2018. "How Do You Rebuild Your Life After Leaving a Polygamous Sect?" BuzzFeed News, January 18. https://www.buzzfeednews.com/article/annehelenpetersen/ex-flds-new-chapter.

Pilkington, Ed. 2008. "Children Removed from Sect in Texas Tell of Girls Forced into Sex with Older Men." *The Guardian*, April 10.

Plante, Stephie Grob. 2015. "NYC Electronics Store Earns Gelt with Orthodox Business Model." *Times of Israel*, January 15. http://www.timesofisrael.com/nyc-electronics-store-earns-gelt-with-orthodox-business-model/.

Poll, Solomon. 1971. *The Hasidic Community of Williamsburg*. New York: Schocken Books.

Popper, Nathanial. 2006. "One Rebbe or Two? As Heirs Feud, Satmar Sect Slides Toward Schism." *Forward*, May 5. https://forward.com/news/1341/one-rebbe-or-two-as-heirs-feud-satmar-sect-slide/.

Potok, Chaim. n.d. "Ultra-Orthodox Jewish Groups." Cult Education Institute. https://culteducation.com/group/1276-ultra-orthodox-jewish-groups.html.

Powell, Michael. 2006a. "Hats On, Gloves Off." *New York Magazine*, April 28. http://nymag.com/news/cityside/16864/.

Powell, Michael. 2006b. "Sons of the Father After the Satmar Grand Rebbe's Death, a Tzimmes Grows in Brooklyn." *Washington Post*, June 4. https://www.washingtonpost.com/archive/lifestyle/2006/06/04/sons-of-the-father-span-classbankheadafter-the-satmar-grand-rebbes-death-a-tzimmes-grows-in-brooklynspan/aa308dc5-c333-4b0f-bb9b-31ca9ac1f4dd/.

Quinn, D. Michael. 1993. "Plural Marriage and Mormon Fundamentalism." In *Fundamentalisms and Society: Reclaiming the Sciences, the Family, and Education*, edited by Martin E. Marty and R. Scott Appleby, 240–93. Chicago: University of Chicago Press.

Quinn, D. Michael. 1998. "Plural Marriage and Mormon Fundamentalism." *Dialogue: A Journal of Mormon Thought* 31, no. 2: 1–68.

Quinn, D. Michael. 2010. "Afghan Women Fear Loss of Modest Gains." *New York Times*, July 31, p. 1.

Quinn, D. Michael. 2013. "Painful Payment for Afghan Debt: A Daughter, 6." *New York Times*, March 31, p. 1.

Rahm, Najim, and David Zucchino. 2019. "'All of Us Have Lost Our Hope': Attacks Hit Girls' Schools as Taliban Ascend." *New York Times*, May 23, p. 10.

Raphelson, Samantha. 2018. "When Leaving Your Religion Means Losing Your Children." National Public Radio, June 14. https://www.npr.org/2018/06/14/619997099/when-leaving-your-religion-means-losing-your-children.

Ravitzky, Aviezer. 1994. "The Contemporary Lubavitcher Hasidic Movement: Between Conservatism and Messianism." In *Accounting for Fundamentalisms: The Dynamic Character of Movements*, edited by Martin E. Marty and R. Scott Appleby, 303–27. Chicago: University of Chicago Press.

Reavy, Pat. 2012. "Texas Seeks to Seize YFZ Ranch from FLDS Church." *Deseret News*, November 28. https://www.deseretnews.com/article/865567677/Texas-seeks-to-seize-YFZ-Ranch-from-FLDS-Church.html.

Revolutionary Association of the Women of Afghanistan. n.d. "Some of the Restrictions Imposed by Taliban on Women in Afghanistan." http://www.rawa.org/rules.htm.

Roberts, Sam. 2011. "A Village with the Numbers, Not the Image, of the Poorest Place." *New York Times*, April 20, p. 1.

Roy, Olivier. 1994. *The Failure of Political Islam*. Cambridge, MA: Harvard University Press.

Rubin, Alissa J. 2015a. "Dangerous Culture Clash for Afghan Policewomen." *New York Times*, March 2, pp. 1, 10.

Rubin, Alissa J. 2015b. "A Thin Line of Defense Against 'Honor Killings.'" *New York Times*, March 3, pp. 1, 14–15.

Rubin, Alissa J., and Habid Zahori. 2012. "Afghan Women's Affairs Aide Shot Months After Killing of Predecessor." *New York Times*, December 11, p. 14.

Rubin, Elizabeth. 2005. "Women's Work." *New York Times Magazine*, October 9. www.nytimes.com/2005/10/09/magazine/09afghan.html.

Rubin, Israel. 1972. *Satmar: An Island in the City*. Chicago: Quadrangle Books.

Rubin, Israel. 1997. *Two Generations of an Urban Island*. 2nd ed. New York: Peter Lang.

Sable, Ahuva. 2013. "The Frum Pedophile." Unpious.com, January 15. http://www.unpious.com/2013/01/the-frum-pedophile/.

Saleh, Amrullah. 2012. "The Crisis and Politics of Ethnicity in Afghanistan." Aljazeera.com, June 26. https://www.aljazeera.com/indepth/opinion/2012/06/201262013830446913.html.

Salt Lake Tribune. 2013. "Alcohol, Coffee and Why the FLDS Drink Them." March 1. https://archive.sltrib.com/article.php?id=55924890&itype=cmsid.

Samaha, Albert. 2014. "All the Young Jews: In the Village of Kiryas Joel, New York, the Median Age Is 13." *Village Voice*, November 12. http://blogs.villagevoice.com/runninscared/2014/11/kiryas_joel_new_york.php.

Sanders, Ash. 2018. "From Polygamy to Democracy: Inside a Fundamentalist Mormon Town." *Rolling Stone*, May 23. https://www.rollingstone.com/culture/culture-news/from-polygamy-to-democracy-inside-a-fundamentalist-mormon-town-628204/.

Schmidt, Susan Ray. 2006. *His Favorite Wife*. Twin Falls, ID: Kassidy Lane Publishing.

Scott, George. 2017. "Creekers Foundation Empowers FLDS Women to Take Control of Rights and Freedom Within." *Desert Pulse*, February 26. http://www.thedesertpulse.com/creekers-foundation-empowers-flds-women-take-control-rights-freedom-within/.

Seierstad, Asne. 2003. *The Bookseller of Kabul*. New York: Back Bay Books.

Selengut, Charles. 1994. "By Torah Alone: Yeshiva Fundamentalism in Jewish Life." In *Accounting for Fundamentalisms: The Dynamic Character of Movements*, edited by Martin E. Marty and R. Scott Appleby, 236–63. Chicago: University of Chicago Press.

Shaffir, William. 1995. "Boundaries and Self-Presentation among the Hasidim: A Study in Identity Maintenance." In *New World Hasidim: Ethnographic Studies of Hasidic Jews in America*, edited by Janet S. Belcove-Shalin, 31–68. Albany: SUNY Press.

Shein, Leah. 2006. "That's the Way It Goes." In *Hide & Seek: Jewish Women and Hair Covering*, edited by Lynne Schreiber, 47–49. Jerusalem, Israel: Urim Publications.

Siddique, Abubakar. 2012. "'Ghagh': The Pashtun Custom of Men Forcing Marriage Proposals on Women." *The Atlantic*, December 9. https://www.theatlantic.com/international/archive/2012/12/ghagh-the-pashtun-custom-of-men-forcing-marriage-proposals-on-women/266059.

Simms, Molly. 2019. "This Organization Helps People Who've Left the Orthodox Jewish Community." *O: The Oprah Magazine*, June 18. https://www.oprahmag.com/life/a27925298/help-leaving-orthodox-jewish-community-footsteps/.

Singular, Stephen. 2008. *When Men Become Gods*. New York: St. Martin's Press.

Skaine, Rosemarie. 2002. *The Women of Afghanistan in the Post-Taliban Era*. Jefferson, NC: McFarland & Company.

Skaine, Rosemarie. 2008. *Women of Afghanistan Under the Taliban*. Jefferson, NC: McFarland & Company.

Sokol, Sam. 2015. "Satmar Hasidic School Bans Mothers from Owning Smartphones." *Jerusalem Post*, August 4. http://www.jpost.com/Diaspora/Satmar-hasidic-school-bans-mothers-from-owning-cellphones-411110.

Sorush, Rohullah. 2019. "What's in a Woman's Name? No Name, No Public Persona." Afghanistan Analysts Network, March 8. http://www.afghanistan-analysts.org/whats-in-a-womans-name-no-name-no-public-persona/.

Sparks, Muriel. 1961. *The Prime of Miss Jean Brodie*. New York: Macmillan.

Spencer, Irene. 2007. *Shattered Dreams*. New York: Center Street.

Spencer, Irene. 2009. *Cult Insanity: A Memoir of Polygamy, Prophets, and Blood Atonement*. New York: Center Street.

Stewart, Sara. 2012. "I Was a Hasidic Jew—but I Broke Free." *New York Post*, February 7. https://nypost.com/2012/02/07/i-was-a-hasidic-jew-but-i-broke-free/.

Stott, Rebecca. 2017. *In the Days of Rain: A Daughter, A Father, A Cult*. New York: Spiegel & Grau.

Szep, Jason. 2007. "Polygamist Community Faces Rare Genetic Disorder." Reuters, June 14. http://www.reuters.com/article/us-usa-mormons-genes-idUSN0727298120070614.

Sztokman, Elana. 2014. "It's Time to Tell the Truth about Kallah Teachers." JewFem.com, April 29. http://www.jewfem.com/index.php?option=com_easyblog&view=entry&id=424&Itemid=513.

Tannenbaum, Gershon. 2014. "Bloomingburg Shtetl Overcomes Obstacles." *5 Towns Jewish Times*, July 10. http://5tjt.com/bloomingburg-shtetl-overcomes-obstacles/.

Taylor, Kate. 2017. "Critics Say City Has Stalled on Investigating Yeshivas." *New York Times*, September 7, p. 22.

Times of Israel. 2016. "Satmar Decree Bars Women from Higher Education." August 24. https://www.timesofisrael.com/satmar-decree-bars-women-from-higher-education/.

Times of Israel. 2019. "Palm Tree Becomes First Official Ultra-Orthodox Town in America." January 6. https://www.timesofisrael.com/palm-tree-becomes-first-official-ultra-orthodox-town-in-america/.

Tolentino, Jia. 2017. "Mike Pence's Marriage and the Beliefs That Keep Women from Power." *New Yorker*, March 31. http://www.newyorker.com/culture/jia-tolentino/mike-pences-marriage-and-the-beliefs-that-keep-women-from-power.

Trencher, Mark L. 2016. "Starting a Conversation: A Pioneering Survey of Those Who Have Left the Orthodox Community." *Nishma Research*, June 19.

Tristam, Pierre. 2019. "Taliban Rules, Decrees, Laws and Prohibitions." ThoughtCo, May 25. https://www.thoughtco.com/taliban-rules-decrees-laws-and-prohibitions-2352763.

Turkewitz, Julie. 2014. "Hasidic Williamsburg, as Seen by One Who Left Sect." *New York Times*, July 10, p. 23.

Unger-Sargon, Batya. 2016. "Healing Hasidic Masturbators and Adulterers—With Psychiatric Drugs." Narratively, August 23. https://narratively.com/healing-hasidic-masturbators-and-adulterers-with-psychiatric-drugs/.

USAID. 2017. "Afghanistan's Maternal Mortality Rate Addressed at National Health Conference." April 6. https://www.usaid.gov/afghanistan/news-information/press-releases/afghanistan%E2%80%99s-maternal-mortality-rate-addressed-national.

Verdon, Amy. 2005. "Rebbe to Wear." FancyMag.com. http://fancymag.com/hasidic.html.

Vizel, Frieda. 2012. "On Women Shaving All Their Hair." Oy Vey Cartoons: Doodles and Other Missives, October 2. http://www.oyveycartoons.com/2012/10/02/women-shaving-all-their-hair/.

Vizel, Frieda. 2014. "A List of Hasidic Female Headgear, with Illustrations." Tours by Frieda, May 27. https://friedavizel.com/2014/05/27/a-list-of-hasidic-female-headgear-with-illustrations/.

Vizel, Frieda. 2017. "The Smartphone War at KJ Is Directed Especially at Women." *In Censorship, Sociology*. https://friedavizel.com/category/sociology/page/7/.

Vizel, Frieda. 2018. "The Truth about Hasidic Education." *Tablet*, April 16. https://www.tabletmag.com/scroll/259976/the-truth-about-hasidic-education.

Wagner, Meg. 2015. "Warren Jeffs' Polygamist Cult Forced Men to Watch 'Seed Bearers' Rape Their Wives in 'Ritualistic Procreation': Investigator." *New York Daily News*, October 1. http://www.nydailynews.com/news/national/warren-jeffs-cult-forced-men-watch-wives-raped-article-1.2381086.

Wakin, Daniel J. 2002. "The Heir Unapparent; Brothers' Feud Fractures a Hasidic Community." *New York Times*, January 24, pp. B1, 6.

Waldman, Amy. 2003. "Meeting on New Constitution, Afghan Women Find Old Attitudes." *New York Times*, December 16, p. 13.

Wall, Elissa, with Lisa Pulitzer. 2008. *Stolen Innocence: My Story of Growing Up in a Polygamous Sect, Becoming a Teenage Bride, and Breaking Free of Warren Jeffs*. New York: William Morrow.

Walters, Joanna. 2015a. "Fleeing the FLDS: Followers Are Abandoning the Notorious Sect in Droves." Aljazeera America, March 16. http://america.aljazeera.com/multimedia/2015/3/fleeing-the-flds-sect.html.

Walters, Joanna. 2015b. "'Deprogramming' from the FLDS, Warren Jeffs' Secretive Cult." Aljazeera America, March 17. http://america.aljazeera.com/multimedia/2015/3/deprogramming-from-the-flds-warren-jeffs-cult.html.

Walters, Joanna. 2016a. "Towns Home to Polygamist Sect Accused of Discrimination as Arizona Trial Begins." *The Guardian*, January 25. https://www.theguardian.com/us-news/2016/jan/25/mormon-polygamist-sect-arizona-utah-trial-fundamentalist-church-jesus-christ-latter-day-saints.

Walters, Joanna. 2016b. "Is the End of Days Looming for Fundamentalist Sect in Utah?" *The Guardian*, April 3. https://www.theguardian.com/us-news/2016/apr/03/utah-fundamentalist-sect-latter-day-saints-end.

Weichselbaum, Lehman. 2010. "Chulent to Go?" *New York Jewish Week*, July 27. https://jewishweek.timesofisrael.com/chulent-to-go/.

Weichselbaum, Simone. 2012. "After Nechemya Weberman, Hasidic Satmar Sect Considers Sending Rebel Teens Away." *New York Daily News*, December 10. http://www.nydailynews.com/new-york/satmar-sect-considers-sending-rebel-teens-article-1.1216642.

Weiss, Maud B., Michel Neumeister, and Jerome Mintz. 1995. *The Challenge of Piety: The Satmar Hasidim in New York*. Munich: Gina Kehayoff.

Weyermann, Debra. 2011. *Answer Them Nothing: Bringing Down the Polygamous Empire of Warren Jeffs*. Chicago: Chicago Review Press.

Winslow, Ben. 2019. "FLDS Leader Served with Lawsuit Papers in Minnesota." Fox News, January 22. https://fox13now.com/2019/01/22/flds-leader-served-with-lawsuit-papers-in-minnesota/.

Winston, Hella. 2005. *Unchosen: The Hidden Lives of Hasidic Rebels*. Boston: Beacon Press.

Winston, Hella. 2006–2007. "So Many Rules, So Little Protection: Sex and Suppression Among Ultra Orthodox Jews." *Lilith*, Winter: 10–14.

Woods, Alden. 2018. "Outsiders, FLDS Battle for Control of Towns Warren Jeffs Left Behind." *USA Today*, April 4. https://www.usatoday.com/story/news/local/arizona/2018/04/04/outsiders-flds-warren-jeffs-believers-battle-control-short-creek-hildale-colorado-city/359309002/.

Wuthnow, Robert, and Matthew P. Lawson. 1994. "Sources of Christian Fundamentalism in the United States." In *Accounting for Fundamentalisms: The Dynamic Character of Movements*, edited by Martin E. Marty and R. Scott Appleby, 18–56. Chicago: University of Chicago Press.

Yarrow, Allison. 2012. "At Orthodox Sex-Abuse Trial, Little-Known Enforcement Group Comes to Light." *Daily Beast*, December 8. https://www.thedailybeast.com/at-orthodox-sex-abuse-trial-little-known-enforcement-group-comes-to-light.

Yerushalmi, Miriam. n.d. "OCD Mikvah Preparation Checklist." Mikvah.org. https://www.mikvah.org/article/ocd_mikvah_preparation_checklist.

Yeshiva World News. 2018. "Satmar Rebbe of Kiryas Joel Declares War against NYS Education Department." November 29. https://www.theyeshivaworld.com/news/general/1632829/satmar-rebbe-of-kiryas-joel-declares-war-against-nys-education-department-full-audio-clip.html.

Zakutinsky, Rivka, and Yaffa Leba Gottlieb. 2001. *Around Sarah's Table: Ten Hasidic Women Share Their Stories of Life, Faith, and Tradition*. New York: The Free Press.

Zalcberg, Sara. 2017. "The Place of Culture and Religion in Patterns of Disclosure and Reporting Sexual Abuse of Males: A Case Study of Ultra Orthodox Male Victims." *Journal of Child Sexual Abuse* 26, no. 5: 590–607.

Index

burqa, 79, 80, 100, 147, 151
buses, 63–64
Bush, George W., 15

"a call" (*ghagh*), 100–101
Carlson, Tucker, 38–39
"casual incest," 134
"Celestial Marriage." *See* polygamy
cell phones, 155–156
Chesler, Phyllis, 76
childbirth, 127. *See also* procreation
child marriage, 6
children, 11, 121–122; divorce and, 107, 180–181. *See also* education
children, FLDS, 114; danger for, 115; Jeffs, Warren, extremes for, 144
civil rights, 44–45
Clinton, Hillary, 62, 146, 185
Cohen, Philip, 159
control of women, 1, 85, 86, 118–119; in motherhood, FLDS, 112; Pashtun modesty as, 59; in Pashtun modesty separation, 66–67; in procreation, 13–14, 111
cosmetics, 73–74, 148
courage (*nang*), 49–50, 50, 52
cultural similarities, 2; arranged marriages as, 3; community separation as, 5; dress codes as, 3; government funding as, 6, 19; household duties in, 4; information restriction as, 4–5; paternity as, 3; proper place as, 3, 5–6, 6n1; recent strictures as, 6; reproduction as, 3; sexual ignorance as, 5

decision-making, 30, 87, 99, 173
Deen, Shulem, 27–28
"destruction lectures," 40–41
dignity (*nang*), 49–50, 50, 52
dispute settlement (*baad*), 7, 99–100
"divine revelations," 34n3, 40, 88, 144–145
division of labor, 14, 141
divorce, 92–93; children and, 107, 180–181; in Pashtun marriage, 107–108; in Satmar marriage, 98; stigma of, 107
dress codes, 3; in FLDS, 59, 76–78, 77, 144. *See also* Pashtun modesty dress;

Satmar dress
"dressed up as a boy" (*bacha posh*), 129
dress of women: Pashtun extremes on, 147–148. *See also* dress codes; Pashtun modesty dress; Satmar dress

economics, 15, 163–164; of divorce, 107–108; of Satmar Hasidim, 30–31, 31n2, 33–34. *See also* government funding
education, 15; in FLDS, 41, 42n5, 170; Pashtun marriage and suffering and, 105–106; in Pashtun recent developments, 161–162; for Satmar children, 121. *See also* girls' education; Satmar marriage, women's education and; sex education
Elimination of Violence Against Women Act (EVAW), 160–161
employment for women: in Pashtun ethnic group, 48; Pashtun marriage and, 105, 105–106; in Pashtun modesty separation, 67, 148; in Satmar Hasidim, 27, 32–33
ethnic groups, 8. *See also* Pashtun ethnic group
EVAW. *See* Elimination of Violence Against Women Act
exercise, Satmar dress for, 70, 75
extremes. *See* Jeffs, Warren, extremes; Pashtun extremes; Satmar extremes

Fascinating Womanhood: A Guide to a Happy Marriage (Andelin), 139
FBI's Ten Most Wanted, 31n2, 38
female mannequins, 70, 75
feminism, 87. *See also* Pashtun recent developments
FLDS. *See* Fundamentalist Church of Jesus Christ of Latter-Day Saints
FLDS recent developments, 165; Creekers Foundation for, 173–175, 174n3; culture shock in, 172–174; education related to, 170; escape from, 171, 171–172, 172n2; evictions in, 167–168; exodus in, 168–169; fraud in, 166; Internet in, 168–169; local government in, 170–171; outsiders in, 169–170; police force in, 171; self-destructive

9 781538 134023